Success in Math

Basic Geometry

Student Edition

Executive Editor: Barbara Levadi
Market Manager: Sandra Hutchison
Senior Editor: Francie Holder
Editors: Karen Bernhaut, Douglas Falk, Amy Jolin
Editorial Assistant: Kris Shepos-Salvatore
Editorial Consultant: Harriet Slonim
Production Manager: Penny Gibson
Production Editor: Walt Niedner
Interior Design: The Wheetley Company
Electronic Page Production: The Wheetley Company
Cover Design: Pat Smythe

ISBN 0-8359-1191-8
Printed in the United States of America
    9 10 11   05

1-800-321-3106
www.pearsonlearning.com

Contents

Chapter 1

Introduction to Basic Elements

OBJECTIVES:

In this chapter, you will learn

- *To recognize a point, a line, and a plane*
- *To recognize line segments and rays*
- *To recognize an angle and its parts*
- *To recognize parallel and perpendicular lines*
- *To recognize angles formed by intersecting lines*
- *To recognize adjacent angles and linear pairs*
- *To recognize intersecting planes, parallel planes, skew lines, and half planes*

Geometry is the study of the relationships of some basic elements called points, lines, and planes. The history of geometry began with the early Babylonians and the ancient Egyptians. They were the first to use the basic ideas of geometry. However, a Greek mathematician named Euclid, who lived around 300 B.C., developed the foundations for geometry as it is studied today. His writings, called *The Elements*, allowed the study of geometry to become a true branch of mathematics.

◀1•1 Points, Lines, Planes

IN THIS LESSON, YOU WILL LEARN

To recognize a point, a line, and a plane

WORDS TO LEARN

Point *a location in space represented by a dot*

Line *a set of many points that extends with no end in opposite directions*

Plane *a flat surface that extends in all directions with no end*

Collinear points *three or more points that lie in a straight line*

Noncollinear points *points that do not lie in a straight line*

Coplanar points *points that lie in the same plane*

Noncoplanar points *points that lie in different planes*

Ury built this cage for her new pet. Imagine that the nail heads show points. What parts of the cage show lines? What parts show planes?

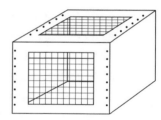

New Idea

The basic terms of geometry are **point** (point), **line** (lyn), and **plane** (playn). These three words are used to describe and define other terms in geometry. A point is a location in space. It can be represented by a dot. A line is made up of many points that extend in opposite directions without ending. A plane is a flat surface that does not end.

Example: Name two points, a line, and a plane in this figure.

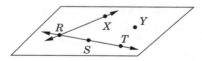

A point is named by a capital letter. Two of the points in the figure are point X and point Y.

A line is named by any two points on it and the symbol $\longleftrightarrow$. One of the lines in the figure is $\overleftrightarrow{RT}$. Read $\overleftrightarrow{RT}$ as "line RT."

A plane is named by any three points that do not all lie in a straight line. One way to name the plane represented by the figure is plane RYT.

1. A line is named $\overleftrightarrow{MN}$. What are the names of two points on the line? How do you know?

_____

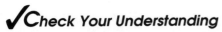

Focus on the Idea

A point is shown by a dot. A line is made up of many points that lie in a straight line. A plane is a flat surface that has no end.

Practice

Draw the two points on a line. Then name the line. The first one is done for you.

2. point P and point Q

$\overleftrightarrow{PQ}$

3. point E and point F

_____

4. point Z and point W

5. point B and point C

_____   _____

Name the points in the plane. Then name the plane. The first one is done for you.

6.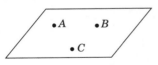

points A, B, C

plane ABC

7.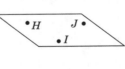

_____

_____

8.

_____

_____

9.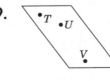

_____

_____

10. Draw a figure showing at least three points.

   a. Name the points and the plane that contain them.

   _____

   b. In your figure, how many lines can you draw containing two points?

   _____

   c. Draw the lines. Name them.

   _____

11. Draw a figure showing at least four points.

   a. Name the points and the plane.

   _____

   b. How many lines can you draw containing the points?

   _____

   c. Draw the lines. Name them.

   _____

Extend the Idea

Three or more points that can be connected with one straight line are called **collinear points** (coh-LIHN-ee-er points). Points that cannot be connected with a straight line are called **noncollinear points** (nahn-coh-LIHN-ee-er points).

Example: Name the collinear points. Then name the noncollinear points.

Points *A*, *B*, and *C* are collinear.

Points *A*, *B*, and *D* are noncollinear.

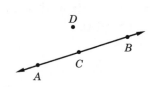

Points that lie on one plane are called **coplanar points** (coh-PLAY-ner points). Points that lie on different planes are called **noncoplanar points** (nahn-coh-PLAY-ner points).

Example: Name the coplanar points. Then name the noncoplanar points.

Points *X*, *Y*, *Z*, and *Q* are coplanar.

Points *M*, *N*, *P*, and *Q* are noncoplanar.

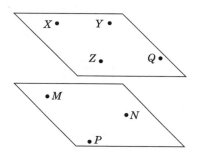

✓Check the Math

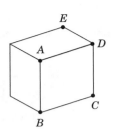

12. Ruby drew this picture. She said points *A*, *B*, and *D* are collinear and coplanar. Is she right? Explain.

_____

Practice

13. Draw three collinear points *D, E,* and *F*. Name the line they form.

_____

14. Draw a picture that shows coplanar points and noncoplanar points.

   a. Name the plane. _____

   b. Name three coplanar points. _____

   c. Name three collinear points. _____

Apply the Idea

15. Think about the cage that Ury is building.

   a. Draw a picture of a cage. Show three noncollinear points on the cage. Label the points *A, B,* and *C*. Is there a plane that contains the three points? If so, name the plane.

   _____

   b. On your cage, draw a fourth point that is not in the same plane as points *A, B,* and *C*. Label the new point *D*. Name all planes formed by any three of the points.

   _____

16. Work in a small group. Find a way to draw four segments that will pass through every point shown on the right. As you draw, do not take your pencil off the paper.

Write About It

17. Draw two points. Can more than one line be drawn through your two points? Why or why not? Draw a picture to prove your answer.

_____

18. Can two lines intersect in two points? Why or why not? Draw a picture to prove your answer.

_____

▶1•2 Line Segments and Rays

IN THIS LESSON, YOU WILL LEARN

To recognize line segments and rays

WORDS TO LEARN

Line segment *a part of a line that consists of two points and all the points between them*

Endpoints *points that represent the starting point of a ray or one of the two points that represent the ends of a line segment*

Ray *the part of a line that starts at one point and extends endlessly in one direction*

The lights went out in Arianne's apartment building. She is using a flashlight to find her way to her friend Joanna's apartment. Each narrow beam of light from the flashlight is an example of a ray. Arianne's straight path from her apartment to her friend's is an example of a line segment since it has a beginning and an end.

New Idea

A **line segment** (lyn SEHG-mehnt) is part of a line. A line segment consists of two **endpoints** (ehnd-points) and all the points between them. A **ray** (ray) is also part of a line. It has one endpoint and extends in one direction without ending.

A line segment is named by its two endpoints. The two endpoints are two points that represent the ends of a line segment. Line segment XY ($\overline{XY}$) or YX ($\overline{YX}$) is shown at the right.

A ray is named by its endpoint, the point that represents the starting point of a ray, and another point. The endpoint of a ray is always named first. Ray YZ ($\overrightarrow{YZ}$) is shown.

✓Check the Math

1. In $\overrightarrow{NM}$, is the endpoint of the ray point N? How do you know?

_____

_____

Focus on the Idea

A line segment is part of a line. It consists of two endpoints and all points between them. A ray is part of a line that begins at one endpoint and extends endlessly in one direction.

Practice

Draw the following figures. Name the endpoint or endpoints of each figure. The first one is done for you.

2. line segment *RS*

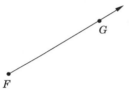

<u>point R, point S</u>

3. ray *GF*

_____

4. $\overline{MN}$

_____

Name each figure. Tell whether it is a *line segment* or a *ray*.

5.

_____

_____

6.

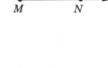

_____

_____

7.

_____

_____

Apply the Idea

8. Arianne and her friends are decorating the gym with crepe paper for a dance. Draw line segments to show at least two different ways Arianne can leave her spot and connect with all of her friends just once.

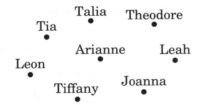

Write About It

9. How are a line, a line segment, and a ray alike? How are they different?

_____

_____

◀1•3 Angles

No matter where you are—in a classroom, at home, or walking down the street—angles of many sizes are part of the things that surround you. As long ago as 300 B.C., angles and their parts were identified by the same words that we use for them today.

New Idea

An **angle** (AN-guhl) is a figure formed by two rays that have the same endpoint. The rays that form the angle are called the **sides of an angle** (sydz). The endpoint is called the **vertex of an angle** (VER-tehks).

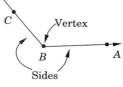

An angle can be named by three letters and the symbol ∠. The angle shown at the right can be called ∠ABC or just ∠B. The sides of the angle are $\overrightarrow{BA}$ and $\overrightarrow{BC}$. The vertex is point B. When you use three letters to name an angle, the letter at the vertex should be the middle letter.

✓Check Your Understanding

An angle is named ∠HIJ.

1. Is point I the vertex of the angle? How do you know?

   _____

2. Are $\overrightarrow{IH}$ and $\overrightarrow{IJ}$ the sides of the angle? How do you know?

   _____

◀Focus on the Idea

An angle is formed by two rays that have the same endpoint. The sides of an angle are the two rays that form the angle. The vertex of an angle is the point at which the sides meet.

Practice

Draw a figure to represent each angle. Name the vertex and the sides of each angle. The first one is done for you.

3. ∠*FGH*

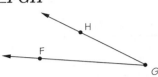

sides: <u> $\overrightarrow{GF}$ and $\overrightarrow{GH}$ </u>

vertex: <u>   point G   </u>

4. ∠*LMP*

sides: _____

vertex: _____

5. ∠*HJK*

sides: _____

vertex: _____

6. ∠*WXY*

sides: _____

vertex: _____

Write the letter of the correct name for each figure.

a. ∠*BAC* **b.** ∠*PQR*

c. ∠*ABC* **d.** ∠*TUV*

e. ∠*QRS*

7.

_____

8.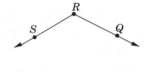

_____

9.

_____

10.

_____

11.

_____

Apply the Idea

12. Look around you and find examples of angles. In the margin, draw pictures of the examples you found and show the angles.

✏ Write About It

13. Suppose a friend was absent from today's math class. Describe what you think your friend needs to know about this lesson. Make any drawings you need for illustration.

_____

_____

1•4 Parallel and Perpendicular Lines

IN THIS LESSON, YOU WILL LEARN

To recognize parallel lines and perpendicular lines

WORDS TO LEARN

Intersecting lines *two lines that meet, or cross, at exactly one point*

Parallel lines *lines in the same plane that do not meet; they are always the same distance apart*

Right angle *an angle with a measure of 90°*

Perpendicular lines *lines that meet at a right angle*

Examples of parallel lines are all around you. The lines on notebook paper are all parallel, so are the crosswalks on streets, and the top and bottom of a window. Perpendicular lines are also all around you. The corner of a room where a wall meets the ceiling, the margin line and the writing lines on notebook paper, and the top and sides of your math book are all examples of perpendicular lines. Look around you. Where else do you see parallel and perpendicular lines right now?

New Idea

Lines that meet at exactly one point are called **intersecting lines** (ihn-ter-SEHKT-ihng lynz). Lines in the same plane that do not intersect are called **parallel lines** (PA-ruh-lehl lynz). The symbol ∥ means "is parallel to."

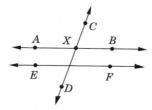

Examples: Name two intersecting lines. Then name two parallel lines.

$\overleftrightarrow{AB}$ and $\overleftrightarrow{CD}$ intersect at point X.
$\overleftrightarrow{AB}$ and $\overleftrightarrow{EF}$ do not intersect.
They are parallel lines.
$\overleftrightarrow{AB} \parallel \overleftrightarrow{EF}$

1. Julio said that $\overleftrightarrow{CD}$ and $\overleftrightarrow{CB}$ are parallel. Marie said that she knew he was wrong without seeing a diagram of these lines. How did Marie know Julio was wrong?

_____

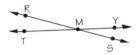

Focus on the Idea

Lines intersect if they meet at exactly one point. Lines are parallel if they are in the same plane and do not meet.

Practice

Draw a label a pair of intersecting lines so that they intersect at the given point. The first one is done for you.

2. $\overleftrightarrow{RS}$ and $\overleftrightarrow{TY}$ intersect at point M.

3. $\overleftrightarrow{XY}$ and $\overleftrightarrow{ZY}$ intersect at point Y.

4. $\overleftrightarrow{RS}$ and $\overleftrightarrow{TU}$ intersect at point V.

5. $\overleftrightarrow{IJ}$ and $\overleftrightarrow{KL}$ intersect at point I.

Name each pair of parallel lines, first with words and then with symbols. The first one is done for you.

6.

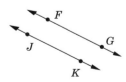

Line FG is parallel to line JK.

$\overleftrightarrow{FG} \parallel \overleftrightarrow{JK}$

7.

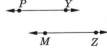

_____

_____

8.

_____

_____

9.

_____

_____

Write the letter of the correct description for each figure.

10.   _____

11. 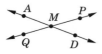 _____

12.   _____

13.   _____

a. $\overleftrightarrow{QM} \parallel \overleftrightarrow{AD}$

b. $\overleftrightarrow{AD}$ and $\overleftrightarrow{PQ}$ intersect at point M.

c. $\overleftrightarrow{RT}$ and $\overleftrightarrow{XU}$ intersect at point V.

d. $\overleftrightarrow{RT} \parallel \overleftrightarrow{QV}$

Extend the Idea

You know that angles are measured in degrees. The symbol for degrees is °. Where lines intersect, angles are formed. An angle with a measure of 90° is called a **right angle** (reyet AN-guhl). Lines that meet at a right angle are called **perpendicular lines** (per-pehn-DIHK-yoo-ler lynz).

Since $\angle ABC$ has a measure of 90°, it is a right angle. $\angle ABD$ is also a right angle. The symbol at the vertex of each angle indicates a right angle.

The symbol ⊥ means "is perpendicular to." In the drawing, $\overleftrightarrow{AB} \perp \overleftrightarrow{DC}$.

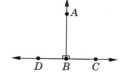

✓Check Your Understanding

14. Draw a pair of perpendicular lines. Be sure to use a ruler or straightedge to help you draw, so you can be sure that your lines are perpendicular.

Practice

For exercises 15 to 17, use the letters and symbols in this figure to name each pair of lines.

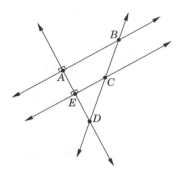

15. Name two pairs of intersecting lines.

_____

16. Name two pairs of perpendicular lines.

_____

17. Name two parallel lines.

_____

Apply the Idea

18. Think about the different types of lines that are painted on streets.

    a. Which of them are examples of parallel lines?

    _____

    b. Which of them are examples of perpendicular lines?

    _____

✏ Write About It

19. Can two parallel lines be perpendicular to the same line? Why or why not? Draw a picture as part of your answer.

_____

_____

◢1•5 Angles Formed by Intersecting Lines

◢ IN THIS LESSON, YOU WILL LEARN

To recognize angles formed by intersecting lines

WORDS TO LEARN

Vertical angles *pairs of angles formed by lines that intersect*

Transversal *a line that intersects two or more lines*

Interior angles *angles that are enclosed between two parallel lines crossed by a transversal*

Exterior angles *angles that lie outside two lines crossed by a transversal*

Alternate interior angles *angles that lie on opposite sides of a transversal and are enclosed between two lines*

Alternate exterior angles *two exterior angles that lie on opposite sides of a transversal and are outside two lines*

The building across from Kendall's doctor's office has an unusual design on the outside. Kendall tried to draw a picture of it. He noticed that the design had some parallel lines and some intersecting lines. The lines formed many different angles.

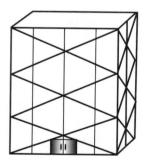

New Idea

When any two lines intersect, they form two pairs of **vertical angles** (VER-tih-kuhl AN-guhl) across from each other. A **transversal** (trans-VER-suhl) is a line that intersects two or more lines. When two lines are crossed by a transversal, the four angles that lie between the two lines are **interior angles** (ihn-TEER-ee-er AN-guhlz). The four angles that lie outside of the two lines crossed by the transversal are **exterior angles** (ehks-TEER-ee-er AN-guhlz).

Examples: $\overleftrightarrow{XY}$ is a transversal that crosses $\overleftrightarrow{AB}$ and $\overleftrightarrow{CD}$.

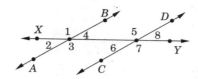

a. Name the angles formed where $\overleftrightarrow{XY}$ crosses $\overleftrightarrow{AB}$.

The four angles formed where $\overleftrightarrow{XY}$ crosses $\overleftrightarrow{AB}$ are $\angle 1$, $\angle 2$, $\angle 3$, and $\angle 4$.

b. Name two pairs of vertical angles formed where $\overleftrightarrow{XY}$ and $\overleftrightarrow{AB}$ intersect.

$\angle 1$ and $\angle 3$ are vertical angles. $\angle 2$ and $\angle 4$ are vertical angles.

c. Name the angles that lie between $\overleftrightarrow{AB}$ and $\overleftrightarrow{CD}$.

The four angles that lie between $\overleftrightarrow{AB}$ and $\overleftrightarrow{CD}$ are $\angle 3$, $\angle 4$, $\angle 5$, and $\angle 6$. These angles are called interior angles.

d. Name the four angles that lie outside $\overleftrightarrow{AB}$ and $\overleftrightarrow{CD}$.

The four angles that lie outside $\overleftrightarrow{AB}$ and $\overleftrightarrow{CD}$ are $\angle 1$, $\angle 2$, $\angle 7$, and $\angle 8$. These angles are called exterior angles.

Focus on the Idea

A transversal is a line that intersects two or more lines. Where two lines cross, the opposite angles they form are called vertical angles. Where two lines are crossed by a transversal, the four angles formed between the two lines are called interior angles. The four angles formed on opposite sides of the two lines are called exterior angles.

Practice

Draw and label two lines that intersect at the given point. Name two pairs of vertical angles. The first one is done for you.

1. $\overleftrightarrow{MN}$ and $\overleftrightarrow{TV}$ intersect at point X.

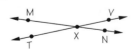

$\angle MXT$ and $\angle VXN$

$\angle MXV$ and $\angle TXN$

2. $\overleftrightarrow{LK}$ and $\overleftrightarrow{GH}$ intersect at point M.

_____

_____

3. $\overleftrightarrow{CD}$ and $\overleftrightarrow{EF}$ intersect at point P.

4. $\overleftrightarrow{ST}$ and $\overleftrightarrow{QR}$ intersect at point U.

_____

_____

_____

_____

5. Draw two parallel lines, $\overleftrightarrow{MN}$ and $\overleftrightarrow{OP}$. Draw a transversal that intersects both lines. Number all the angles that are formed.

a. Use the numbers to name four interior angles.

_____

b. Use the numbers to name all four exterior angles.

_____

Use the figure for exercises 6 to 8.

6. Name all pairs of vertical angles.

_____

7. Name all four interior angles.

_____

8. Name all four exterior angles.

_____

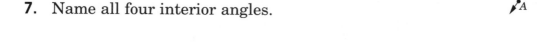

Extend the Idea

Interior angles that lie on opposite sides of a transversal are called **alternate interior angles** (AWL-ter-niht ihn-TEER-ee-er AN-guhlz). Exterior angles that lie on opposite sides of a transversal are called **alternate exterior angles** (AWL-ter-nuht ehks-TEER-ee-er AN-guhlz).

Example: Use the figure below. Name all pairs of alternate interior angles and alternate exterior angles.

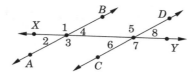

$\angle 4$ and $\angle 6$ are alternate interior angles.

$\angle 3$ and $\angle 5$ are alternate interior angles.

$\angle 1$ and $\angle 7$ are alternate exterior angles.

$\angle 2$ and $\angle 8$ are alternate exterior angles.

9. Draw two lines. Then draw a transversal that crosses both of them. Number all the angles that are formed.

   a. Name both pairs of alternate interior angles.

   _____

   b. Name both pairs of alternate exterior angles.

   _____

Practice

Use the figure for exercises 10 and 11.

10. Name both pairs of alternate interior angles.

    _____

11. Name both pairs of alternate exterior angles.

    _____

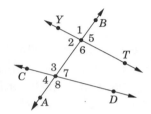

Apply the Idea

12. Number the angles in the picture of the building that Kendall drew. Use the numbers to name:

    a. all pairs of vertical angles. _____

    b. all interior angles. _____

    c. all pairs of alternate interior angles. _____

    d. all exterior angles. _____

    e. all pairs of alternate exterior angles. _____

✏ Write About It

13. Explain how to draw two lines and a transversal so that the following are formed: six pairs of vertical angles, six pairs of alternate interior angles, six pairs of alternate exterior angles. Draw a picture at the right as part of your answer.

    _____

    _____

14. How many transversals can you draw that cross two lines? How do you know? Draw a picture at the right to prove your answer.

    _____

    _____

► IN THIS LESSON, YOU WILL LEARN

To recognize adjacent angles and linear pairs

WORDS TO LEARN

Adjacent angles *two angles with one vertex and a common side*

Linear pair *two adjacent angles whose noncommon sides form a straight line*

The hands on a clock form pairs of angles. Two of the angles shown by the hands on this clock are adjacent angles. One angle is formed by the minute hand and the hour hand. The other is formed by the hour hand and the second hand. These angles have the same vertex. The hour hand is their common side. The minute hand and the second hand together form a straight line, so the angles are also a linear pair.

3:08 and 38 seconds

New Idea

Two angles with the same vertex and a common side are **adjacent angles** (uh-JAY-sehnt AN-guhlz). Two adjacent angles whose noncommon sides form a straight line are a **linear pair** (LIHN-ee-er pair).

Examples: ∠ABC and ∠CBD are adjacent angles. Name their their common side and their vertex.

$\overrightarrow{BC}$ is a side of both angles.
Point B is the vertex of both angles.
Since $\overrightarrow{BA}$ and $\overrightarrow{BD}$ form a straight line, ∠ABC and ∠CBD are adjacent angles and a linear pair.

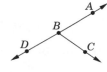

✓Check the Math

1. Circle the adjacent angles in the figures below.
2. Put a box around the linear pairs.

  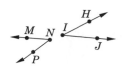

Focus on the Idea

Two angles that share a vertex and one side are called adjacent angles. Adjacent angles whose noncommon sides form a straight line are called a linear pair.

Practice

Tell whether each pair of adjacent angles is also a linear pair. Write *yes* or *no*. The first one is done for you.

3.    _____yes_____

4.    _____

5. 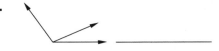   _____

6.   _____

For exercises 7 to 9, draw and label a figure that matches the description.

7. Two angles that are not adjacent

8. Two angles that are adjacent but are not a linear pair

9. Two angles that form a linear pair

Apply the Idea

10. On page 18 you saw an example of a time at which the minute and second hands on a clock form a straight line. At what time would the hour hand and the second hand form a straight line? Draw a picture at the right to prove your answer.

_____

Write About It

11. Can angles that are not adjacent form a linear pair? Explain why or why not. Draw a picture at the right to prove your answer.

_____

_____

_____

Intersecting and Parallel Planes

↰ IN THIS LESSON, YOU WILL LEARN

To recognize intersecting planes, parallel planes, skew lines, and half planes

WORDS TO LEARN

Intersecting planes *planes that meet in one line*

Parallel planes *planes that do not intersect*

Skew lines *lines that do not intersect and are not in the same plane*

Half plane *part of a plane made up of one line, called the edge, and all points on one side of the edge*

Lamar has built four steps up to the front of a house. He nailed boards together to make each stair. Each board represents part of a plane. Some of the boards meet in one line. Some of the boards never intersect.

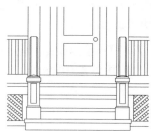

New Idea

Planes that meet are called **intersecting planes** (ihn-ter-SEHKT-ihng playnz). Where they meet, they form a line. Planes that do not intersect are called **parallel planes** (PA-ruh-lehl playnz). Lines that do not intersect and are not in the same plane are called **skew lines** (skyoo lynz).

Example: In the figure below, which planes intersect? Which planes are parallel?

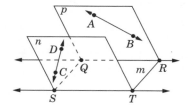

Planes p and m intersect to form line $\overleftrightarrow{QR}$. Planes m and n intersect to form line $\overleftrightarrow{ST}$. Planes n and p are parallel.

$\overleftrightarrow{AB}$ and $\overleftrightarrow{CD}$ are in different planes and so, will not intersect. They are skew lines.

✓**Check Your Understanding**

Use figures a to d for exercises 1 and 2.

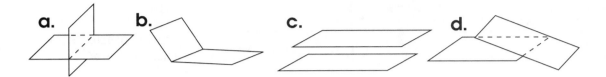

1. Circle the intersecting planes.
2. Put a box around the parallel lines.

Focus on the Idea

Planes that meet along one line are called intersecting planes. Planes that do not intersect are called parallel planes. Lines that do not intersect and are not in the same plane are skew lines.

Practice

Write whether each figure shows *intersecting planes* **or** *parallel planes.* **The first one is done for you.**

3.

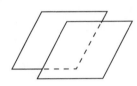

_____parallel planes_____

4.

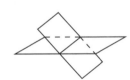

_____

5.

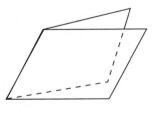

_____

6.

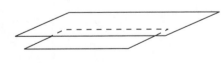

_____

Write the letter of the correct description for each figure.

7.

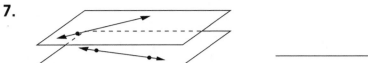

_____

a. planes intersecting at $\overleftrightarrow{LK}$

b. parallel planes and parallel lines

8.

_____

c. planes intersecting at $\overleftrightarrow{TR}$

d. planes intersecting at $\overleftrightarrow{DF}$

9.

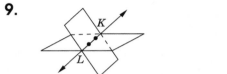

_____

e. parallel planes and skew lines

10.

_____

11.

_____

Extend the Idea

Part of a plane made up of a line and all points on one side of the line is called a **half plane** (haf playn). The line is called the edge of the half plane.

Example: Name the line that is the edge of the half plane.

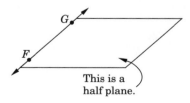

This is a half plane.

$\overleftrightarrow{FG}$ is the edge of the half plane.

Practice

Name the edge of the half plane shown in each figure.

12.

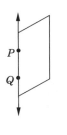

_____

13.

_____

14.

_____

15.

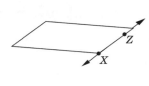

_____

Identify the half planes in the figure.

16. How many half planes are shown with edge $\overleftrightarrow{TR}$?_____

17. How many half planes are shown with edge $\overleftrightarrow{AB}$?_____

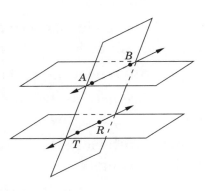

Apply the Idea

18. Look back at the four steps Lamar built.

  a. How many half planes will the steps form?_____

  b. How many boards did he use to build the steps?_____

⟋ Write About It

19. Give an example of more than two planes meeting at a single line. Draw a picture to illustrate your example.

_____

_____

_____

_____

Chapter 1 Review

In This Chapter, You Have Learned

- To recognize a point, a line, a plane, a line segment, and a ray
- To recognize an angle and its parts
- To recognize parallel and perpendicular lines
- To recognize angles formed by intersecting lines, adjacent angles, and linear pairs
- To recognize intersecting planes, parallel planes, skew lines, and half planes

Words You Know

From the lists of "Words To Learn," choose the word or phrase that best completes each statement.

1. A(n) _____ is made up of two rays that have the same endpoint.

2. Lines with one point that are the same are called _____ lines.

3. An angle with a measure of 90° is a(n) _____ angle.

4. Lines that are not parallel and are in parallel planes are called _____ lines.

5. Two angles with sides that form straight lines are _____ angles.

6. A(n) _____ is a flat surface that has no end.

7. Lines that intersect to form a right angle are _____ lines.

More Practice

Use the figure below for exercises 8 to 10.

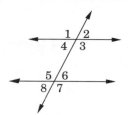

8. Name all vertical angles.

   _____

9. Name both pairs of alternate interior angles.

   _____

10. Name both pairs of alternate exterior angles.

    _____

Write the letter of the best name for each of exercises 11 to 19.

a. point   **b.** linear pair of angles   **c.** line

d. line segment   **e.** parallel lines   **f.** ray

g. vertical angles 1 and 2   **h.** perpendicular lines   **i.** right angle

11.

12.

13.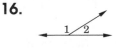

_____

14.

15.

16.

_____

17.

18.

19.

_____

Problems You Can Solve

20. The roads in Birmingham, Alabama, are shown at the right. The roads running north and south are called streets. The roads running east and west are called avenues.

   a. What can you say about all of the avenues?

   _____

   b. What can you say about all of the streets?

   _____

   c. What can you say about the intersection of any street and avenue?

   _____

21. For Your Portfolio Suppose you draw three lines. Describe the different ways the three lines can relate to each other. Draw pictures to prove your answers.

_____

_____

Chapter 1 Practice Test

Use the figure at the right for exercises 1 to 15.

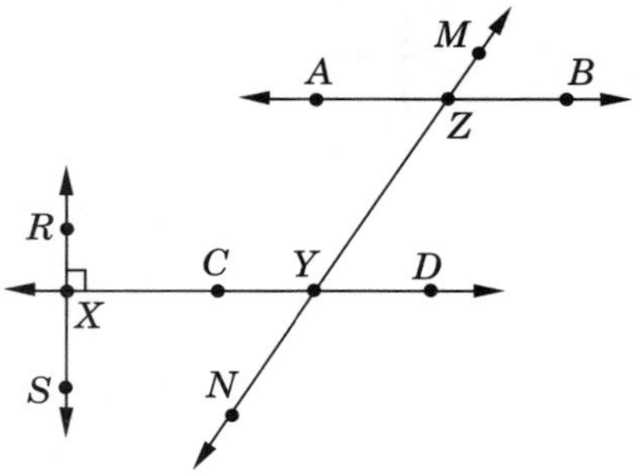

1. Name three points. ____________
2. Name two line segments. ____________
3. Name two lines. ____________
4. Name two rays. ____________
5. Name a pair of adjacent angles. ____________
6. Name a pair of vertical angles. ____________
7. Name a linear pair of angles. ____________
8. Name a right angle. ____________
9. Name a pair of perpendicular lines.
____
10. Name a pair of parallel lines. ____________
11. Name a pair of intersecting lines. ____________
12. Name a transversal. ____________
13. Name a pair of alternate interior angles. ____________
14. Name a pair of alternate exterior angles. ____________
15. Name a pair of intersecting lines. ____________
16. Name three collinear points. ____________

Solve.

17. Laverne's uncle builds skyscrapers. He tells Laverne that the vertical sides of a skyscraper are not parallel. Why do you think this is true?

____

18. Think of the floors of a skyscraper as planes. Are the planes parallel or perpendicular to each other?

____

19. If the floors of a skyscraper are planes, what kind of angles do they form with the sides of the building?

____

20. Draw a picture to illustrate your answers to exercises 17 and 18.

Chapter 2
Angles

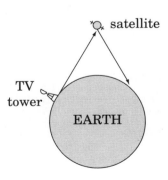

OBJECTIVES:

In this chapter, you will learn

- *To recognize straight, right, acute, and obtuse angles*
- *To recognize complementary and supplementary angles*
- *To measure angles with a protractor*
- *To draw angles with a protractor*
- *To recognize congruent line segments and congruent angles*
- *To recognize and draw the midpoint of a line segment*
- *To draw the bisector of a line segment*
- *To recognize and draw the bisector of an angle*
- *To recognize congruent angles formed by parallel lines and a transversal*
- *To recognize supplementary angles formed by parallel lines and a transversal*

The ancient Greeks used angle measurement and ratio to estimate the distance from Earth to each planet. Today, engineers, astronomers, and workers in the communications industry use angle measure for the same purpose. The principle on which cable television works depends on angle measurement.

Ray works for a cable television company that uses a satellite to transmit its programs across the country. Programs are first transmitted to the satellite, and then they are transmitted back to Earth at the same angle. If they are transmitted from Earth at an angle of 60°, at what angle is the transmission returned?

satellite

TV
tower

EARTH

↘2•1 Classifying Angles

Triangles are important in construction because they are rigid. The supports for this iron bridge form many types of angles. How are the angles different from each other?

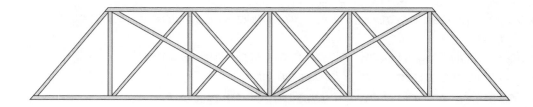

New Idea

Angles are grouped, or classified, by their size. An angle that measures less than 90° is an **acute angle** (uh-KYOOT AN-guhl). An angle that is greater than 90° and less than 180° is an **obtuse angle** (ahb-TOOS AN-guhl). An angle that measures 180° is a **straight angle** (strayt AN-guhl). The sides of a straight angle form a straight line.

Examples: An acute angle is smaller than a right angle.

∠*ABC* measures less than 90°. So, ∠*ABC* is an acute angle.

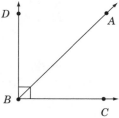

⤺**Remember**

A right angle measures 90°.

An obtuse angle is greater than a right angle and less than a straight angle.

∠*PQR* is greater than 90° and less than 180°. So, ∠*PQR* is an obtuse angle.

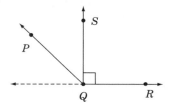

The sides of a straight angle are rays that extend in opposite directions. ∠*LMN* measures 180°. So, ∠*LMN* is a straight angle.

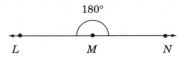

✓**Check the Math**

1. Karla drew ∠*ABC*, which measured 73°. She said it was an acute angle. Is Karla correct? Explain.

_____

**Focus on the Idea**

An acute angle is greater than 0° and less than 90°. An obtuse angle is greater than 90° and less than 180°. A straight angle measures 180°. It has sides that form a straight line.

Practice

Tell whether each angle is *right*, *straight*, *acute*, or *obtuse*. The first one is done for you.

2.

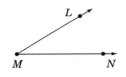

_____acute_____

3.

_____

4.

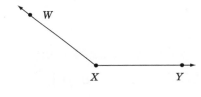

_____

5.

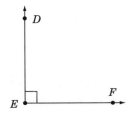

_____

6.

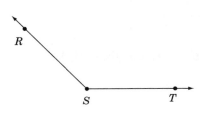

_____

7.

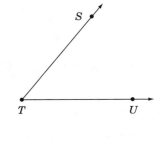

_____

Draw an example of each type of angle.

   8. acute angle   **9.** obtuse angle

   10. right angle   **11.** straight angle

Extend the Idea

This figure shows many different angles. Each of the angles can be classified as straight, right, acute, or obtuse.

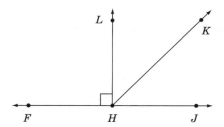

Examples: $\angle FHJ$ is a straight angle.

                     $\angle LHK$ is an acute angle.

                     $\angle FHL$ is a right angle.

                     $\angle FHK$ is an obtuse angle.

✓ Check Your Understanding

   12. Two adjacent angles have non-common sides that form a straight line. If one angle is acute, what kind of angle is the other one? How do you know?

_____

Practice

Use the figure above to answer exercises 13 to 16. If the angle is not shown, write *none*.

   13. If another obtuse angle is shown, name it. _____

   14. If another right angle is shown, name it. _____

   15. If another straight angle is shown, name it. _____

   16. How many angles are shown? _____

Use the figure to answer exercises 17 to 20.

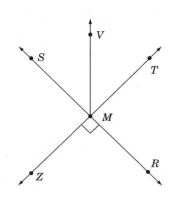

17. Name all straight angles.

_____

18. Name all right angles.

_____

19. Name all acute angles.

_____

20. Name all obtuse angles.

_____

Apply the Idea

Look back at the picture of the bridge supports on page 28. Label and name one of each type of angle shown.

21. straight angle _____

22. right angle _____

23. acute angle _____

24. obtuse angle _____

Write About It

25. Draw a pair of perpendicular lines.

a. What kinds of angles are formed by the lines you drew?

_____

b. How do you know?

_____

_____

_____

►2•2 Recognizing Complementary and Supplementary Angles

► IN THIS LESSON, YOU WILL LEARN
To recognize complementary and supplementary angles

WORDS TO LEARN
Complementary angles *two angles whose measures have a sum of 90°*
Supplementary angles *two angles whose measures have a sum of 180°*

Alejandro designs fences for a landscaping company. He uses the support boards for strength and for visual interest. The boards that support the fence form different angles. What kind of angles do they form?

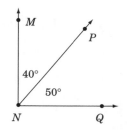

New Idea
Sometimes two angles can be grouped, or classified, by their sum. If the sum of the measures of two angles is 90°, the angles are called **complementary angles** (cahm-plu-MEHN-tah-ree AN-guhlz). If the sum of the measures of two angles is 180°, the angles are called **supplementary angles** (sup-luh-MEHN-tah-ree AN-guhlz).

Examples: The sum of the measures of complementary angles is 90°. So, two complementary angles that are adjacent form a right angle.

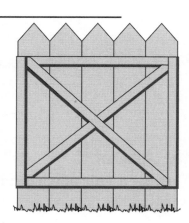

In this figure, ∠*MNP* measures 40° and ∠*PNQ* measures 50°. Since 40° + 50° = 90°, ∠*MNP* and ∠*PNQ* are complementary.

The sum of the measures of supplementary angles is 180°. So, two supplementary angles that are adjacent form a straight angle.

In this figure, ∠*XYZ* measures 110°
and ∠*ZYW* measures 70°. Since
110° + 70° = 180°, ∠*XYZ* and
∠*ZYW* are supplementary.

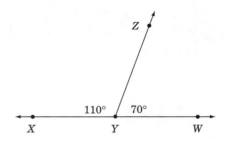

✓*Check Your Understanding*

1. Are two right angles supplementary? How do you know?

_____

_____

◢ Focus on the Idea

*Complementary angles are two angles whose
measures have a sum of 90°.*
*Supplementary angles are two angles whose
measures have a sum of 180°.*

Practice

**Tell whether each pair of angles is *complementary* or
supplementary. The first one is done for you.**

2.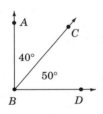

   complementary

3.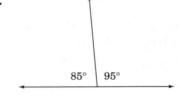

   _____

4.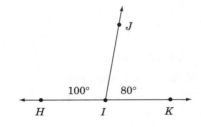

   _____

5.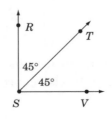

   _____

Use the figure at the right. Write a letter, *a*, *b*, or *c*, to correctly identify each pair of angles.

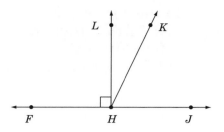

6. ∠*FHL* and ∠*LHJ* _____

7. ∠*FHK* and ∠*KHJ* _____

8. ∠*LHK* and ∠*KHJ* _____

a. supplementary angles
b. complementary angles
c. right, supplementary angles

Extend the Idea

Two angles can be complementary or supplementary, even if they are not adjacent angles.

Examples: In this figure, ∠1 has a measure of 25° and ∠2 has a measure of 65°. Since 25° + 65° = 90°, ∠1 and ∠2 are complementary.

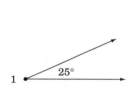 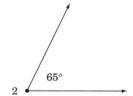

In this figure, ∠3 has a measure of 115° and ∠4 has a measure of 65°. Since 115° + 65° = 180°, ∠3 and ∠4 are supplementary.

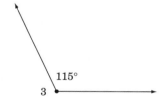 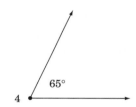

✓ Check the Math

9. Consuela measures a pair of angles as 44° and 46°. She says they are complementary. Is she correct? Explain your answer.

_____

_____

_____

Practice

10. Draw and label two angles that are both adjacent and complementary.

11. Draw and label two angles that are supplementary.

12. If the measure of $\angle ABC = 35°$, what is the measure of its complement? _____

13. If the measure of $\angle DEF = 115°$, what is the measure of its supplement? _____

Use the angles below for exercises 14 to 15.

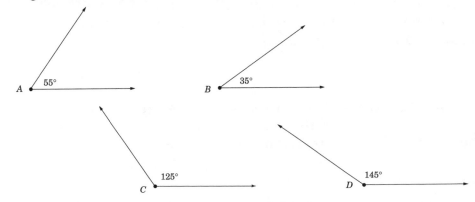

14. Name one pair of complementary angles. _____
15. Name two pairs of supplementary angles. _____

Apply the Idea

Look back at the supports on the fence on page 32. Label and name a pair of each kind of angle.

16. complementary angles _____
17. supplementary angles _____

Write About It

18. **a.** Can two acute angles be supplementary? Explain.

_____

b. Draw a picture to prove your answer.

◄2•3 Using a Protractor to Measure Angles

IN THIS LESSON, YOU WILL LEARN

To measure angles with a protractor

WORDS TO LEARN

Protractor *a tool that is used to measure angles in degrees*

Ms. Aunko is a surveyor. Some of her responsibilities include mapping streets, highways, building sites, and bridges. Part of her job is to find the measures of angles of streets where buildings are about to be built. She measures angles in degrees.

New Idea

A **protractor** (PROH-trak-ter) is a tool used to measure an angle in degrees. Use the inner scale of the protractor to measure an acute angle. Use the outer scale to measure an obtuse angle.

☞Remember

The vertex of an angle is the point where the rays, or sides, of the angle meet.

Example: To measure $\angle RST$, first find the center point at the bottom of the protractor. Put this point on top of vertex S.

Position the 0° line on the protractor on $\overrightarrow{ST}$.

Find the point where $\overrightarrow{SR}$ intersects the protractor. Read the number on the inner scale at this point.

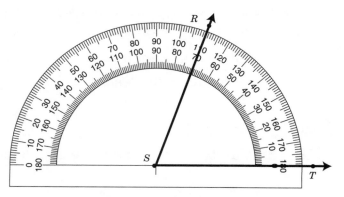

The number on the inner scale is 70. So the measure of $\angle RST$ is 70°. This can be written using symbols. The symbol for size or measure is m. The symbol for angle is $\angle$.

The measure of $\angle RST$ is 70°. Write: $m\angle RST = 70°$.

Focus on the Idea

A protractor is a tool for measuring angles in degrees.

Practice

Find the measure of each angle. Use symbols to write the measure. The first one is done for you.

1.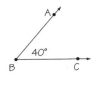

2.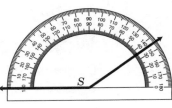

3.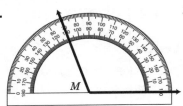

$m\angle ABC = 40°$ _____

_____

_____

Use a protractor to find the measure of each angle. (You may use a straightedge to extend the angle rays before you measure.)

4.

5.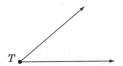

6.

G T K

_____

_____

_____

Apply the Idea

7. Ms. Aunko is making a map of several streets she is surveying. What is the measure of each angle formed by each street corner?

4th Avenue

Main Street   Elm Street

1st Avenue

  a. Main St. and 1st Ave. _____

  b. Elm St. and 1st Ave. _____

  c. Elm St. and 4th Ave. _____

  d. Main St. and 4th Ave. _____

Write About It

8. Do you think the angles at the right have equal measures? Why? Use a protractor to measure the angles to prove your answer.

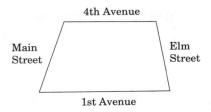

A B

_____

_____

Using a Protractor to Draw Angles

▼ **IN THIS LESSON, YOU WILL LEARN**

To draw angles with a protractor

WORDS TO LEARN

Degrees *units of measure for angles, each of which is equal to $\frac{1}{360}$ of a circle*

Marcus is in charge of assigning locations for his neighborhood art fair. To make a map of the area, Marcus must draw all the street corners at the correct angles. How can he do this?

New Idea

A protractor can be used to draw an angle with a given measure. An angle is measured in **degrees**, units of measure, each of which is equal to $\frac{1}{360}$ of a circle.

Example: Draw $\angle MNP$ that measures 50°.

Step 1 Draw a ray and label it $\overrightarrow{NP}$.

Step 2 Put the center point of the protractor on point N.

Step 3 Line up the 0° line on the inner scale of the protractor with $\overrightarrow{NP}$.

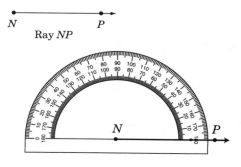

Step 4 Find the point on the inner scale labeled 50. Mark point M at this point.

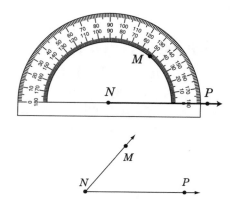

Step 5 Remove the protractor and draw $\overrightarrow{NM}$.

The measure of $\angle MNP$ is 50°.

Focus on the Idea

A protractor can be used to draw an angle with a given measure or size.

Practice

Draw and label each angle. The first one is done for you.

1. $m\angle ABC = 100°$

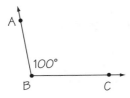

2. $m\angle RST = 80°$

3. $m\angle LMN = 150°$

4. $m\angle HIJ = 95°$

5. $m\angle QRS = 20°$

6. $m\angle WXY = 170°$

Apply the Idea

7. The measure of $\angle DEF$ is 40°.

   a. How can you draw an angle that is adjacent to $\angle DEF$ and that has the same measure?

   _____

   b. Draw a picture to prove your answer.

8. On his map of the art fair, Marcus draws four streets at an intersection. The streets intersect at angles of 60°, 90°, 110°, and 100°. Use the margin to draw the intersection.

Write About It

9. a. How can you use a protractor to divide a right angle into two angles with measures of 30° and 60°?

   _____

   b. Draw a picture in the margin to prove your answer.

▸2•5 Recognizing Congruent Line Segments and Angles

▸ **IN THIS LESSON, YOU WILL LEARN**

To recognize congruent line segments and congruent angles

WORDS TO LEARN

Congruent *figures that have the same size and shape*

Congruent angles *angles that have the same measure or size*

Congruent line segments *line segments that are the same length*

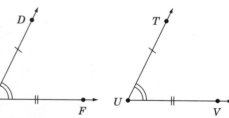

Marita built this trellis. Some of the lines and angles of the trellis have the same measure. Can you find them?

New Idea

Congruent (KAHN-groo-uhnt) figures have the same size and shape. If two shapes are exactly the same, they are congruent. Angles that have the same measure are called **congruent angles** (KAHN-groo-uhnt AN-guhlz). Line segments that have the same length are called **congruent line segments** (KAHN-groo-uhnt leyen SEHG-mehnts). This symbol is used to show congruent angles and congruent line segments: ≅ . It means "is congruent to."

Examples: $\angle DEF$ and $\angle TUV$ each measure 65°. Since they have the same measure, they are congruent angles. We write this using symbols.

$\angle DEF \cong \angle TUV$

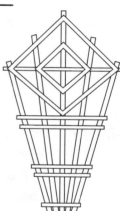

In a drawing, we use arcs or curves to show that angles are congruent. Because $\angle DEF \cong \angle TUV$, both angles are marked with two arcs.

In the figure, $\overline{UV}$ and $\overline{EF}$ have the same length. They are congruent line segments. Because $\overline{UV} \cong \overline{EF}$, both segments are marked with two hatch marks.

◢ Focus on the Idea

Congruent figures have the same size and shape. Congruent angles are angles that have the same measure. Congruent line segments are line segments that have the same length.

Practice

Use symbols to name the congruent line segments or congruent angles shown in each figure. The first two are done for you.

1.

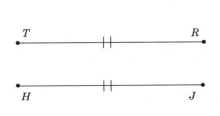

$\overline{TR} \cong \overline{HJ}$

2.

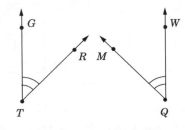

$\angle GTR \cong \angle MQW$

3.

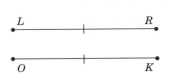

_____

4.

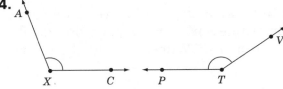

_____

Use the figure at the right for exercises 5 and 6.

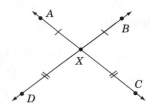

5. Use symbols to name all pairs of congruent line segments. _____

6. Use symbols to name all pairs of congruent angles. _____

Apply the Idea

7. Look back at Marita's trellis on page 40. Label two line segments that you think are congruent. Describe how you can check to see if they are congruent.

_____

✎ Write About It

8. Two angles are both supplementary and congruent. What are the measures of the angles? Explain your answer.

_____

_____

◢2•6 Bisecting Line Segments

◢ **IN THIS LESSON, YOU WILL LEARN**

To recognize and draw the midpoint of a line segment

To draw the bisector of a line segment

WORDS TO LEARN

Midpoint a point that divides a line segment into two equal parts

Bisects divides into two equal parts

Bisector a line that divides an angle or a line segment into two equal parts

Compass a tool used to draw circles and arcs

Straightedge a tool used to draw straight lines

Tia wants to make a clay sculpture in her art class. She first must build a wire framework for the clay. She needs to cut a piece of wire into two equal pieces. Where should she cut the wire?

New Idea

The **midpoint** (MIHD-point) is a point on a line segment that divides the line segment into two equal parts. The midpoint **bisects** (beye-SEHKTS) the line segment because it divides the line segment into two equal parts.

Example: In this figure, point P divides $\overline{XY}$ into two equal parts. So point P is the midpoint of $\overline{XY}$. We can also say that point P bisects $\overline{XY}$. $\overleftrightarrow{MN}$ is called a **bisector** (BY-sehkt-er) of $\overline{XY}$ because $\overleftrightarrow{MN}$ contains point P.

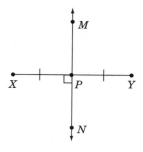

✓Check Your Understanding

1. $\overline{JK}$ and $\overline{RS}$ intersect at point T. If $\overline{JT} \cong \overline{TK}$ and $\overline{RT} \cong \overline{TS}$, what can you call point T? How do you know?

Focus on the Idea

A midpoint is a point on a line segment that bisects the line segment, or divides it into two equal parts.

Practice

Name the midpoint of each line segment. The first one is done for you.

2.

F   H   G

_____point H_____

3.

P   R   Q

_____

4.

X   Y   W

_____

5.

C   E   B

_____

Write a congruence statement for each line segment shown in exercises 2 to 5. The first one is done for you.

6. $\overline{FG}$ _____$\overline{FH} \cong \overline{HG}$_____

7. $\overline{PQ}$ _____

8. $\overline{XW}$ _____

9. $\overline{CB}$ _____

Extend the Idea

A **compass** (KUM-puhs) is a tool we use to draw circles and arcs. A **straightedge** (STRAYT-ehj), is a tool used to draw straight lines. We can use a compass and a straightedge to construct the bisector of a line segment without measuring the segment.

Example: Use a compass and a straightedge to bisect $\overline{LJ}$.

Step 1 Put the compass point at point L.

Step 2 Open the compass so that it makes an arc that is more than half the length of $\overline{LJ}$.

Step 3 Draw two arcs, one above $\overline{LJ}$, and one below it.

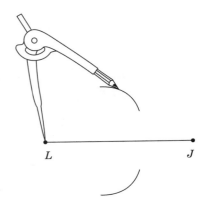

Step 4   Keep the compass setting the same.
Move the compass point to point *J*. Draw
another pair of arcs that cross the first
arcs you drew.

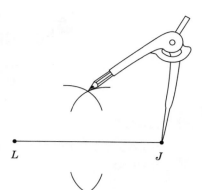

Step 5   Use a straightedge to draw a line
segment through the points where the arcs
intersect. The point where this line
segment intersects $\overline{LJ}$ is the midpoint
of $\overline{LJ}$. Label the midpoint *P*.

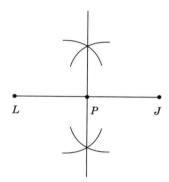

✓Check Your Understanding

10. Explain why, in the construction above, the midpoint of a
line segment is the point where the arcs intersect.

_____

_____

_____

Practice

**Answer these questions about some of the steps needed to bisect a
line segment *AB*. The first question has been answered for you.**

11. Name one point on which the compass point is placed.

_____A_____

12. Name another point on which the compass point is placed.

_____

13. How wide should the compass be opened to draw an arc on
$\overline{AB}$ from point *A*?

_____

_____

Construct the bisector of each line segment. Label the midpoint *P*, and write a congruence statement.

14.

A •———————————• B

_____

15.

• T

• R

_____

16.

_____

17.

_____

Apply the Idea

18. Tia needs to cut another piece of wire into four equal pieces. Her teacher asks her to make a drawing to show how she can do this. What can Tia draw?

_____

_____

Write About It

19. How can you use line bisectors to divide a square into two rectangles of the same size?

_____

_____

↲2•7 Bisecting Angles

WORDS TO LEARN

Angle bisector *a ray that divides an angle into two congruent angles*

Tyrone cuts a piece of pizza into two equal parts. He cuts the piece of pizza down the middle. The cut he makes is the bisector of the angle formed at the pointed end of the piece of pizza.

New Idea

A ray that divides an angle into two congruent angles is called the **angle bisector** (AN-guhl BY-sehkt-er).

In this figure, $\angle XYT \cong \angle TYZ$. So $\overrightarrow{YT}$ is the angle bisector of $\angle XYZ$. We say that $\overrightarrow{YT}$ bisects $\angle XYZ$. The arcs show that the angles are congruent.

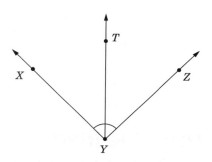

✓Check Your Understanding

1. $\angle KLM$ is a right angle. $\overrightarrow{LR}$ bisects $\angle KLM$.

    a. What is the measure of $\angle KLR$ and $\angle RLM$?

    _____

    b. How do you know?

    _____

    _____

↰Focus on the Idea

An angle bisector is a ray that divides an angle into two congruent angles.

Practice

Name the angle bisector of each angle. The first one is done for you.

2.

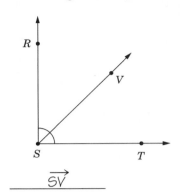

<u> $\overrightarrow{SV}$ </u>

3.

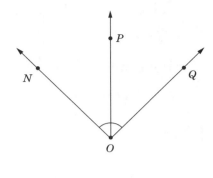

_____

4.

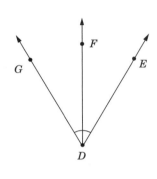

_____

5.

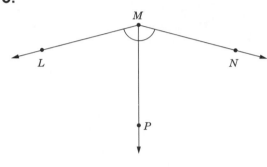

_____

Write a congruence statement for each angle shown in
exercises 2 to 5. The first one is done for you.

6. $\angle RST$ _____<u>$\angle RSV \cong \angle VST$</u>_____

7. $\angle NOQ$ _____

8. $\angle GDE$ _____

9. $\angle LMN$ _____

Extend the Idea

You can use a protractor to find an angle bisector.

Example: Use a protractor to bisect $\angle RST$.

Step 1 First find the measure of the
angle. The measure of $\angle RST$
is 80°.

Step 2 Then find half of the angle
measure. Half of 80° is 40°.
Draw a point at
the mark labeled 40.
Label this point W.

Step 3 Draw $\overrightarrow{SW}$, the angle bisector
of $\angle RST$.

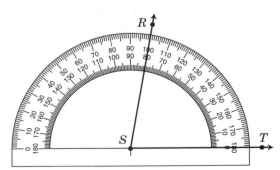

You can also use a compass and a straightedge to construct the angle bisector of an angle.

Example: Use a compass and straightedge to bisect ∠N.

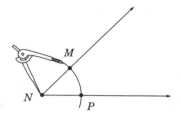

Step 1 Put the compass point at point N.

Step 2 Open the compass and draw an arc that intersects both sides of the angle. Label the points of intersection M and P.

Step 3 Place the compass point at point M and draw an arc within ∠N.

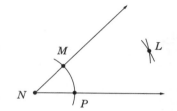

Step 4 Keep the compass setting the same. Move the compass point to point P. Draw an arc that intersects the arc you drew in Step 3. Label the point of intersection L.

Step 5 Use a straightedge to draw $\overrightarrow{NL}$. $\overrightarrow{NL}$ is the angle bisector of ∠N.

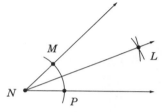

✓**Check Your Understanding**

10. If $\overrightarrow{BD}$ bisects ∠ABC and m∠ABD = 31°, how many degrees are in ∠DBC? (Remember what happens when an angle is bisected.) Draw a picture as part of your answer.

_____

Practice

Use a protractor to draw the bisector of each angle.

11.

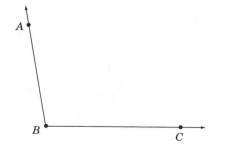

12.

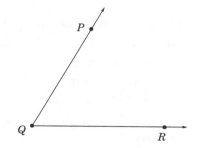

Construct the angle bisector of each angle, using a straightedge and compass. Check by measuring with a protractor.

13.

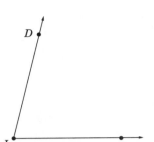

14.

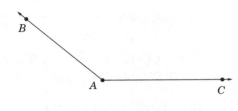

Apply the Idea

15. Sophie is constructing a wheel for a miniature merry-go-round. She has four spokes in the circle that form right angles. How can she decide where to put two more spokes so that the new spokes bisect each right angle? Draw a picture as part of your answer.

_____

_____

_____

✏ Write About It

16. An acute angle is bisected. Are the two angles formed acute or obtuse? How do you know?

_____

_____

_____

17. Do you prefer to use a compass and straightedge or a protractor to bisect an angle? Explain your choice.

_____

_____

_____

⬛2•8 Using Parallel Lines

The map of a city shows some streets that you can think of as parallel lines and other streets that are transversals. Many different angles are formed where the lines intersect. Which pairs of angles do you think are congruent?

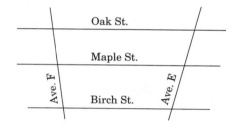

New Idea

Two parallel lines and a transversal form many pairs of congruent angles. Each pair of alternate interior angles is congruent. Each pair of **corresponding angles** (kawr-uh-SPAHN-dihng AN-guhlz) is congruent. Corresponding angles are a pair of angles on the same side of the transversal; one angle is an interior angle, and the other is an exterior angle.

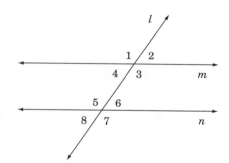

Another way to name a line is with a small letter. The lines in this figure are named line m, line n, and line l. Line m and line n are parallel. Line l is a transversal.

∠4 and ∠6 are alternate interior angles. Since they are formed by parallel lines and a transversal, they are congruent. $\angle 4 \cong \angle 6$

∠1 and ∠5 are corresponding angles. Since they are formed by parallel lines and a transversal, they are congruent. $\angle 1 \cong \angle 5$

1. Name a pair of alternate interior angles in the figure at the right.

   _____

2. Name a pair of corresponding angles in the figure at the right.

   _____

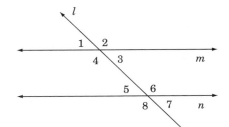

▸ **Focus on the Idea**

Each pair of alternate interior angles formed by two parallel lines and a transversal is congruent. Each pair of corresponding angles formed by two parallel lines and a transversal is congruent.

Practice

In the figure at the right, line *r* is parallel to line *s*.

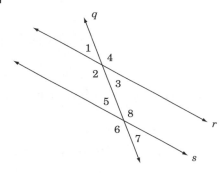

Use the figure to answer exercises 3 to 5.
Part of exercise 3 is done for you.

3. Use symbols to name two pairs of congruent alternate interior angles. _____ $\angle 3 \cong \angle 5$; _____

4. Use symbols to name four pairs of congruent corresponding angles.

   _____

5. Suppose $m\angle 2 = 140°$ and $m\angle 5 = 40°$. Without using a protractor, find the measures of all of the other angles shown.

   a. $m\angle 8 =$ _____   **b.** $m\angle 1 =$ _____

   c. $m\angle 3 =$ _____   **d.** $m\angle 4 =$ _____

   e. $m\angle 6 =$ _____   **f.** $m\angle 7 =$ _____

In this figure, $r \parallel s$, $m\angle 1 = 80°$, and $m\angle 2 = 100°$. Find the measure of each angle.

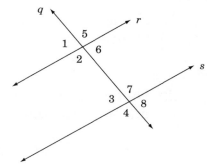

6. $m\angle 3 =$ _____

7. $m\angle 4 =$ _____

8. $m\angle 6 =$ _____

9. $m\angle 8 =$ _____

10. $m\angle 7 =$ _____

11. $m\angle 5 =$ _____

Extend the Idea

Vertical angles and supplementary angles also are formed by parallel lines and a transversal. All pairs of vertical angles are congruent. In the figure above, one pair of vertical angles is $\angle 1$ and $\angle 6$.

⤾Remember

Where two lines intersect, two of the angles formed are vertical angles. Two angles with a sum of 180° are supplementary angles.

✓Check Your Understanding

12. Are $\angle 5$ and $\angle 6$ vertical angles? Explain your answer.

_____

13. Name two other pairs of vertical angles in the figure above.

_____

14. Name two pairs of supplementary angles in the figure above.

_____

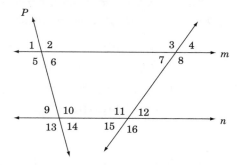

Practice

In this figure, $m \parallel n$, $m\angle 1 = 75°$, and $m\angle 4 = 55°$

Find the measure of each angle.

15. $m\angle 2 =$ _____   16. $m\angle 10 =$ _____

17. $m\angle 3 =$ _____   18. $m\angle 11 =$ _____

19. $m\angle 5 =$ _____   20. $m\angle 12 =$ _____

21. $m\angle 6 =$ _____   22. $m\angle 13 =$ _____

23. $m\angle 7 =$ _____   24. $m\angle 14 =$ _____

25. $m\angle 8 =$ _____   26. $m\angle 15 =$ _____

27. $m\angle 9 =$ _____   28. $m\angle 16 =$ _____

Apply the Idea

29. Look back at the street map on page 50. Label all lines and angles.

a. Name all parallel lines.

_____

b. Name all transversals.

_____

c. Name all pairs of alternate interior angles.

_____

d. Name all pairs of corresponding angles.

_____

e. Name all pairs of vertical angles.

_____

f. Name all pairs of supplementary angles.

_____

Write About It

30. Can all alternate interior and corresponding angles formed by two parallel lines and a transversal be congruent? How do you know?

_____

_____

_____

Draw a picture to prove your answer.

In This Chapter, You Have Learned:

- To recognize straight, right, acute, and obtuse angles
- To recognize complementary and supplementary angles
- To measure and draw angles with a protractor
- To recognize congruent line segments and congruent angles
- To recognize and draw the midpoint of a line segment, the bisector of a line segment, and the bisector of an angle
- To recognize congruent angles and supplementary angles formed by parallel lines and a transversal

Words You Know

From the lists of "Words to Learn," choose the word or phrase that best completes each statement.

1. Angles are measured in _____.
2. A(n) _____ angle has a measure between 0° and 90°.
3. A ray that divides an angle into two congruent angles is called the angle _____.
4. Congruent angles are angles with the same _____.
5. Two angles with a sum of 90° are _____ angles.
6. Two angles with a sum of 180° are _____ angles.
7. An angle with a measure of 180° and sides that are opposite rays is called a(n) _____ angle.
8. A(n) _____ is an instrument used to measure angles.
9. To _____ means to divide into two equal parts.
10. A(n) _____ is an instrument used to draw circles and arcs.
11. A point that divides a line segment into two equal parts is called a(n) _____.

More Practice

Use a protractor to find the measure of each angle. Then classify the angle as *acute, right,* or *obtuse.*

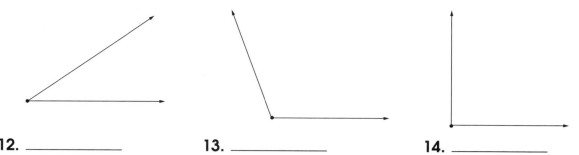

12. _____   13. _____   14. _____

15. Use a protractor to draw an angle with a measure of 80°. Then use a compass and a straightedge to construct the angle bisector.

16. Draw a line segment FG. Then use a ruler to find the midpoint of FG.

In the figure at the right, $x \parallel y$ and $m\angle 1 = 55°$. Find the measure of each angle.

17. $m\angle 3 = $ _____

18. $m\angle 5 = $ _____

19. $m\angle 7 = $ _____

20. $m\angle 6 = $ _____

21. $m\angle 4 = $ _____

22. $m\angle 2 = $ _____

23. $m\angle 8 = $ _____

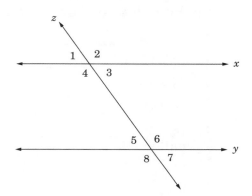

Problems You Can Solve

24. Miriam is a carpenter. She needs to cut a board into two equal pieces. Use some terms you have learned in this chapter to describe what she needs to do.

_____

_____

25. Timi has one piece of pie left. She wants to split it evenly with a friend. How can she be sure they each get exactly half of the piece?

_____

_____

26. For Your Portfolio Name at least two letters in the alphabet that contain congruent angles. Explain how you know the angles are congruent. Draw a picture to prove your answers.

_____

_____

Use the figure at the right to answer exercises 1 to 6.

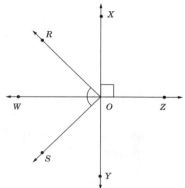

1. Name a straight angle. _____

2. Name an acute angle. _____

3. Name an obtuse angle. _____

4. Name a pair of complementary angles.
   _____

5. Name a pair of supplementary angles.
   _____

6. Name a pair of congruent angles.
   _____

**In the figure at the right, $q \parallel r$ and $m\angle 8 = 120°$.
Find the measure of each angle.**

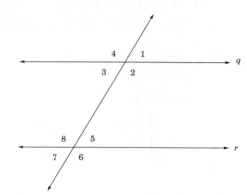

7. $m\angle 4 =$ _____

8. $m\angle 1 =$ _____

9. $m\angle 2 =$ _____

10. $m\angle 3 =$ _____

11. $m\angle 5 =$ _____

12. $m\angle 6 =$ _____

13. $m\angle 7 =$ _____

14. Draw the midpoint of $\overline{DW}$.

15. Draw the angle bisector of $\angle ABC$.

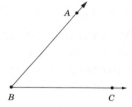

16. Suppose a billiard ball is hit from point X. It hits the side cushion of the billiard table without a spin. Two congruent angles are formed by the path of the ball. The diagram at the right shows the path of a ball.

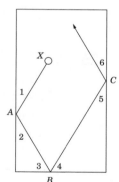

   a. Name all pairs of congruent angles shown.

   _____

   _____

   b. How do you think the function of congruent angles in this way might help you play the game?

   _____

   _____

Chapter 3

Triangles

OBJECTIVES:

In this chapter, you will learn

- *To recognize line segments that form a triangle*
- *To recognize parts of a triangle*
- *To classify a triangle according to its sides or angles*
- *To recognize congruent triangles*
- *To recognize corresponding parts of congruent triangles*
- *To use the SSS, SAS, and ASA congruence postulates to prove triangles congruent*
- *To find missing measures of angles of a triangle*
- *To use the Pythagorean Theorem to find the missing length of a side of a right triangle*
- *To find the lengths of corresponding sides of similar triangles*
- *To use inequalities to express the relationship between the sides and angles of a triangle*

In 2600 B.C., the Egyptians built the Pyramid of Snefu. They used many concepts from geometry to do their work. They began by shaping the base of the pyramid like a right triangle. They did this by first tying knots equal distances apart along the length of a rope. This divided the rope into 12 equal sections. After sticking three pegs into the ground, they wrapped the rope around the pegs. The right triangle formed by the rope had sides of three, four, and five sections. How did this rope help them know they had formed a right triangle?

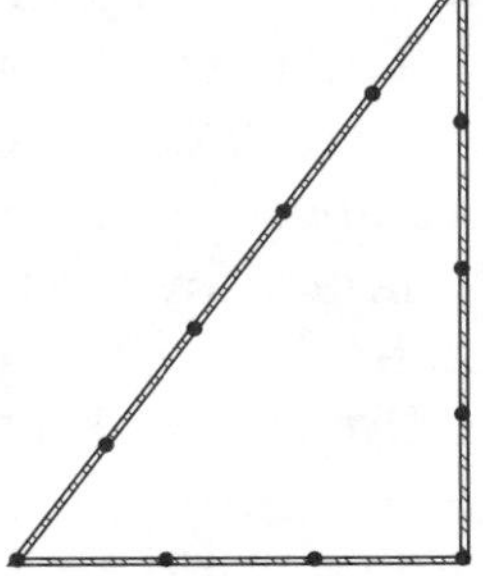

3•1 Identifying the Line Segments That Form Triangles

IN THIS LESSON, YOU WILL LEARN

To recognize line segments that form a triangle

To recognize parts of a triangle

WORDS TO LEARN

Triangle *figure formed by three line segments*

Sides *the line segments that form a figure*

Vertex *the point at which two line segments intersect*

Vertices *more than one vertex*

Interior *all points inside a figure*

Exterior *all points outside a figure*

R. Buckminster Fuller was an architect who developed the geodesic dome. The triangle is one of the basic structures of the dome. The triangle's three sides make it stronger and more stable than other geometric shapes.

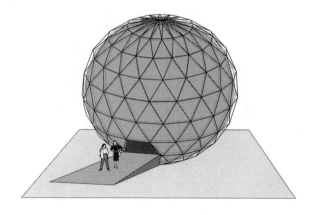

New Idea

A **triangle** (TRY-ang-guhl) is formed by three line segments called **sides** (sydz). The point at which two of the line segments intersect is called a **vertex** (VER-tehks). The three points where the line segments intersect are the **vertices** (VER-teh-seez) of the triangle. A triangle is named by its vertices. A triangle divides a plane into three parts. The three parts are the triangle itself, the points in the **interior** (ihn-TIHR-ee-uhr), or inside, the triangle, and the points in the **exterior** (ehk-STIHR-ee-uhr), or outside, the triangle.

Example: The figure at the right is $\triangle RST$.
The sides of $\triangle RST$ are $\overline{RS}$, $\overline{ST}$, and $\overline{TR}$.
The vertices of $\triangle RST$ are points R, S, and T.
Point A is in the interior of $\triangle RST$.
Point X is in the exterior of $\triangle RST$.

Focus on the Idea

A triangle is a figure formed by three line segments called sides. The sides join three points, called the vertices of the triangle.

Practice

Complete the following exercises.

1. Name the triangle, its sides, and its vertices. The first part is done for you.

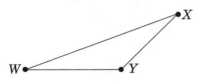

△WXY _____

sides = _____

vertices = _____

2. Draw a △*FGH*. Draw point *P* in the interior of △*FGH*. Draw point *Q* in the exterior of △*FGH*.

3. A figure is named △*DFN*.
   a. What are the sides of the triangle? _____
   b. What are the vertices of the triangle? _____

4. A triangle has sides $\overline{LM}$, $\overline{MN}$, and $\overline{NL}$.
   a. Draw and label the triangle.

   b. What is a name for the triangle?

   _____

Apply the Idea

5. List three ways triangles are used in businesses and industries.

   _____

   _____

   _____

✎ Write About It

6. Can a triangle be formed by three line segments that intersect other than at their endpoints? Why or why not?

   _____

   _____

▸ **IN THIS LESSON, YOU WILL LEARN**

To classify a triangle according to its sides or angles

WORDS TO LEARN.

Equilateral triangle *a triangle with three sides of equal length*

Isosceles triangle *a triangle with at least two sides of equal length*

Scalene triangle *a triangle with no equal sides*

Right triangle *a triangle with one right angle*

Acute triangle *a triangle with three acute angles*

Obtuse triangle *a triangle with one obtuse angle*

Some patchwork quilts are made up of many triangles. How many different kinds of triangles can you find in the quilt square? What kind of triangles are they?

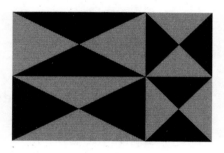

New Idea

A triangle can be classified by its number of congruent sides.

An **equilateral triangle** (ee-kwih-LAT-uhr-uhl TRY-ang-guhl) has three congruent sides.

An **isosceles triangle** (eye-SAHS-uh-leez) has at least two congruent sides.

A **scalene triangle** (SKAY-leen) has no congruent sides.

To show which sides of a triangle are congruent, mathematicians draw hatch marks on the sides. The sides with the same number of hatch marks are congruent.

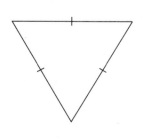

Equilateral Triangle

Isosceles Triangle

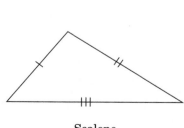

Scalene Triangle

1. Roberto said a triangle in which all the sides were equal to 10 cm was an isosceles triangle. Was he right? Explain.

_____

Focus on the Idea

Triangles can be classified by their sides as equilateral, isosceles, *or* scalene.

Practice

Classify each triangle as *equilateral, isosceles,* or *scalene*. The first one is done for you.

2.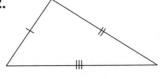

<u>   scalene   </u>

3.

_____

4.

_____

Classify each triangle as *equilateral, isosceles,* or *scalene*. Then find each indicated measurement.

5.

$\overline{AB} \cong \overline{BC}$
$\overline{AB} = 5$ m

$\overline{BC} =$ _____

6.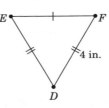

$\overline{DE} \cong \overline{EF} \cong \overline{FD}$
$\overline{FD} = 4$ in.

$\overline{EF} =$ _____

$\overline{DE} =$ _____

Draw a triangle of each kind.

7. an isoceles triangle

8. a scalene triangle

Extend the Idea

A triangle can also be classified by the measure of its angles. Small arcs drawn inside the angles show which angles are congruent. Angles with the same number of arcs are congruent.

⌒Remember

An acute angle has a measure of less than 90°. An obtuse angle has a measure greater than 90° and less than 180°. A right angle has a measure of 90°.

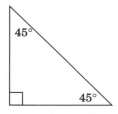

Right Triangle

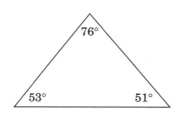

Acute Triangle

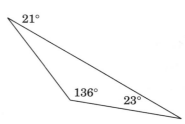

Obtuse Triangle

| A **right triangle** (reyet TRY-ang-guhl) has one right angle. | An **acute triangle** (uh-KYOOT) has all acute angles. | An **obtuse triangle** (ahb-TOOS) has one obtuse angle. |

✓Check Your Understanding

9. If a triangle has all sides equal to 12 cm and all angles equal to 60°, what words can be used to classify it?

_____

Practice

Classify each triangle as *right*, *acute*, or *obtuse*. The first one is done for you.

10.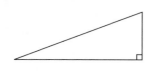

_____obtuse_____

11.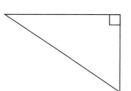

_____

12.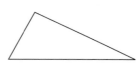

_____

13.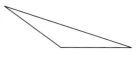

_____

14.

_____

15.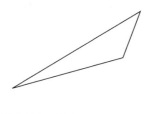

_____

Use a protractor to measure the angles of each triangle. Then classify the triangle as *right*, *acute*, or *obtuse*.

16.

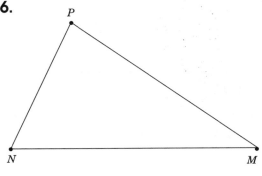

$m\angle M =$ _____

$m\angle N =$ _____

$m\angle P =$ _____

_____

17.

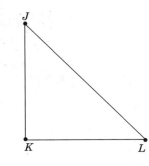

$m\angle J =$ _____

$m\angle K =$ _____

$m\angle L =$ _____

_____

Apply the Idea

18. Look at the quilt pattern on page 60. Label the angles and name the different types of triangles shown.

_____

_____

Write About It

19. Think about whether a triangle can be classified in more than one way.

a. Can an isosceles triangle also be a right triangle? Why or why not?

_____

_____

_____

b. Draw a picture to support your answer.

Identifying Congruent Triangles

Mandy and her friend are window dressers. They are painting a backdrop for a window display using congruent triangles. How can they be sure that the triangles are congruent?

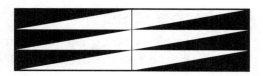

New Idea

Congruent triangles (KAHN-groo-uhnt TRY-ang-guhlz) are triangles with the same size and shape. If two triangles are congruent, the matching sides or angles are called **corresponding parts** (kawr-uh-SPAHN-ding pahrts). If two triangles are congruent, corresponding angles are congruent (indicated by the same number of arcs) and corresponding sides are congruent (same number of slash marks).

Example: $\triangle QRS$ and $\triangle TUV$ are congruent.

Corresponding angles: Q and T; R and U; and S and V.
Corresponding sides: $\overline{QR}$ and $\overline{TU}$; $\overline{RS}$ and $\overline{UV}$; and $\overline{SQ}$ and $\overline{VT}$.
Corresponding parts must be in the same order for both triangles.
  $\triangle QRS \cong \triangle TUV$

Corresponding angles are congruent:
  $\angle Q \cong \angle T$; $\angle R \cong \angle U$; $\angle S \cong \angle V$

Corresponding sides are congruent:
  $\overline{QR} \cong \overline{TU}$; $\overline{RS} \cong \overline{UV}$; $\overline{SQ} \cong \overline{VT}$

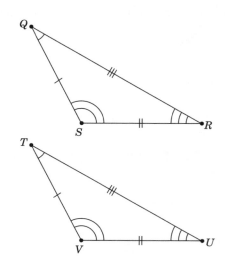

◆ Focus on the Idea

Two triangles that have the same size and shape are called congruent triangles. Corresponding parts of congruent triangles are congruent.

Practice

Complete to name the congruent triangle. The first one is done for you.

1.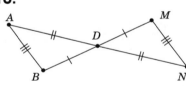

2.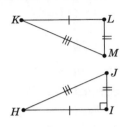

3.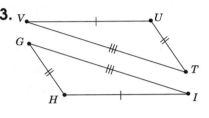

$\Delta DEF \cong \Delta$ _ABC_____

$\Delta HIJ \cong \Delta$ _____

$\Delta GHI \cong \Delta$ _____

△JLM is congruent to △RST. Name their corresponding sides and angles.

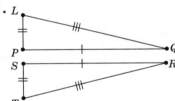

4. $\overline{MJ} \cong$ _____

5. $\angle L \cong$ _____

6. $\overline{ML} \cong$ _____

7. $\angle M \cong$ _____

8. $\angle J \cong$ _____

9. $\overline{JL} \cong$ _____

Use symbols to write a statement that names the pair of congruent triangles.

10.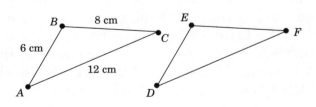

11.

12.

_____

_____

_____

Apply the Idea

13. $\triangle ABC \cong \triangle DEF$.
If $\overline{AB} = 6$ cm, $\overline{BC} = 8$ cm,
and $\overline{AC} = 12$ cm,
find $\overline{DE}$, $\overline{EF}$, and $\overline{DF}$.

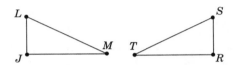

_____

✎ Write About It

14. Why do you think Mandy and her friend used congruent triangles in their pattern?

_____

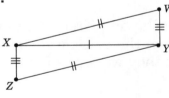

3•4 Proving Triangles Congruent

Natasha and Gregory are playing a game. Natasha says Gregory has broken the rules of the game. Gregory says he has not. They realized that they were playing by different rules.

New Idea

A rule in mathematics is called a **postulate** (PAHS-tyoo-liht). There are postulates about corresponding parts of triangles that can be used to show that the triangles are congruent.

If all three sides of one triangle are congruent to the three corresponding sides of another triangle, then the two triangles are congruent. This is called the **Side-Side-Side Postulate** (syd syd syd PAHS-tyoo-liht) and is abbreviated **SSS**.

Example: In the triangles at the right, $\overline{AB} \cong \overline{DE}$, $\overline{BC} \cong \overline{EF}$, and $\overline{CA} \cong \overline{FD}$. According to the SSS postulate, the triangles are congruent.

$$\triangle ABC \cong \triangle DEF$$

1. Circle the pairs of triangles that can be shown to be congruent according to the SSS postulate.

a. 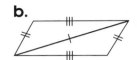 b.  c. d.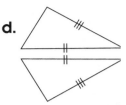

◄ **Focus on the Idea**

A postulate is a rule in mathematics. Postulates can be used to show that two triangles are congruent.

Practice

Write the three statements that must be true for the triangles to be congruent according to SSS. The first one is done for you.

2.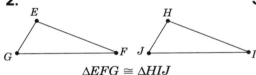

$\triangle EFG \cong \triangle HIJ$

$\overline{EF} \cong \overline{HI}, \overline{FG} \cong \overline{IJ}, \overline{GE} \cong \overline{JH}$

3.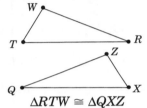

$\triangle RTW \cong \triangle QXZ$

_____

4.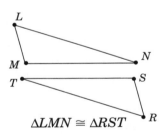

$\triangle LMN \cong \triangle RST$

_____

5.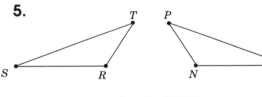

$\triangle RST \cong \triangle NOP$

_____

Tell if each pair of triangles can be shown to be congruent using the SSS postulate. If they can, write a statement showing that they are congruent.

6.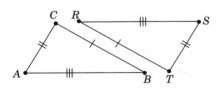

_____

7.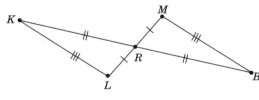

_____

8.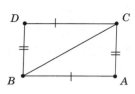

9.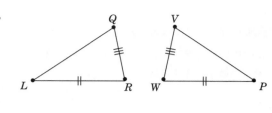

_____ _____

Extend the Idea

If two sides and the angle formed by the two sides of one triangle are congruent to the corresponding parts of a second triangle, then the triangles are congruent. This is called the **Side-Angle-Side Postulate** and is abbreviated **SAS**.

If two angles and their common side in one triangle are congruent to the corresponding parts of a second triangle, then the triangles are congruent. This is called the **Angle-Side-Angle Postulate** and is abbreviated **ASA**.

Example: In the triangles at the right,

$\overline{LM} \cong \overline{PQ}$, $\overline{MN} \cong \overline{QR}$, and $\angle M \cong \angle Q$.

$\angle M$ is the angle formed by $\overline{LM}$ and $\overline{MN}$.

$\angle Q$ is the angle formed by $\overline{PQ}$ and $\overline{QR}$.

According to the SAS postulate, the triangles are congruent.

$$\triangle LMN \cong \triangle PQR$$

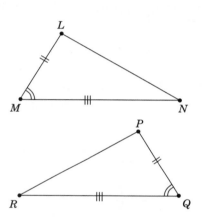

Practice

Tell if each pair of triangles is congruent according to the SAS Postulate or the ASA Postulate. The first one is done for you.

10.

_____ASA_____

11.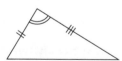

_____

12.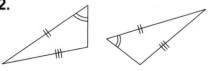

_____

13.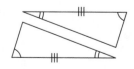

_____

Name the corresponding parts that must be congruent in order to show that the triangles are congruent according to the given postulate.

14.

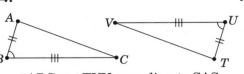

$\triangle ABC \cong \triangle TUV$ according to SAS

_____

_____

15.

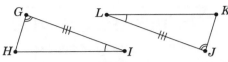

$\triangle GHI \cong \triangle JKL$ according to ASA

_____

_____

16.

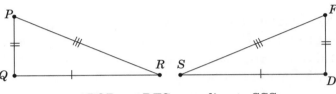

$\triangle PQR \cong \triangle DFS$ according to SSS

_____

17.

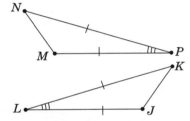

$\triangle MNP \cong \triangle JKL$ according to SAS

_____

Apply the Idea

18. Vaughn wants to find out if any of the shapes in a pattern he is drawing are congruent. His pattern is shown at the right. Use letters to label the triangles. Then use a protractor, a ruler, and the postulates you have learned to find all of the congruent triangles.

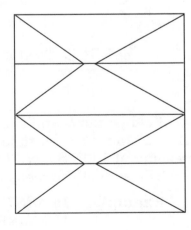

_____

_____

_____

✏ Write About It

19. Describe how you found the congruent triangles in exercise 18.

_____

_____

3•5 Angles of a Triangle

In this lesson, you will learn

To find missing measures of angles of a triangle

Words to learn

Interior angles of a triangle *angles formed by the sides in the interior of the triangle*

Quincy makes kites in the shape of triangles. He sells them by mail. If he can fold the kites to fit in an envelope, he can save money. Quincy found a system for folding his triangles. Will his system work for every triangle?

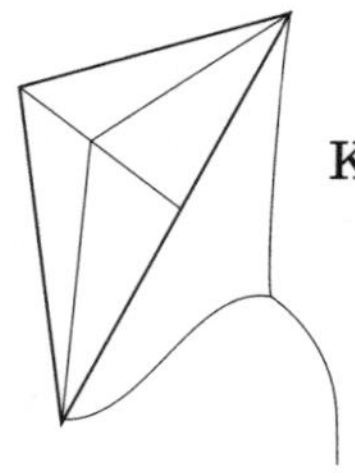

Kite

New Idea

A piece of paper shaped like a triangle is shown below. The **interior angles** (ihn-TIHR-ee-uhr ANG-guhlz) of the triangle are the angles formed by the sides of the triangle in the interior of the triangle. The triangle can be folded to find the sum of the measures of the interior angles, using the following steps:

Fold point A down to meet $\overline{BC}$.

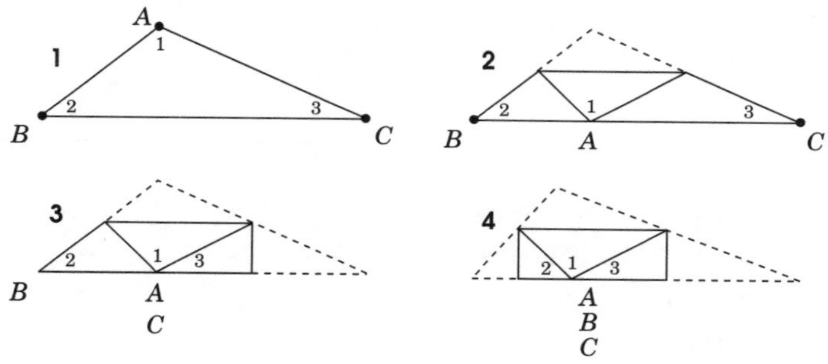

Fold points B and C in to meet point A. Notice that $\angle 2$, $\angle 1$, and $\angle 3$ meet to form a straight angle, which has a measure of 180°. So, $m\angle 1 + m\angle 2 + m\angle 3 = 180°$.

The sum of the measures of the angles of a triangle is 180°.

Example: In ΔRST at the right, $m\angle R = 35°$ and $m\angle S = 85°$. Use the fact that the sum of the measures of the angles of a triangle is 180° to find $m\angle T$.

$$m\angle R + m\angle S + m\angle T = 180°$$
$$35° + 85° + m\angle T = 180°$$
$$120° + m\angle T = 180°$$
$$m\angle T = 180° - 120°$$
$$m\angle T = 60°$$

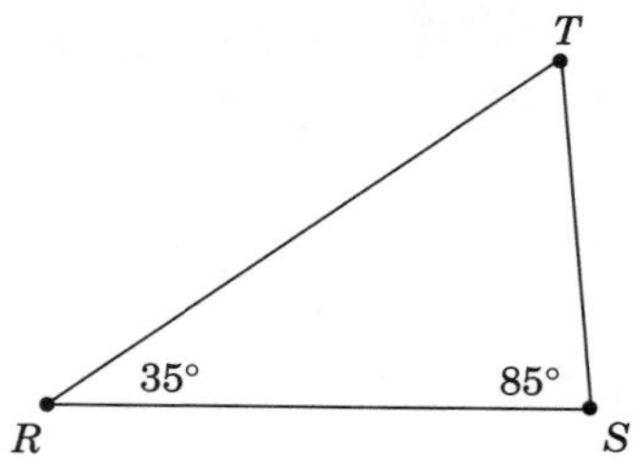

Focus on the Idea

The sum of the measures of the angles of a triangle is 180°.

Practice

Complete the statements to find the missing angle measure in each triangle. The first one is done for you.

1.

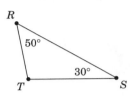

$m\angle R + m\angle S + m\angle T = \underline{180°}$

$50° + \underline{30°} + m\angle T = \underline{180°}$

$\underline{80°} + m\angle T = \underline{180°}$

$m\angle T = \underline{180°} - \underline{80°} = \underline{100°}$

2.

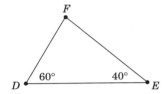

$m\angle D + m\angle E + m\angle F = \underline{\hphantom{xxxx}}$

$60° + \underline{\hphantom{xxxx}} + m\angle F = \underline{\hphantom{xxxx}}$

$\underline{\hphantom{xxxx}} + m\angle F = \underline{\hphantom{xxxx}}$

$m\angle F = \underline{\hphantom{xxxx}} - \underline{\hphantom{xxxx}} = \underline{\hphantom{xxxx}}$

3.

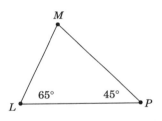

$m\angle L + m\angle M + m\angle P = \underline{\hphantom{xxx}}$

$65° + m\angle M + 45° = \underline{\hphantom{xxxx}}$

$\underline{\hphantom{xxxx}} + m\angle M = \underline{\hphantom{xxxx}}$

$m\angle M = \underline{\hphantom{xx}} - \underline{\hphantom{xx}} = \underline{\hphantom{xx}}$

4.

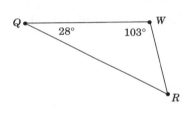

$m\angle R + m\angle W + m\angle Q = \underline{\hphantom{xxxx}}$

$m\angle R + \underline{\hphantom{xxxx}} + \underline{\hphantom{xxxx}} = \underline{\hphantom{xxxx}}$

$m\angle R + \underline{\hphantom{xxxx}} = \underline{\hphantom{xxxx}}$

$m\angle R = \underline{\hphantom{xxxx}} - \underline{\hphantom{xxxx}} = \underline{\hphantom{xxxx}}$

5. If $\triangle ABC$ is a right triangle, what is the sum of the two acute angles in the triangle? How do you know?

_____

_____

_____

_____

_____

Find the missing angle measure in each triangle.

6.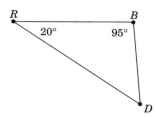

$m\angle D =$ _____

7.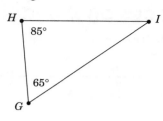

$m\angle I =$ _____

8.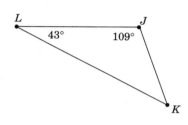

$m\angle K =$ _____

9.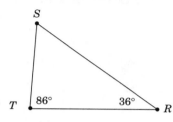

$m\angle S =$ _____

Extend the Idea

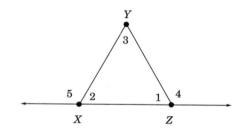

The figure at the right shows some of the different angles of triangle *XYZ*. If you know the measure of $\angle 3$ and the measure of $\angle 1$, then you can find the measure of $\angle 2$.

$$m\angle 1 + m\angle 2 + m\angle 3 = 180°$$

Now look at $\angle 2$ and $\angle 5$. They form a linear pair. You can find the measure of $\angle 5$ if you know the measure of $\angle 2$ because $m\angle 5 + m\angle 2 = 180°$.

Example: In $\triangle ABC$, the measures of two interior angles are 60° and 50°.

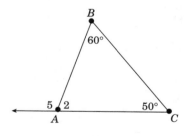

$$m\angle 2 + 60° + 50° = 180°$$

$$m\angle 2 + 110° = 180°$$

$$m\angle 2 = 180° - 110° = 70°$$

$m\angle 5 + m\angle 2 = 180° \leftarrow$ These angles form a linear pair.

$m\angle 5 + 70° = 180° \leftarrow$ Substitute 70° for $\angle 2$.

$$m\angle 5 = 180° - 70° = 110°$$

Practice

Complete the statements to find the missing angle measures in △NMP.

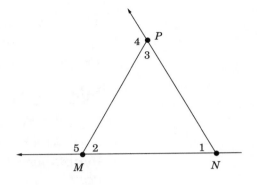

10. $m\angle 3 = 60°$ and $m\angle 1 = 40°$

$m\angle 2 = 180° -$ _____ $=$ _____

$m\angle 5 = 180° - m\angle 2 =$ _____

11. $m\angle 2 = 80°$ and $m\angle 1 = 40°$

$m\angle 3 = 180° -$ _____ $=$ _____

$m\angle 4 = 180° - m\angle 3 =$ _____

**In △MKL, $m\angle 5 = 100°$ and $m\angle 1 = 25°$.
Find the missing angle measures.**

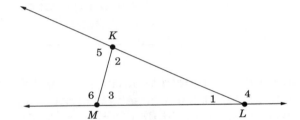

12. $m\angle 3 =$ _____

13. $m\angle 2 =$ _____

14. $m\angle 4 =$ _____

15. $m\angle 6 =$ _____

Apply the Idea

16. When the door to Tomás's bathroom is completely open, it forms an angle of 145°. Two walls meet to form a right angle. What angle does the back of the door form with each wall when it is completely open? _____

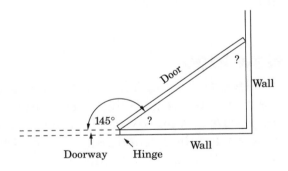

Write About It

17. Draw and label a triangle of your own. Show at least two interior angles. Write two problems about the measures of the angles of your triangle.

_____

_____

_____

_____

▸3•6 Right Triangles

IN THIS LESSON, YOU WILL LEARN

To use the Pythagorean Theorem to find the missing length of a side of a right triangle

WORDS TO LEARN

Legs *the two sides of a right triangle that form the right angle*

Hypotenuse *the side of a right triangle opposite the right angle*

Theorem *a mathematical statement that can be proved*

Pythagorean Theorem *theorem that states that in a right triangle, the sum of the squares of the lengths of the two legs equals the square of the length of the hypotenuse*

Julia drew a picture of the baseball field at her school. The angle at each base is a right angle. She drew a line down the middle of the infield from home plate to second base. How long is the line from home plate to second base?

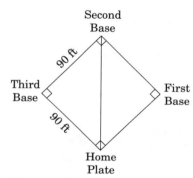

New Idea

In a right triangle, the two sides that form the right angle are called the **legs** (lehgz). The side opposite the right angle is called the **hypotenuse** (hy-PAHT-ih-noos). The length of each side of a right triangle can be named using a small letter. The letter is usually the same as the letter that labels the opposite vertex.

Example: In $\triangle ABC$, $\angle C$ is a right angle, so $\triangle ABC$ is a right triangle. $\overline{AC}$ and $\overline{BC}$ are the legs. $\overline{AB}$ is the hypotenuse.

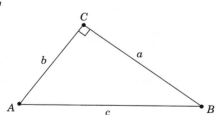

The length of leg $\overline{AC}$ is b.

The length of leg $\overline{BC}$ is a.

The length of hypotenuse $\overline{AB}$ is c.

1. The legs of a right triangle are $\overline{MN}$ and $\overline{PN}$. Is $\overline{MP}$ the hypotenuse? How do you know?

_____

Focus on the Idea

The legs of a right triangle are the sides that form the right angle. The hypotenuse of a right triangle is the side opposite the right angle.

Practice

Name the legs and hypotenuse of each right triangle. The first one is done for you.

2.

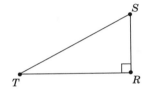

legs: <u>$\overline{SR}$ and $\overline{TR}$</u>

hypotenuse: <u>$\overline{ST}$</u>

3.

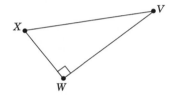

legs: _____

hypotenuse: _____

4.

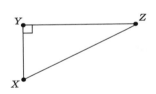

legs: _____

hypotenuse: _____

5.

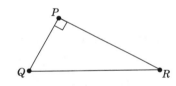

legs: _____

hypotenuse: _____

Label each side of the right triangle with the small letter that names the opposite vertex. Then write the small letters that name the legs and the hypotenuse.

6.

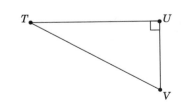

legs: _____

hypotenuse: _____

7.

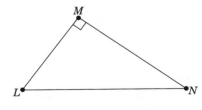

legs: _____

hypotenuse: _____

Extend the Idea

A **theorem** (THEE-uh-ruhm) is a mathematical statement that can be proved. The **Pythagorean Theorem** (pih-thag-uh-REE-uhn THEE-uh-ruhm) states that in a right triangle, the sum of the squares drawn on the lengths of the two legs equals the square drawn on the length of the hypotenuse. According to the Pythagorean Theorem, leg^2 + leg^2 = hypotenuse^2 or $a^2 + b^2 = c^2$. If you know the lengths of any two sides of a right triangle, you can use the Pythagorean Theorem to find the length of the third side.

Examples: $\triangle ABC$ is a right triangle. The lengths of the legs are a and b. The length of the hypotenuse is c.

$$a^2 + b^2 = c^2$$

If $a = 3$ cm and $b = 4$ cm, use the Pythagorean Theorem to find c.

$a^2 + b^2 = c^2$

$3^2 + 4^2 = c^2$ ← Substitute 3 for a and 4 for b.

$9 + 16 = c^2$

$25 = c^2$ ← Solve for c.

$\sqrt{25} = \sqrt{c^2}$

$5 = c$

The measure of c is 5 cm.

↰ Remember

The symbol $\sqrt{}$ means square root. The square root of 25 ($\sqrt{25}$) is 5, because 5 • 5 = 25.

In $\triangle ABC$, the lengths of one leg and the hypotenuse are given. Use the Pythagorean Theorem to find a.

$a^2 + b^2 = c^2$ ← Substitute 6 for b and 9 for c.

$6^2 + a^2 = 9^2$

$36 + a^2 = 81$

$a^2 = 81 - 36$

$a^2 = 45$

$\sqrt{a^2} = \sqrt{45}$

$a = \sqrt{45}$

$a \approx 6.7$ in. (rounded to the nearest tenth)

✓Check Your Understanding

8. In a right triangle, is the hypotenuse always longer than the sum of the lengths of legs? Explain your answer.

Practice

For each right triangle, find the length of the missing side. The first one is done for you.

9.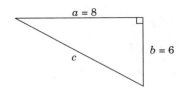

$a^2 + b^2 = c^2$

$\underline{\quad 8^2 \quad} + \underline{\quad 6^2 \quad} = c^2$

$\underline{\quad 64 \quad} + \underline{\quad 36 \quad} = c^2$

$\underline{\quad 100 \quad} = c^2$

$\sqrt{100} = \sqrt{c^2}$

$\underline{\quad 10 \quad} = c$

10.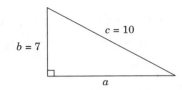

$a^2 + b^2 = c^2$

$a^2 + \underline{\qquad}^2 = \underline{\qquad}^2$

$a^2 + \underline{\qquad} = \underline{\qquad}$

$a^2 = \underline{\qquad} - \underline{\qquad}$

$a^2 = \underline{\qquad}$

$\sqrt{a^2} = \underline{\qquad}$

$a \approx 7.1$

For △*ABC*, use the Pythagorean Theorem to find the missing length for the given measures. Round each length to the nearest tenth.

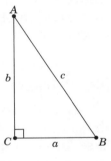

11. $a = 4, b = 8, c = $ _____

12. $a = 5, c = 10, b = $ _____

13. $b = 9, c = 18, a = $ _____

14. $a = 6, c = 12, b = $ _____

15. $a = 13, b = 13, c = $ _____

16. $a = 15, c = 20, b = $ _____

Apply the Idea

17. Look back at the baseball field on page 74.

    a. In the right triangle that contains first base, label the legs a and b. Label the hypotenuse c.

    b. If the distance between each base is 90 feet, find c to the nearest tenth. _____

Write About It

18. Suppose the Pythagorean Theorem is true for a given triangle. Do you think the triangle is a right triangle? Why or why not?

_____

_____

_____

3•7 Similar Triangles

IN THIS LESSON, YOU WILL LEARN

*To find the lengths of corresponding sides of
similar triangles*

WORDS TO LEARN

Scale drawing *a drawing of a structure that is too big
or too small to be drawn actual size*

Similar triangles *triangles that are the same shape but
not necessarily the same size*

Ratio *comparison of two numbers*

Proportion *a statement that two ratios are equal*

André is a construction worker. He uses a scale drawing to guide the
construction of a building. How can a scale drawing be used to build a
larger structure?

New Idea

A **scale drawing** (skayl DRAW-ihng) is a drawing of a structure
that is too big or too small to be drawn actual size. Scale drawings are
based on similar figures. **Similar triangles** (SIHM-uh-luhr
TRY-ang-guhlz) are triangles that are the same shape but not
necessarily the same size. In two similar triangles, the corresponding
angles are congruent. The corresponding sides are not congruent. The
symbol ~ means "is similar to." The symbol → shows correspondence.

Remember

Corresponding parts are a side or angle of one triangle that
matches a side or angle of another triangle.

Examples: △*ABC* and △*DEF* are similar. The corresponding
vertices are *A* and *D*, *B* and *E*, and *C* and *F*. It is
important to write the corresponding vertices
in the same order when using symbols for
the similarities. We write △*ABC* ~ △*DEF*
to show corresponding parts. Corresponding
angles are congruent. Corresponding
sides are in proportion.

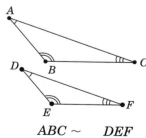

$$\angle A \cong \angle D \qquad \angle B \cong \angle E \qquad \angle C \cong \angle F$$

$$\overline{AB} \to \overline{DE} \qquad \overline{BC} \to \overline{EF} \qquad \overline{CA} \to \overline{FD}$$

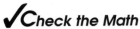

1. If $\triangle HJK \sim \triangle XYZ$, is $\angle K \cong \angle Z$? How do you know?

_____

_____

Focus on the Idea

Similar triangles are the same shape but may not be the same size.

Practice

Complete each statement of similarity so that the statement matches the corresponding parts. The first one is done for you.

2.
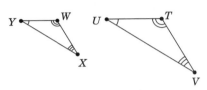

$\triangle WXY \sim \triangle$ _____TVU_____

3.
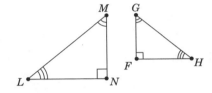

$\triangle MNL \sim \triangle$ _____

4.
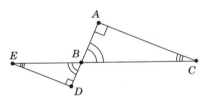

$\triangle ABC \sim \triangle$ _____

5.
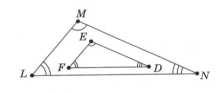

$\triangle NLM \sim \triangle$ _____

Draw two triangles that match the similarity statement given. Then name the three pairs of corresponding sides.

6. $\triangle DEF \sim \triangle RQP$

7. $\triangle GHI \sim \triangle CDB$

_____   _____

8. $\triangle CDE \sim \triangle CAB$

9. $\triangle MNP \sim \triangle QNR$

_____   _____

Extend the Idea

When two triangles are similar, the **ratios** (RAY-shee-ohz) formed by corresponding sides are equal. The corresponding sides of similar triangles are said to be proportional. You can write a **proportion** (proh-POR-shuhn) using the length of the sides of similar triangles.

Examples: $\triangle ABC$ and $\triangle XYZ$ are similar:

$\triangle ABC \sim \triangle XYZ$

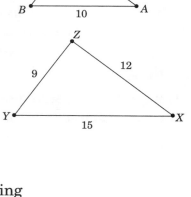

Corresponding sides:

$$\overline{AB} \rightarrow \overline{XY}$$

$$\overline{BC} \rightarrow \overline{YZ}$$

$$\overline{CA} \rightarrow \overline{ZX}$$

$\frac{AB}{XY} = \frac{10}{15} = \frac{2}{3}$
$\frac{BC}{YZ} = \frac{6}{9} = \frac{2}{3}$
$\frac{CA}{ZX} = \frac{8}{12} = \frac{2}{3}$

Since each ratio equals $\frac{2}{3}$, the corresponding sides are proportional: $\frac{AB}{XY} = \frac{BC}{YZ} = \frac{CA}{ZX}$

$\triangle MNL \sim \triangle IJK$

The lengths of some of the sides are given. Use proportions to find the length of i.

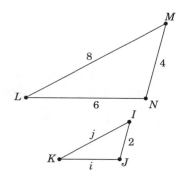

$\frac{MN}{IJ} = \frac{NL}{JK}$	Set up a proportion with corresponding sides.
$\frac{4}{2} = \frac{6}{i}$	Substitute.
$4 \cdot i = 2 \cdot 6$	Find the cross-products.
$4i = 12$	Simplify.
$\frac{4i}{4} = \frac{12}{4}$	Divide both sides by 4.
$i = 3$	Simplify.

The length of $\overline{JK}$ is 3.

✓ Check Your Understanding

10. Explain how congruent and similar triangles are alike. Then explain how they are different.

_____

_____

Practice

Use these triangles to answer exercises 11 and 12.

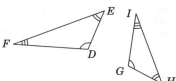

$$\triangle DEF \sim \triangle GHI$$

11. Name all corresponding sides. The first one is done for you.

$\overline{DE} \rightarrow \overline{GH}$ $\overline{EF} \rightarrow$ _____ $\overline{FD} \rightarrow$ _____

12. Give all of the proportions formed by the sides of the two triangles. The first one is done for you.

$\dfrac{DE}{GH} = \dfrac{EF}{HI}$ $\dfrac{EF}{HI} =$ _____ $\dfrac{DE}{GH} =$ _____

Use proportions to find the missing lengths in each triangle.

13.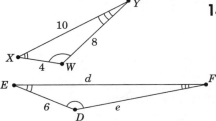

_____   _____

14.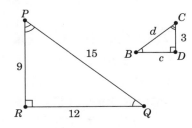

_____   _____

15.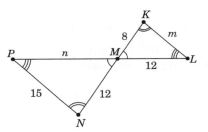

_____   _____

16.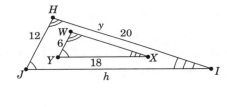

_____   _____

Apply the Idea

17. Waylon is designing a triangular flower bed. The sides of the flower bed are to measure 5 feet, 5 feet, and 3 feet. In his scale drawing, the 3-foot side measures 1.5 inches.

   a. What is the length of the other two sides on the scale drawing?

   _____

   b. Draw the scale drawing.

Write About It

18. Are congruent triangles also similar triangles? Why or why not?

_____

3.8 Using Inequalities for Sides and Angles of a Triangle

> ### IN THIS LESSON, YOU WILL LEARN
> To use inequalities to express the relationship between the sides and angles of a triangle
>
> ### WORDS TO LEARN
> **Inequality** *a statement that two expressions are not equal*
> **Triangle Inequality Theorem** *states that for any triangle, the sum of the lengths of any two sides is greater than the length of the remaining side*

Marta measured the distance she had to walk from her house to her school, then to her job at the bank and back home. No matter how she measured the distances, the sum of any two parts of her route was greater than the remaining part.

New Idea

An **inequality** (ihn-ee-KWAWL-uh-tee) states that two expressions are not equal. An inequality can be used to describe the relationship between the lengths of the sides of any triangle. The **Triangle Inequality Theorem** (TRY-ang-guhl ihn-ee-KWAWL-uh-tee thee-uh-ruhm) states that for any triangle, the sum of the lengths of any two sides is greater than the length of the remaining side.

Examples: You can write three inequalities for $\triangle ABC$.

$$\overline{AB} + \overline{BC} > \overline{CA}$$
$$9 + 15 > 16$$
$$24 > 16$$

$$\overline{AB} + \overline{CA} > \overline{BC}$$
$$9 + 16 > 15$$
$$25 > 15$$

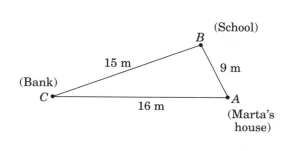

$$\overline{BC} + \overline{CA} > \overline{AB}$$
$$15 + 16 > 9$$
$$31 > 9$$

Example: Can a triangle have sides of 12, 30, and 17 inches?
Use the Triangle Inequality Theorem to find out.
Check all possible inequalities.

$12 + 30 > 17$	$12 + 17 > 30$	$30 + 17 > 12$
$42 > 17$ Yes	$29 > 30$ No	$47 > 12$ Yes

The second inequality is not true, so 12, 30, and 17
cannot be the correct lengths of the sides of a triangle.

✓ Check the Math

1. Lee said that he could draw a triangle with sides of 14 cm,
15 cm, and 18 cm. Can he do this? Explain your answer.

_____

◀ Focus on the Idea

*In a triangle, the sum of the lengths of any two sides is
greater than the length of the third side.*

Practice

**Complete each statement to write all possible inequalities for each
triangle. The first one is done for you.**

2.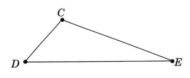

$\overline{CD}$	+	$\overline{DE}$	$> \overline{EC}$
$\overline{DE}$	+	$\overline{EC}$	$> \overline{CD}$
$\overline{CD}$	+	$\overline{EC}$	$> \overline{DE}$

3.

_____	+	_____	$> \overline{MO}$
_____	+	_____	$> \overline{MN}$
_____	+	_____	$> \overline{ON}$

4.

_____ + _____ $> \overline{SR}$

_____ + _____ $> \overline{RQ}$

_____ + _____ $> \overline{QS}$

5.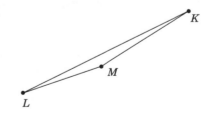

_____ + _____ $> \overline{MK}$

_____ + _____ $> \overline{LM}$

_____ + _____ $> \overline{KL}$

Tell if the given numbers can be the lengths of the three sides of a triangle. Write *yes* or *no*.

6. 7, 8, 5 _____

7. 19, 10, 6 _____

8. 12, 8, 13 _____

9. 25, 28, 22 _____

10. 15, 29, 30 _____

11. 3, 20, 26 _____

12. 100, 5, 100 _____

13. 19, 19, 19 _____

14. 2.5, 8.5, 3.5 _____

Extend the Idea

The angles and the sides of a triangle have a special relationship. If two sides are not equal, then the angles opposite those sides are not equal. Also, the greater of those two angles is opposite the longer side.

Examples: In $\triangle XYZ$, $\angle X$ is opposite $\overline{YZ}$, $\angle Y$ is opposite $\overline{XZ}$, and $\angle Z$ is opposite $\overline{XY}$.

If $m\angle X > m\angle Y$, then $YZ > XZ$.

If $m\angle Y > m\angle Z$, then $XZ > XY$.

If $YZ > XY$, then $m\angle X > m\angle Z$.

In $\triangle MNP$, $\overline{MN}$ is opposite $\angle P$, $\overline{NP}$ is opposite $\angle M$, and $\overline{PM}$ is opposite $\angle N$.

$MN = 8$, $NP = 2$, and $PM = 7$. Which angle has the greatest measure? Since $8 > 7 > 2$, then $\overline{MN} > \overline{PM} > \overline{NP}$. So, $m\angle P > m\angle N > m\angle M$. Therefore, $\angle P$ has the greatest measure.

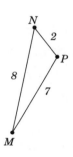

✓Check Your Understanding

15. Is the relationship between angles in a triangle also true for an equilateral triangle? _____

Practice

For each triangle, name the opposite angles or sides. The first one is done for you.

16.

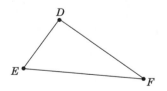

$\overline{ED}$ is opposite ____$\angle F$____.

$\overline{DF}$ is opposite ____$\angle E$____.

$\overline{EF}$ is opposite ____$\angle D$____.

17.

$\overline{SR}$ is opposite _____.

$\overline{RQ}$ is opposite _____.

$\overline{SQ}$ is opposite _____.

18.

19.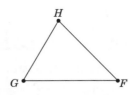

∠B is opposite _____.   ∠F is opposite _____.

∠D is opposite _____.   ∠H is opposite _____.

∠C is opposite _____.   ∠G is opposite _____.

Use △RST for exercise 20.

20. If $\overline{TR} > \overline{ST}$, what do you know about the relationship between ∠S and ∠R?

_____

Use the diagrams to help you answer exercises 21 and 22.

21.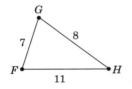

22.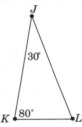

In △FGH, which angle has the greatest measure? _____

In △KJL, which side is the shortest? _____

Apply the Idea

23. This map shows the number of blocks between places in Morte's neighborhood. Morte walks from school to the library to the skating path. He claims that he walks 22 blocks. Is this possible? Why or why not?

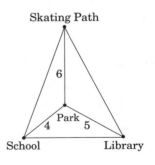

_____

✏ Write About It

24. An isosceles triangle has two equal sides. What do you know about the relationship between the angles opposite these sides? How do you know?

_____

_____

Chapter 3   Review

In This Chapter, You Have Learned

- To recognize line segments that form a triangle
- To classify a triangle according to its sides or angles
- To recognize congruent triangles and corresponding parts
- To use the SSS, SAS, and ASA congruence postulates
- To use the Pythagorean Theorem to find the missing length of a side
- To find the lengths of corresponding sides of similar triangles
- To use inequalities to express relationships between sides and angles

Words You Know

From the lists of "Words To Learn," choose the word or phrase to complete each statement.

1. A triangle with three congruent sides is a(n) _____ triangle.

2. Congruent triangles have the same _____ and _____ .

3. A triangle with no congruent sides is a(n) _____ triangle.

4. The pairs of sides or angles of two congruent triangles that are congruent are called _____ .

5. A(n) _____ triangle has one obtuse angle.

6. The sides of a right triangle are called the _____ .

7. Triangles that are the same shape but not the same size are _____ triangles.

8. A triangle with at least two congruent sides is a(n) _____ triangle.

More Practice

Name the corresponding parts needed to show that the triangles are congruent according to the given postulate.

9.

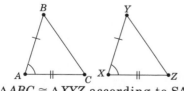

$\triangle ABC \cong \triangle XYZ$ according to SAS

_____

10.

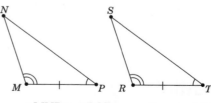

$\triangle MNP \cong \triangle RST$ according to ASA

_____

Tell if the given numbers can be the measures of the sides of a triangle. Write *yes* or *no*.

11. 8, 9, 13 _____   12. 15, 25, 7 _____   13. 2, 8, 4 _____

In the figure at the right, $m\angle 2 = 95°$ and $m\angle 5 = 135°$. Find the missing measures.

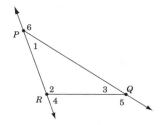

14. $m\angle 4 =$ _____

15. $m\angle 3 =$ _____

16. $m\angle 6 =$ _____

17. $m\angle 1 =$ _____

Use the Pythagorean Theorem and a calculator to find each measure to the nearest tenth.

18.

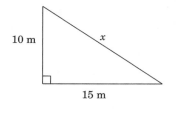

_____

19.

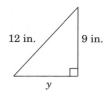

_____

Use a proportion to find the missing measure in each pair of similar triangles.

20.

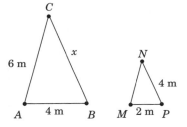

_____

21.

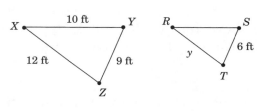

_____

Use △*NMJ* at the right for exercises 22 and 23.

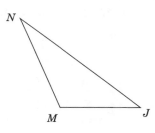

22. If $\overline{NM} > \overline{MJ}$, what can you say about the relationship between $\angle N$ and $\angle J$? _____

23. If $\overline{NJ} < \overline{NM}$, what can you say about the relationship between $\angle J$ and $\angle M$? _____

Problems You Can Solve

24. A diagram of the front of a tent is shown at the right. The pole at the front of the tent is 8 feet high. What is the distance along the ground? _____

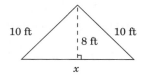

25. **For Your Portfolio**   Make a scale drawing of a structure that is shaped like a triangle, or that has a triangle as part of the structure. For example, the roofs of many houses are shaped like triangles. Estimate the actual measurements or use measurements that you think are possible for the real structure.

Classify each triangle as *acute, obtuse, right, scalene, isosceles,* or *equilateral.* Use as many terms as apply to each triangle.

1.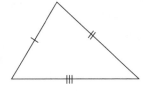

_____

2.

_____

3.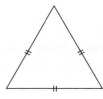

_____

4.

_____

5.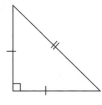

_____

6.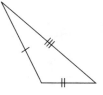

_____

7. Name the congruent, corresponding parts needed to show that $\triangle ABC$ and $\triangle ABD$ are congruent according to the SSS postulate.

_____

8. Use the Pythagorean Theorem to find the hypotenuse of the triangle at the right to the nearest tenth. _____

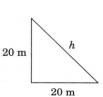

In $\triangle DEF$, $m\angle 2 = 60°$ and $m\angle 3 = 80°$.
Find the missing measures.

9. $m\angle 4 = $ _____

10. $m\angle 1 = $ _____

11. $m\angle 5 = $ _____

12. $m\angle 6 = $ _____

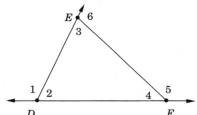

$\triangle LMN$ is similar to $\triangle QRS$.
Use proportions to find the missing sides.

13. $\overline{QS} = $ _____

14. $\overline{RS} = $ _____

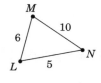

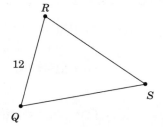

15. Can 4 cm, 8 cm, and 12 cm be the measures of the sides of a triangle? Why or why not?

_____

Chapter 4

Polygons

OBJECTIVES:

In this chapter, you will learn

- *To identify figures as polygons*
- *To name polygons according to their number of sides*
- *To identify and use properties of parallelograms*
- *To identify and use properties of rectangles*
- *To identify and use properties of rhombuses and squares*
- *To identify and use properties of trapezoids*
- *To identify regular polygons*
- *To find the measure of the angles of a regular polygon*
- *To identify congruent polygons*
- *To find the lengths of corresponding sides of similar polygons*
- *To draw polygons on the coordinate plane*
- *To identify a tessellation*
- *To create a tessellation using transformations*

A design made by covering figures is called a mosaic (moh-ZAY-ihk). Small tiles are often used in mosaics. Mosaics can decorate walls, floors, and the outside of buildings. One building that is decorated by a mosaic is the stadium at the University of Mexico. The mosaic is made of small geometric figures and was designed by the artist, Diego Rivera (DYEH-goh ree-VEH-rah).

4•1 Types of Polygons

IN THIS LESSON, YOU WILL LEARN

To identify figures as polygons

To name polygons according to the number of sides

WORDS TO LEARN

Polygon *a closed figure formed by joining three or more line segments at their endpoints*

Non-consecutive vertices *any two vertices that are not next to one another*

Diagonal *a line segment that joins two nonconsecutive vertices of a polygon*

Soccer balls are covered with geometric figures called polygons. Look at the drawing to the right. How many different kinds of figures can you find on the soccer ball?

New Idea

A soccer ball is covered with two kinds of figures, 5-sided figures and 6-sided figures. A closed figure formed by joining three or more line segments is called a **polygon** (PAHL-ih-gahn). The line segments form the sides of the polygon. The endpoints of the line segments meet to form the vertices of the polygon. A line segment that joins two **non-consecutive vertices** is called a **diagonal** (dy-AG-uh-nuhl).

Example: Name the figure.

Figure *GHIJ* is formed by line segments, so it is a polygon.

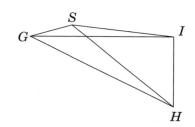

Sides: $\overline{GH}, \overline{HI}, \overline{IJ}, \overline{JG}$

Vertices: *G, H, I, J*

Diagonals: $\overline{GI}, \overline{JH}$

A polygon can be classified by its number of sides. The common names for some polygons are shown in the chart.

Number of Sides	Common Name	Number of Sides	Common Name
3	triangle	8	octagon
4	quadrilateral	9	nonagon
5	pentagon	10	decagon
6	hexagon	for more than 10	*n*-gon
7	heptagon	(*n* sides)	

Focus on the Idea

A polygon is a closed figure formed by three or more line segments. The diagonal is a line segment drawn to connect two non-consecutive sides. A polygon is named by its number of sides.

Practice

Name the sides, the vertices, and the diagonals of each polygon. Part of the first one is done for you.

1.

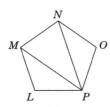

sides: $\overline{LM}, \overline{MN}, \overline{NO}, \overline{OP}, \overline{PL}$

vertices: _____

diagonals: _____

2.

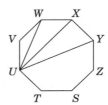

sides: _____

vertices: _____

diagonals: _____

Draw each polygon.

3. triangle   **4.** heptagon   **5.** decagon   **6.** hexagon

Apply the Idea

7. Look around your classroom. Find examples of two different polygons. Draw and name the polygons.

✏ Write About It

8. Two non-regular quadrilaterals do not overlap, but they share one side. (In other words, two points are vertices of both quadrilaterals.) If you ignore the shared side, what polygon do they form? Explain. Then draw a picture to prove your answer.

4•2 Properties of Parallelograms

Euclid (YOO-klihd) was a Greek mathematics teacher who lived about 300 B.C. He wrote the first known geometry textbook, most of which was based on research by earlier mathematicians. Even today, his book called the *Elements* is one of the most widely read books in the world. In the book, Euclid expressed his ideas about geometric properties. One of his most important ideas has to do with parallel lines. Euclid said there is only one line through a given point that is parallel to any other line. Many mathematicians have developed their own ideas about geometry while trying to prove this idea of Euclid's to be wrong.

Remember

Parallel lines are lines in the same plane that do not intersect. The symbol ∥ means "is parallel to." Congruent line segments have the same length. Congruent angles have the same measure.

New Idea

A quadrilateral with two pairs of parallel sides is called a **parallelogram** (par-uh-LEHL-uh-gram). In a quadrilateral, the sides that do not meet are called opposite sides. The angles that do not share a side are called opposite angles. The opposite sides of a parallelogram are congruent. The opposite angles of a parallelogram are congruent.

Example: Name the opposite sides, opposite angles, and parallel sides of this figure. Then name the figure.

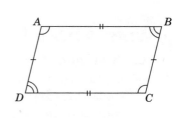

Opposite sides: $\overline{AB}$ and $\overline{CD}$; $\overline{BC}$ and $\overline{DA}$

Opposite angles: $\angle A$ and $\angle C$; $\angle B$ and $\angle D$

In quadrilateral *ABCD*, $\overline{AB} \parallel \overline{CD}$ and $\overline{BC} \parallel \overline{DA}$. *ABCD* is a parallelogram.

In a parallelogram, the opposite sides are congruent and the opposite angles are congruent, so $\overline{AB} \cong \overline{CD}$, $\overline{BC} \cong \overline{DA}$, $\angle A \cong \angle C$, and $\angle B \cong \angle D$.

✓Check the Math

1. Adrian says that if one pair of opposite sides of a quadrilateral are parallel, then the quadrilateral is a parallelogram. Rico says that both pairs of opposite sides must be parallel for it to be a parallelogram.

    a. Who is correct? Why?

    _____

    b. Draw a picture to prove your answer.

Focus on the Idea

A parallelogram is a quadrilateral with two pairs of parallel sides. Opposite sides and opposite angles of a parallelogram are congruent.

Practice

Name the congruent sides and congruent angles of each parallelogram. Part of the first one is done for you.

2.

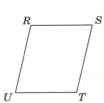

sides: ___$\overline{RS} \cong \overline{TU},$___

angles: ___$\angle R \cong \angle T,$___

3.

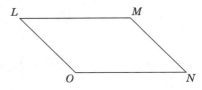

sides: _____

angles: _____

Use parallelogram *LMNO* in exercise 3 for exercises 4 to 7.

4. If $\overline{LM} = 8$ cm, then $\overline{ON} = $ _____.

5. If $\overline{OL} = 5$ cm, then $\overline{NM} = $ _____.

6. If $m\angle N = 45°$, then $m\angle L = $ _____.

7. If $m\angle O = 135°$, then $m\angle M = $ _____.

⤶Remember

A diagonal of a quadrilateral is a line segment that joins two non-consecutive vertices. To bisect means to divide into two equal parts.

Extend the Idea

The diagonals of parallelogram $RSTU$ are $\overline{RT}$ and $\overline{SU}$. The diagonals of a parallelogram have special properties:

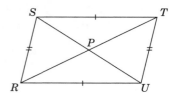

- Each diagonal of a parallelogram divides the parallelogram into two congruent triangles.

- The diagonals of a parallelogram bisect each other.

Example: If $RT = 10$ in. and $SU = 9$ in., find RP, PT, SP, and PU.

Since the diagonals of a parallelogram bisect each other, RP and PT are half of RT, and SP and PU are half of SU.

$$\tfrac{1}{2}(RT) = RP = PT \qquad \tfrac{1}{2}(SU) = SP = PU$$
$$\tfrac{1}{2}(10) = RP = PT \qquad \tfrac{1}{2}(9) = SP = PU$$
$$5 = RP = PT \qquad \tfrac{9}{2} = SP = PU$$
$$4\tfrac{1}{2} = SP = PU$$

Line segments RP and PT are each 5 inches long. Line segments SP and PU are each $4\tfrac{1}{2}$ inches long.

✓Check Your Understanding

8. $\overline{JL}$ and $\overline{MK}$ are diagonals of a parallelogram intersecting at point N.

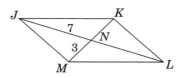

   a. If the measure of $\overline{JN}$ is 7, what is the measure of $\overline{NL}$? _____

   b. If the measure of $\overline{MN}$ is 3, what is the measure of $\overline{NK}$? _____

Practice

Name four pairs of congruent line segments and two pairs of congruent triangles for each parallelogram. The first one is done for you.

9. line segments: _____$\overline{XY} \cong \overline{ZW},$_____

   _____$\overline{YZ} \cong \overline{WX}, \overline{XA} \cong \overline{AZ}, \overline{YA} \cong \overline{AW}$_____

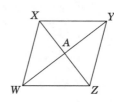

   triangles: _____$\triangle YXW \cong \triangle WZY,$_____

   _____$\triangle XYZ \cong \triangle ZWX$_____

10.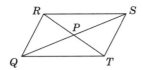

line segments: _____

_____

triangles: _____

_____

11.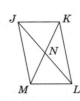

line segments: _____

_____

triangles: _____

_____

Apply the Idea

12. Irami is making a kite shaped like a parallelogram. She makes one side 1.5 feet and another side 1 ft. One cross bar is 2 feet and the other is 1.5 feet. How many sticks does she need? How long is each one?

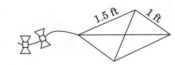

_____

Write About It

13. Suppose you know the measure of one side of a parallelogram. Can you find the measure of the other three sides without measuring them? Why or why not?

_____

_____

_____

14. Draw a scalene triangle. Draw a second scalene triangle congruent to the first. How many different parallelograms can you form with your two triangles? Draw pictures to illustrate your answer. (Hint: For each parallelogram you discover, flipping it over does not give you a new, different parallelogram.)

_____

4•3 Rectangles

IN THIS LESSON, YOU WILL LEARN

To identify and use properties of rectangles

WORDS TO LEARN

Rectangle *a parallelogram with four right angles*

Several people in Vinnie's apartment building are working together to make some repairs. Vinnie is repairing a door frame. He needs to construct the frame so that the sides intersect to form right angles. Sari is repairing the window frames. She notices that the sides of a window meet the top and bottom at right angles. In this lesson, you too will work with four-sided figures whose sides form right angles.

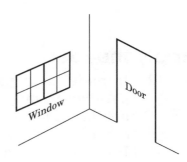

New Idea

A **rectangle** (REHK-tang-guhl) is a parallelogram with four right angles. A right angle measures exactly 90°. A rectangle has all the properties of a parallelogram. In addition, the two diagonals of a rectangle are congruent.

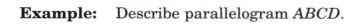

Example: Describe parallelogram *ABCD*.

Because *ABCD* is a parallelogram:
- its opposite sides are parallel and congruent. $\overline{AB} \parallel \overline{CD}, \overline{BC} \parallel \overline{DA}$
  $\overline{AB} \cong \overline{CD}, \overline{BC} \cong \overline{DA}$
- its diagonals bisect each other. $\overline{AF} \cong \overline{FC}, \overline{BF} \cong \overline{FD}$

Parallelogram *ABCD* has four right angles, so it is a rectangle. Because it is a rectangle:
- its angles are right angles. $\angle A = \angle B = \angle C = \angle D = 90°$
- its diagonals are congruent. $\overline{AC} \cong \overline{BD}$

Focus on the Idea

A parallelogram with four right angles is called a rectangle. The diagonals of a rectangle are congruent.

Practice

Tell whether each figure is a rectangle. Write *yes* or *no*, then explain your answer. The first one is done for you.

1.

  No, it is not a rectangle.

  It is not a parallelogram.

2.

  _____

  _____

3.

  _____

  _____

4.

  _____

  _____

5. Hank says that the following statement is true about the diagonals of rectangle *WXYZ*. Is Hank correct? Explain. $\overline{YA} \cong \overline{AW} \cong \overline{ZA} \cong \overline{AX}$

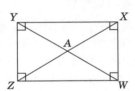

_____

Use rectangle *CDEF* for exercises 6 to 8.

6. If $\overline{CD}$ = 6 in., $\overline{FE}$ = _____.

7. If $\overline{CF}$ = 8 in., $\overline{DE}$ = _____.

8. If $\overline{CE}$ = 10 in., $\overline{DF}$ = _____,
  $\overline{CG}$ = _____, $\overline{GE}$ = _____,
  $\overline{DG}$ = _____, and $\overline{GF}$ = _____.

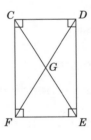

Apply the Idea

9. Vinnie measures one side of a doorway to be 8 feet high and the distance across the doorway to be 4 feet wide. What is the height of the other side of the doorway? _____

Write About It

10. A parallelogram has two right angles that are not opposite angles. Is the parallelogram a rectangle? Why or why not?

_____

_____

Rhombuses and Squares

▶ IN THIS LESSON, YOU WILL LEARN

To identify and use properties of rhombuses and squares

WORDS TO LEARN

Rhombus *a parallelogram with four congruent sides*
Square *a rectangle with four congruent sides*

Trina needs to change a flat tire on her car. She attaches a jack and raises the car. Trina notices a shape formed at the center of the jack. The sides of this shape, $\overline{AB}, \overline{BC}, \overline{CD}$, and $\overline{DA}$, remain congruent no matter how high the jack raises the car. What is the shape formed at the center of the jack?

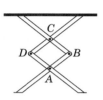

New Idea

A parallelogram with four congruent sides is called a **rhombus** (RAHM-buhs). A rhombus has all the properties of a parallelogram. In addition, the diagonals of a rhombus are perpendicular to each other. Each diagonal bisects two of the angles.

A rectangle with four congruent sides is called a **square** (skwair). A square has all the properties of a rectangle and all the properties of a rhombus.

↰ *Remember*

Where perpendicular lines intersect, they form right angles.

Example: Is parallelogram *ABCD* a rhombus or a square? What are its properties?

In the parallelogram *ABCD*, the diagonals are perpendicular. $\overline{AC} \perp \overline{BD}$
Each diagonal bisects a pair of opposite angles.
$\angle 1 \cong \angle 2, \angle 3 \cong \angle 4, \angle 5 \cong \angle 6, \angle 7 \cong \angle 8$

The parallelogram has four congruent sides that do not meet at right angles, so it is a rhombus.

Rectangle *WXYZ* is shown at the right.

It has all the properties of both a rectangle and a rhombus, so it is a square.

◀ Focus on the Idea

A rhombus is a parallelogram with four congruent sides. A square is a rectangle with four congruent sides. A square is also a rhombus.

Practice

Draw and label a figure for each description. The first one is done for you.

1. a square   2. a rhombus   3. a rectangle   4. a parallelogram

Use square *DEFG* for exercises 5 to 7.

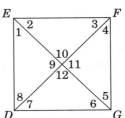

5. $m\angle 9 = m\angle 10 = m\angle$_____ $= m\angle$_____
   Each angle equals _____.

6. $m\angle 1 = m\angle$_____ Each angle equals _____.

7. $m\angle 3 = m\angle$_____ Each angle equals _____.

Use rhombus *HJKL* for exercises 8 to 9.

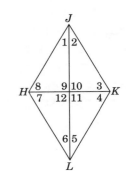

8. $m\angle 9 = m\angle 10 = m\angle$_____ $= m\angle$_____
   Each angle equals _____.

9. $m\angle HJK = 60°$

   a. $m\angle 1 = m\angle$_____ Each angle equals _____.

   b. $m\angle KLH = m\angle$_____ Each angle equals _____.

   c. $m\angle 5 = m\angle$_____ Each angle equals _____.

Apply the Idea

Look back at the jack Trina used.

10. Name the rhombus. Name all congruent angles formed. Use a protractor to find the measures of the angles.

_____

✏ Write About It

11. A parallelogram has two consecutive sides that are congruent. Is the parallelogram a rhombus? Why or why not?

_____

4•5 Trapezoids

In the picture, the roof of a library building appears to be shaped like a quadrilateral. What kind of quadrilateral is it?

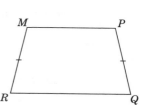

New Idea

A quadrilateral with one pair of parallel sides is called a **trapezoid** (TRAP-ih-zoid). The parallel sides are called the **bases** (bays-uhz) of the trapezoid. The sides that are not parallel are called the **legs** (lehgz). Each angle that has a base as a side is called a **base angle** (bays ANG-guhl). A trapezoid with congruent legs is called an **isosceles trapezoid** (eye-SAHS-uh-leez TRAP-ih-zoid).

Example: List the properties of trapezoid *MPQR*.

$\overline{MP} \parallel \overline{RQ}$ and $\overline{MR}$ and $\overline{PQ}$ are not parallel.

$\overline{MP}$ and $\overline{RQ}$ are the bases.

$\overline{MR}$ and $\overline{PQ}$ are the legs.

$\overline{MR} \cong \overline{PQ}$

Angles R and Q are a pair of base angles.

Angles M and P are another pair of base angles.

MPQR is an isosceles trapezoid.

✓Check Your Understanding

1. What is the difference between a parallelogram and a trapezoid?

Focus on the Idea

A trapezoid is a quadrilateral with exactly one pair of parallel sides called the bases. The sides that are not parallel are called the legs. An isosceles trapezoid has two congruent legs.

Practice

Tell whether each quadrilateral is a *trapezoid*, an *isosceles trapezoid*, or *neither*. Explain your answer. The first one is done for you.

2.

Trapezoid; It has two parallel sides but its legs are not congruent.

3.

_____

_____

_____

4.

_____

_____

_____

5.

_____

_____

_____

Tell whether it is possible to draw a trapezoid with the properties given. Write *yes* or *no*. If your answer is *yes*, draw the trapezoid. If your answer is *no*, explain why it is not possible.

6. a leg that is longer than either base

_____

7. four acute angles

_____

8. two right angles

_____

9. three congruent sides

_____

10. three obtuse angles

_____

11. congruent bases

_____

Extend the Idea

A line segment that connects the midpoints of the legs of a trapezoid is called a **median** (MEE-dee-uhn). A median divides each leg into two equal parts. A median is parallel to the bases of the trapezoid. The length of a median of a trapezoid is one-half the sum of the lengths of the bases.

Example: Name the median of trapezoid $ABCD$.

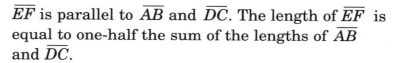

E is the midpoint of leg $\overline{AD}$

F is the midpoint of leg $\overline{BC}$.

$\overline{EF}$ is the median of trapezoid $ABCD$

$\overline{EF}$ is parallel to $\overline{AB}$ and $\overline{DC}$. The length of $\overline{EF}$ is equal to one-half the sum of the lengths of $\overline{AB}$ and $\overline{DC}$.

If $\overline{AB} = 10$ and $\overline{DC} = 14$, you can find the length of $\overline{EF}$ this way:

$\overline{EF} = \frac{1}{2}(\overline{AB} + \overline{DC})$

$\overline{EF} = \frac{1}{2}(10 + 14)$

$\overline{EF} = \frac{1}{2}(24)$

$\overline{EF} = 12$

The length of median $\overline{EF}$ is 12.

✓Check the Math

12. Niki told Kenneth that she can draw a trapezoid with bases that measure 2 inches and 3 inches and a median that measures 3 inches. Is this possible? Why or why not?

_____

_____

Practice

Use trapezoid *HIJK* for exercises 13 to 18.

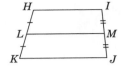

13. If the measure of $\overline{HI}$ = 12 cm and $\overline{JK}$ = 18 cm, what is the measure of $\overline{LM}$?_____

14. If the measure of $\overline{HI}$ = 30 cm and $\overline{JK}$ = 10 cm, what is the measure of $\overline{LM}$?_____

15. If the measure of $\overline{HI}$ = 5 in. and $\overline{JK}$ = 16 in., what is the measure of $\overline{LM}$?_____

16. If the measure of $\overline{HL}$ = 5 in., what is the measure of $\overline{LK}$?

    _____

17. If the measure of $\overline{IJ}$ = 12 in., what is the measure of $\overline{MJ}$?

    _____

18. If the measure of $\overline{HK}$ = 14 in. and the measure of $\overline{LM}$ = 16 in., what is the measure of $\overline{LK}$?_____

Apply the Idea

Look back at the roof of the library building on page 100.

19. Label and name the trapezoid. Name the bases, the legs, and the base angles.

    _____

20. Use a ruler to measure the bases of the trapezoid. What is the sum of the bases?

    _____

21. Use a ruler to find the midpoints of the legs. Then draw the median. Measure the median. How does the length of the median compare to your answer to exercise 20?

    _____

✏ Write About It

22. Tina draws the median of an isosceles trapezoid. Does the median divide the trapezoid into two isosceles trapezoids? Why or why not?

    _____

    _____

    _____

    _____

↴4•6 Regular Polygons

↴IN THIS LESSON, YOU WILL LEARN

To identify regular polygons

To find the measure of the angles of a regular polygon

WORDS TO LEARN

Interior angle of a polygon *angle within a polygon formed by two sides of the polygon*

Regular polygon *polygon with all sides and all angles congruent*

Exterior angle of a polygon *an angle that lies outside a polygon, but forms a linear pair with an interior angle of the polygon*

Carmen wants to put a mirror in her room. She finds four small hexagonal mirrors exactly the same size. She discovers that there are several ways to hang the mirrors so that they fit together to form one large mirror on her wall. Carmen wonders if all hexagons fit together in the same way.

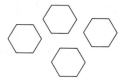

New Idea

Any polygon can be divided into triangles by drawing all the diagonals from one vertex. The number of triangles formed is always two less than the number of sides of the polygon.

An **interior angle of a polygon** (ihn-TIHR-ee-uhr ANG-guhl), or angle within a polygon, is formed by two sides of a polygon. The sum of the measures of the interior angles of any polygon is given by the formula $180°(n - 2)$ where n is the number of sides of the polygon.

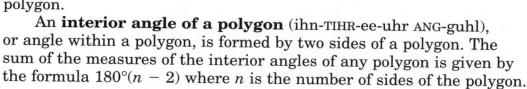

Example: Find the sum of the measures of the interior angles of a hexagon.

$$
\begin{aligned}
\text{Sum of angles} &= 180°(n - 2) \\
&= 180°(6 - 2) \\
&= 180°(4) \\
&= 720°
\end{aligned}
$$

The sum of the measures of the interior angles of a hexagon is 720°.

A polygon with all sides and all angles congruent is called a
regular polygon (REHG-yuh-luhr PAHL-ih-gahn). Since all the angles
of a regular polygon are congruent, you can use this formula to find
the measure of each of its interior angles:

$$\frac{180°(n-2)}{n}$$

Example: Find the measure of each interior angle of a regular hexagon.

Substitute 6 for n in the formula since a hexagon
has 6 sides:

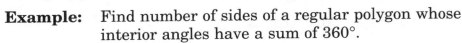

Each angle $= \frac{180°(n-2)}{n} = \frac{180°(6-2)}{6} = \frac{720}{6} = 120°$

The measure of each interior angle is 120°.

The formula $180°(n-2)$ can also be used to find the number of
sides of a polygon whose interior angles have a given sum.

Example: Find number of sides of a regular polygon whose
interior angles have a sum of 360°.

$$180°(n-2) = 360°$$

$$\frac{180(n-2)}{180} = \frac{360}{180} \qquad \leftarrow\text{Divide both sides by 180.}$$

$$n - 2 = 2 \qquad \leftarrow\text{Add 2 to both sides.}$$

$$n = 4$$

This regular polygon has 4 sides.

✓**Check Your Understanding**

1. If all sides of a polygon are congruent, is the polygon
   regular? Why or why not?

   _____

   _____

   _____

   _____

   _____

   _____

◢**Focus on the Idea**

*In a regular polygon, all the sides and all the angles
are congruent. The interior angles are formed by two
sides of the polygon. Use the formula $180°(n-2)$ to
find the sum of the measures of the interior angles of
a polygon. Use the formula $\frac{180°(n-2)}{n}$ to find the
measure of each interior angle of a regular polygon.*

Practice

2. Circle the regular polygons.

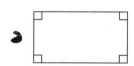   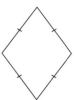

Find the sum of the interior angles of each regular polygon. The first one is done for you.

3. triangle

    $n = 3$
    Sum $= 180(3 - 2)$
    $\quad\quad = 180$

4. quadrilateral
   (4 sides)

   _____

5. pentagon
   (5 sides)

   _____

6. octagon
   (8 sides)

   _____

Find the measure of each interior angle of each regular polygon.

7. triangle _____

8. quadrilateral _____

9. pentagon _____

10. octagon _____

Find the number of sides of each polygon whose interior angles have the given sum. Part of the first one is done for you.

11. 900°

    $180°(n - 2) = 900°$
    $\dfrac{180°(n - 2)}{180°} = \dfrac{900°}{180°}$
    $n - 2 =$
    $\quad\quad n =$

12. 1,260°

Extend the Idea

In this hexagon, $\angle 1$ and $\angle ABC$ form a linear pair. Angle 1 is an **exterior angle of a polygon** (ehk–STIHR–ee ANG guhl), an angle outside a polygon that forms a linear pair with an interior angle of the polygon.

Example: Find the measure of the exterior angle of a regular hexagon.

The measure of the interior angle of a regular hexagon is 120°.

$$\angle 1 + \angle ABC = 180°$$
$$\angle 1 + 120° = 180°$$
$$\angle 1 = 60°$$

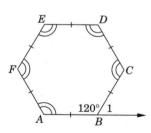

If you know the number of sides of a regular polygon, you can find the sum of the measures of its exterior angles. Multiply the measure of an exterior angle by the number of sides.

Example: Find the sum of the measures of the exterior angles of a hexagon.

$$sum = 6 \cdot 60°$$
$$= 360°$$

✓Check the Math

13. Fran says that you can tell how many sides a regular polygon has by the measure of its exterior angles. Richard says that you need to know the sum of the measures of the interior angles to find the number of sides. Who is correct? How do you know?

_____

Practice

Use the answers from exercises 7 to 10 to find the measure of each exterior angle of each regular polygon. Then find the sum of the exterior angles. The first one has been started for you.

14. triangle: exterior angle = $\underline{180° - 60° =}$ _____

sum of exterior angles = $\underline{3(120) =}$ _____

15. quadrilateral: exterior angle = _____

sum of exterior angles = _____

16. pentagon: exterior angles = _____

interior angle = _____

sum of exterior angles = _____

17. octagon: exterior angles = _____

interior angle = _____

sum of exterior angles = _____

Apply the Idea

18. What have you discovered about the sum of the measures of the exterior angles of a regular polygon?

_____

✏ Write About It

19. Draw an arrangement of Carmen's mirrors. If any of the hexagons have a common vertex, find the sum of the angles at that vertex. Carmen wondered if all hexagons would fit together in the same way. Tell what you think. Explain your answer.

_____

◀4•7 Congruent Polygons

In this lesson, you will learn

To identify congruent polygons

Words to learn

Congruent polygons *polygons that have the same size and shape*

Corresponding parts *the matching pairs of sides and angles of two congruent polygons*

Ned is designing a stained-glass window. He is cutting shapes from different colors of construction paper to use as templates, or patterns. To make sure the shapes fit together, Ned needs to use certain kinds of figures that he learned about in geometry. What is unique about the shapes Ned is using?

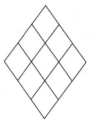

New Idea

Congruent polygons (KAHN-groo-uhnt PAHL-ih-gahnz) are exactly the same size and have exactly the same shape. All the **corresponding parts** (kawr-uh-SPAHN-dihng pahrts), the matching pairs of angles and the matching pairs of sides of congruent polygons, are congruent. When you use symbols to show that two polygons are congruent, you must list the corresponding vertices in the same order.

Example: Label the corresponding parts of these congruent polygons:
$ABCD \cong WXYZ$

The corresponding vertices are A and W, B and X, C and Y, and D and Z.

The corresponding parts that are congruent are:

$\angle A \cong \angle W \quad \angle B \cong \angle X$
$\angle C \cong \angle Y \quad \angle D \cong \angle Z$

$\overline{AB} \cong \overline{WX} \qquad \overline{BC} \cong \overline{XY}$
$\overline{CD} \cong \overline{YZ} \qquad \overline{DA} \cong \overline{ZW}$

◀ Focus on the Idea

Two polygons that have the same size and shape are congruent polygons. The pairs of congruent sides and angles of congruent polygons are corresponding parts.

Practice

Pentagon *FGHJK* is congruent to pentagon *PQRST*. Name the corresponding parts of the pentagons. The first one is done for you.

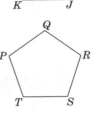

1. $\overline{FG} \cong$ ___PQ___

2. $\overline{GH} \cong$ _____

3. $\overline{HJ} \cong$ _____

4. $\overline{ST} \cong$ _____

5. $\overline{TP} \cong$ _____

6. $\angle F \cong$ _____

7. $\angle G \cong$ _____

8. $\angle R \cong$ _____

9. $\angle S \cong$ _____

10. $\angle K \cong$ _____

Draw and label two congruent polygons for each statement.

11. Parallelogram *MNPQ* is congruent to parallelogram *RSTU*.

12. Hexagon *PQRSTU* is congruent to hexagon *JKLMNO*.

Apply the Idea

13. Look back at the figures Ned used for his stained-glass design on page 108. Label two congruent polygons and write a statement to describe the congruence.

_____

Write About It

14. If two polygons are congruent, must they also be regular polygons? Why or why not?

_____

_____

_____

15. Why do you think Ned used congruent polygons in his pattern?

_____

_____

_____

↴4•8 Similar Polygons

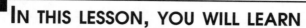

IN THIS LESSON, YOU WILL LEARN

To find the lengths of corresponding sides of similar polygons

WORDS TO LEARN

Similar polygons *polygons that are the same shape and have corresponding sides that are in proportion*

Ms. Nichols is a construction engineer. She is working at the site of a new office building. She depends on special drawings of the building, called blueprints, to direct the construction of each office.

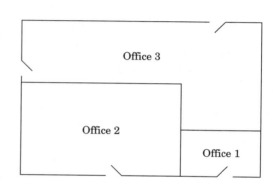

New Idea

Similar polygons (SIHM-uh-luhr PAHL-ih-gahnz) have the same shape but are not the same size. Each pair of corresponding angles of similar polygons is congruent. The corresponding sides of similar polygons are in proportion.

To use symbols to write a similarity, it is important to write the corresponding vertices of both polygons in the same order. The symbol ∼ means "is similar to." The symbol ↔ means "corresponds to."

Examples: Write a similarity statement for these similar parallelograms:

$MNOP \sim RSTU$

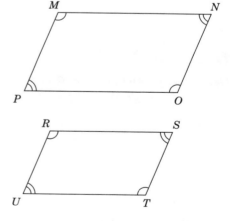

The corresponding vertices of the similar parallelograms are:

M and R, N and S, O and T, and P and U.

The corresponding sides are:

$\overline{MN} \leftrightarrow \overline{RS}$ $\overline{NO} \leftrightarrow \overline{ST}$
$\overline{OP} \leftrightarrow \overline{TU}$ $\overline{PM} \leftrightarrow \overline{UR}$

The congruent parts are:

$\angle M \cong \angle R$ $\angle N \cong \angle S$ $\angle O \cong \angle T$ $\angle P \cong \angle U$

1. Rod says that the statement "quadrilateral *DEFG* ~ quadrilateral *JKLM*" is true. Merry says that the statement "quadrilateral *DEFG* ~ quadrilateral *KJLM*" is true. Can they both be correct? Why or why not?

_____

_____

_____

◣ Focus on the Idea

Similar polygons have the same shape, but not the same size. Corresponding angles of similar polygons are congruent. Corresponding sides are in proportion.

Practice

Write a similarity statement about each pair of similar polygons. Then name the congruent angles and the corresponding sides. Part of the first one is done for you.

2.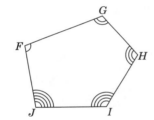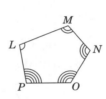

_____ pentagon FGHIJ ~ pentagon LMNOP _____

∠F ≅ ∠L, ∠G ≅ ∠M, ∠H ≅ ∠ _____, ∠I ≅ ∠ _____, ∠J ≅ _____,

$\overline{FG} \leftrightarrow \overline{LM}$, $\overline{GH} \leftrightarrow \overline{MN}$, $\overline{HI} \leftrightarrow$ _____, $\overline{IJ} \leftrightarrow$ _____ , $\overline{JF} \leftrightarrow$ _____

3.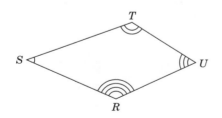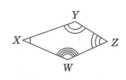

_____

_____

4.

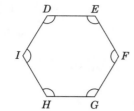

_____

_____

Extend the Idea

An equation stating that two ratios are equal is called a proportion. The corresponding sides of two similar polygons are in proportion. So you can use proportions to find the missing sides of similar polygons.

Example: Find the measures of the missing sides:

trapezoid *RSTU* ~ trapezoid *KLMN*

The measures of $\overline{RS}, \overline{ST}, \overline{RU}, \overline{KL}$, and $\overline{MN}$ are given. Write proportions to find the measures of the missing sides.

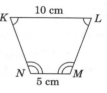

Step 1 Write proportions for corresponding sides.

$$\frac{RS}{KL} = \frac{ST}{LM} \qquad \frac{RS}{KL} = \frac{TU}{MN} \qquad \frac{RS}{KL} = \frac{RU}{KN}$$

Step 2 Substitute the lengths of the sides.

$$\frac{8}{10} = \frac{6}{LM} \qquad \frac{8}{10} = \frac{TU}{5} \qquad \frac{8}{10} = \frac{6}{KN}$$

Step 3 Cross-multiply and solve to find the missing sides.

$$\frac{8}{10} = \frac{6}{LM} \qquad \frac{8}{10} = \frac{TU}{5} \qquad \frac{8}{10} = \frac{6}{KN}$$

Step 4 Solve.

$$8(\overline{LM}) = 60 \qquad 10(\overline{TU}) = 40 \qquad (\overline{KN}) = 60$$

$$\frac{8(LM)}{8} = \frac{60}{8} \qquad \frac{10(TU)}{10} = \frac{40}{10} \qquad \frac{8(KN)}{8} = \frac{60}{8}$$

Missing sides: $\overline{LM} = 7.5$ cm $\qquad \overline{TU} = 4$ cm $\qquad \overline{KN} = 7.5$ cm

✓Check Your Understanding

5. If all pairs of corresponding sides of two polygons form the ratio $\frac{3}{4}$, are the polygons similar? Why or why not?

_____

Practice

6. Circle the pairs of figures that are similar.

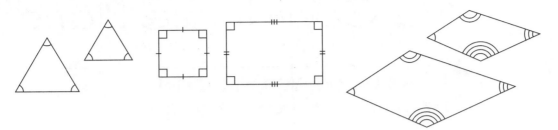

Use proportions to find the missing measures in each pair of similar polygons. The first one is started for you.

7. quadrilateral $RSTU$ ~ quadrilateral $WXYZ$

$$\frac{RS}{WX} = \frac{ST}{XY}$$

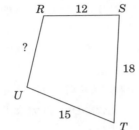
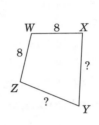

8. pentagon $VWXYZ$ ~ pentagon $ABCDE$

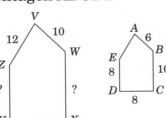

9. rectangle $ABCD$ ~ rectangle $NKLM$

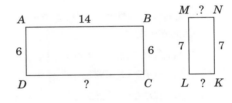

Apply the Idea

10. Look back at the blueprint shown on page 110. Use a metric ruler to find the dimensions of Office 1, Office 2, and the outer walls. Write the lengths directly on the blueprint.

Write About It

11. Each of two polygons is similar to a third polygon. Are the two polygons similar to each other? Why or why not? In the margin, draw a picture to prove your answer.

_____

_____

4•9 Drawing Polygons on the Coordinate Plane

IN THIS LESSON, YOU WILL LEARN

To draw polygons on the coordinate plane

WORDS TO LEARN

Coordinate plane *a grid where every point can be located by using two numbers*

x-axis *the horizontal number line used on a coordinate plane*

y-axis *the vertical number line used on a coordinate plane*

Origin *the meeting point of the x-axis and the y-axis*

Ordered pair *two numbers that tell the x-coordinate and y-coordinate of a point*

Coordinate *one of the numbers in an ordered pair*

x-coordinate *the number of units that a point is right or left of the origin*

y-coordinate *the number of units that a point is up or down from the origin*

Transformations *movements of a figure from one place to another*

Translation *slide of a figure*

Reflection *flip of a figure over a given line*

Rotation *turn of a figure*

Lila uses a map to show Luke how to get to her house. The map is separated into sections by horizontal and vertical dotted lines. How do these lines help Lila show Luke where she lives?

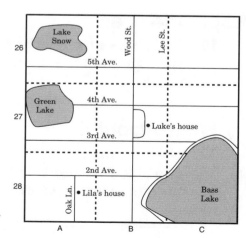

New Idea

Two intersecting number lines form a **coordinate plane** (koh-AWR-duh-niht playn). The horizontal number line is called the **x-axis** (EHKS-ak-sihs). The vertical number line is called the **y-axis** (WY-ak-sihs). The intersection of the x-axis and the y-axis is the **origin**. Pairs of numbers are used to locate points in a coordinate plane. Each is called an **ordered pair** (AWR-dehrd pair). Each number in an ordered pair is called a

coordinate (koh-AWR-duh-niht). The first coordinate of an ordered pair is the **x-coordinate** (EHKS-koh-awr-duh-niht). The second coordinate is the **y-coordinate** (WY-koh-awr-duh-niht).

A polygon can be located on a coordinate plane by assigning an ordered pair to each vertex, then drawing a dot at each point. The dots can then be connected to draw the polygon.

Example: What are the ordered pairs for the vertices of $\triangle DEF$?

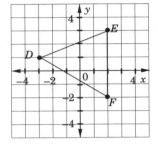

Give the x-coordinate first, then the y-coordinate.
  Point D is at $(-3, 1)$.
  Point E is at $(2, 3)$.
  Point F is at $(2, -2)$.

Ordered pairs can be used to locate the vertices of a polygon.

Example: Draw $\triangle ABC$ with the following vertices: A at $(3, 2)$, B at $(4, -3)$, and C at $(-2, 2)$.

Locate each point by first moving right or left along the x-axis, then up or down along the y-axis. Connect the points to draw $\triangle ABC$.

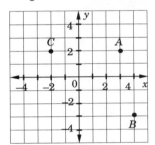
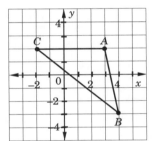

Focus on the Idea

On the coordinate plane, ordered pairs of numbers are used to locate points. Each of the two numbers that make up an ordered pair is called a coordinate. The horizontal number line in a coordinate plane is called the x-axis. The vertical number line is called the y-axis. An ordered pair always lists the x-coordinate first, then the y-coordinate.

✓ Check the Math

1. Hera graphs point M on the coordinate plane. She says that the point is located on the x-axis. Michael says that the y-coordinate must be 0. Is he correct? Why or why not?

_____

_____

Practice

Name the ordered pairs at each vertex of the polygon. The first one is done for you.

2.

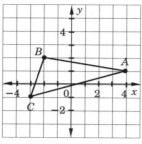

A at (4, 1)

B at (–2, 2)

C at (–3, –1)

3.

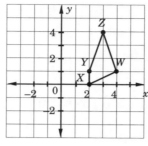

W at _____

X at _____

Y at _____

Z at _____

4.

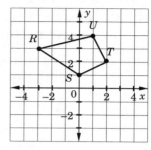

R at _____

S at _____

T at _____

U at _____

Draw a polygon with the given vertices on the coordinate plane. Then give the name of the polygon you have drawn.

5. J at (–4, 3), K at (–2, –2), L at (–2, 3)_____

6. R at (1, 1), T at (2, –4), W at (–3, –1), X at (–3, 3)_____

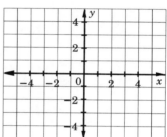

Extend the Idea

A polygon can be moved to a different position on the coordinate plane by sliding, flipping, or turning it. All three movements are called **transformations** (trans-fuhr-MAY-shuhns). A slide is called a **translation** (trans-LAY-shuhn). A flip is called a **reflection** (rih-FLEK-shuhn). A turn is called a **rotation** (roh-TAY-shuhn).

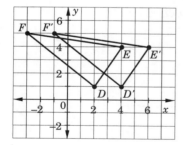

Triangle *DEF* has been *translated* 2 units to the right. The coordinates of the image are *D′*(4, 1), *E′*(6, 4), and *F′*(–1, 5). *D′E′F′* is read as *D* prime, *E* prime, *F* prime.

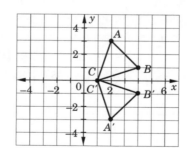

Triangle *ABC* has been *reflected* over the *x*-axis. The coordinates of the image are *A′*(2, –3), *B′*(4, –1), and *C′*(1, 0).

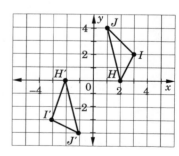

Triangle *HIJ* has been *rotated* 180°. The coordinates of the image are *H′*(–2, 0), *I′*(–3, –3), and *J′*(–1, –4).

✓Check Your Understanding

Identify each transformation as a *translation*, a *reflection*, or a *rotation*.

7.
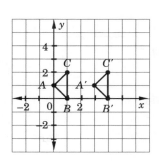

8.
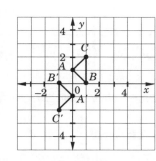

9.
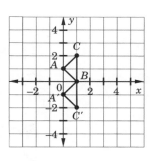

_____   _____   _____

Practice

Graph the image of △*FGH* under the transformation described. Then state the coordinates of the image.

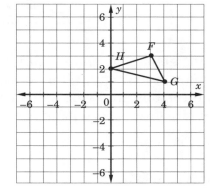

10. Translate △*FGH* 3 units to the right. Label the translated image △*F'G'H'*.

    F' _____   *G'* _____   *H'* _____

11. Reflect △*FGH* over the *x*-axis. Label the reflected image △*F"G"H"*.

    F" _____   *G"* _____   *H"* _____

Apply the Idea

12. Look back at the map on page 114. How can Lila refer to the coordinates on the map to help Luke find her house?

    _____

    _____

    _____

✎ Write About It

13. Look at yourself in a mirror. What transformation can you use to describe your image? Explain your answer.

    _____

    _____

    _____

    _____

◢4•10 Tessellations of Regular Polygons

◢ IN THIS LESSON, YOU WILL LEARN

To identify a tessellation

To create a tessellation using transformations

WORDS TO LEARN

Tessellation *pattern of repeating polygons that completely covers an area without any gaps or overlaps*

Regular tessellation *pattern formed by tessellating one regular polygon*

Some geometric shapes can be used to cover a given area. Square, rectangular, and octagonal tiles can cover kitchen countertops and back splashes. Wood parquet is used for floors. Often, these geometric pieces are set in interesting designs.

New Idea

A pattern of repeating polygons that completely covers an area is called a **tessellation** (tehs-uh-LAY-shuhn). There are no gaps between the polygons that form a tessellation. The polygons do not overlap. A tessellation formed by repeating one regular polygon is called a **regular tessellation** (REHG-yuh-luhr tehs-uh-LAY-shuhn).

⟿Remember

An equilateral triangle is a regular polygon with three congruent sides and three congruent angles.

Examples: What kind of tessellation does each pattern represent?

The pattern at the right is formed by by octagons and squares. It is a tessellation.

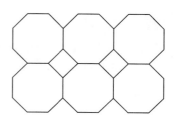

The pattern at the right is formed by equilateral triangles. It is a regular tessellation.

1. Circle the regular tessellations.

◄ **Focus on the Idea**

A pattern of repeating polygons that completely covers an area without any gaps or overlaps is called a tessellation. A regular tessellation is formed by repeating one regular polygon.

Practice

Name the polygon or polygons in each tessellation. The first one is done for you.

2.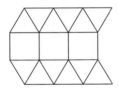

equilateral triangles, squares

3.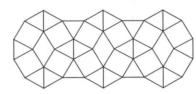

_____

4.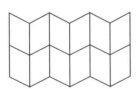

_____

5.

_____

6. Look back at exercises 2 and 3.

   a. Compare your answers. What do you notice?

   _____

   b. Compare the tessellations. What do you notice?

   _____

   c. What conclusions can you draw?

   _____

Extend the Idea

A tessellation is formed by translating, reflecting, or rotating one or more polygons. You can use one or all of these transformations of one or more polygons to make tessellations of your own.

Example: Make a tessellation with a triangle and a trapezoid.

Draw the given polygons (a triangle and a trapezoid) on dot paper.

Then transform the polygons so that they do not overlap and there are no gaps.

✓Check the Math

7. Will said that each of the sides of a polygon in a tessellation must be congruent to a side of another polygon in the tessellation. Is he correct? Why or why not?

_____

_____

_____

Practice

Use the given polygons to make a tessellation that covers the dotted area as completely as possible.

8.

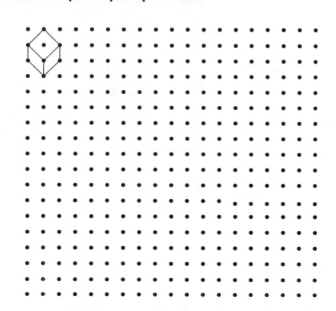

9.

10. Choose polygons to make a tessellation of your own.

Apply the Idea

11. Look back at one of the tiles shown on page 119. How would you describe the pattern? How might it have been formed?

_____

12. Look around you and find other examples of tessellations. Draw pictures of your examples and describe how the tessellations might have been formed.

_____

Write About It

13. Is it possible to make a tessellation with a circle? Why or why not? Draw a picture to support your answer.

_____

_____

In This Chapter, You Have Learned

- To identify and name polygons
- To identify and use properties of parallelograms, rectangles, rhombuses, squares, and trapezoids
- To identify regular polygons and congruent polygons
- To find the measure of the angles of a regular polygon
- To find the lengths of corresponding sides of similar polygons
- To draw polygons on the coordinate plane
- To identify and create a tessellation

Words You Know

From the lists of "Words to Learn," choose the word or phrase that best completes each statement.

1. A(n)_____ is a closed figure with three or more sides.

2. A pattern of repeating polygons that completely covers an area without any gaps or overlaps is called a(n)_____.

3. A rectangle is a(n)_____ with four right angles.

4. A(n)_____ with exactly one pair of parallel sides is called a trapezoid.

5. A parallelogram with four congruent sides is called a(n)_____.

6. _____ polygons have the same size and shape.

7. A(n)_____ of numbers is used to give the location of a point on a coordinate plane.

More Practice

Name each polygon.

8.

9.

10.

11.

_____ _____ _____ _____

Name the quadrilateral. Be as specific as possible.

12.

13.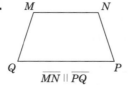
$\overline{MN} \parallel \overline{PQ}$

14.

15.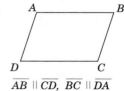
$\overline{AB} \parallel \overline{CD}, \ \overline{BC} \parallel \overline{DA}$

_____ _____ _____ _____

Use parallelogram ABCD for exercises 16 to 19.

16. $m\angle C = $ _____

17. $m\angle B = m\angle D = $ _____

18. $CD = $ _____

19. $\triangle ABD \cong \triangle$ _____

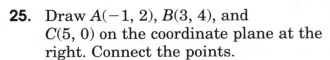

Use rhombus WXYZ for exercises 20 to 23.

20. $YW = $ _____

21. $XQ = QZ = $ _____

22. $XZ = $ _____

23. $m\angle XQY = m\angle$ _____ $= m\angle$ _____ $= m\angle$ _____ $= $ _____

24. **a.** How many interior angles does a regular octagon have?

    _____

    b. What is the measure of each interior angle?

    _____

25. Draw $A(-1, 2)$, $B(3, 4)$, and $C(5, 0)$ on the coordinate plane at the right. Connect the points.

26. Reflect the polygon you drew for excercise 25 over the x–axis. Label the new points A', B', and C'.

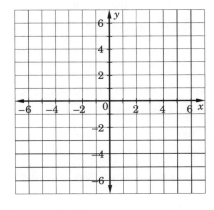

Problems You Can Solve

27. Draw a quadrilateral. Then draw a line segment that could be the side of a similar quadrilateral. Use proportions to find the lengths of the other three sides of the similar quadrilateral. Then finish drawing the similar quadrilateral.

28. **For Your Portfolio**   Work in a small group. Look around for signs that are shaped like polygons. Describe each sign and name each polygon. Why do you think these shapes were chosen for these signs? Present your findings to the class.

Chapter 4   Practice Test

Write the letter to identify each polygon. Use each letter only once.

1. hexagon _____

2. octagon _____

3. trapezoid_____

4. quadrilateral_____

5. rhombus _____

6. rectangle_____

a.

b.

c.

d.

e.

f.

Find the following.

7. The measure of one angle of a parallelogram is 80°. What are the measures of the other angles of the parallelogram?_____

8. The length of a base of a trapezoid is 18. The length of its median is 14. What is the length of the other base? _____

The sum of the measures of the angles of a certain regular polygon is 720°.

9. How many sides does the polygon have? _____

10. What is the name of the polygon? _____

11. What is the measure of each interior angle of the polygon? _____

12. What is the measure of each exterior angle of the polygon? _____

Solve.

13. Adrian is creating a quadrilateral by drawing two congruent equilateral triangles. What kind of quadrilateral did she draw?_____

Use the similar quadrilaterals at the right to answer exercises 14 to 16.

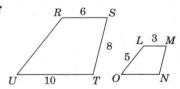

14. *MN* = _____

15. *NO* = _____

16. *RU* = _____

17. Draw the following points *F*(5, 2), *G*(4, −2), *H*(0, −3), and *I*(−2, 1). Connect the points.

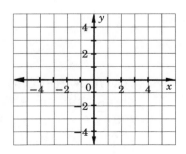

Chapter 5

Area and Perimeter of Polygons

OBJECTIVES:

In this chapter, you will learn

- *To find the perimeter and area of parallelograms and rectangles*
- *To estimate the perimeter and area of polygons*
- *To find the perimeter and area of rhombuses and squares*
- *To find the area of triangles and trapezoids*
- *To find the perimeter and area of irregular polygons*
- *To know when to use perimeter or area to solve problems*

In 1891, Dr. James Naismith invented the game of basketball. The original game used two wooden peach baskets nailed to the balcony of a school gym.

The current game uses backboards, hoops, and nets. It is played on a rectangular court. The court is painted with carefully measured lines, circles, and rectangles. The area and the perimeter of each court must be the same as every other court. To make sure a court is the standard shape and size, it is necessary to know how to find the area and perimeter of several kinds of polygons.

◢5•1 Perimeter of Parallelograms and Rectangles

◢ IN THIS LESSON, YOU WILL LEARN
To find the perimeter of parallelograms and rectangles

WORDS TO LEARN
Perimeter *the distance around a polygon*
Length of a rectangle *the longer pair of sides*
Width of a rectangle *the shorter pair of sides*

The distance around the outside of a basketball court is the perimeter of the court. What is the measure of the perimeter of this court?

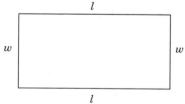

New Idea

The **perimeter** (puh-RIHM-uh-tuhr) of a polygon, or the distance around the polygon, is found by adding the measures of its sides. The **length of a rectangle** (lehngkth) refers to the measure of each of the two longer sides of a rectangle. The **width of a rectangle** (wihdth) refers to the measure of each of the two shorter sides. Find the perimeter, P, of a rectangle, where l is the length and w is the width, by using the formula:

Perimeter = length + length + width + width
$$P = l + l + w + w$$
$$P = 2l + 2w$$

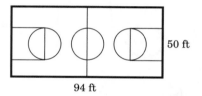

Examples: What is the perimeter of the basketball court? The length of the basketball court is 94 feet and the width is 50 feet.

$P = 2l + 2w$
$P = 2(94) + 2(50)$ ← Substitute 94 for l and 50 for w.
$P = 188 + 100$ ← Simplify.
$P = 288$

The perimeter of the basketball court is 288 feet.

To find the perimeter of the parallelogram at the right, find the total length of the four sides.

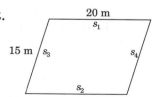

$P = s_1 + s_2 + s_3 + s_4$
$P = 2(20) + 2(15)$ ← Substitute 20 for 2 sides and 15 for 2 sides.
$P = 40 + 30$ ← Simplify.
$P = 70$ m

Focus on the Idea

The perimeter of a polygon is the total length of its sides. Use the formula P = 2l + 2w to find the perimeter of a rectangle. The perimeter of a polygon can be found by adding the measures of all the sides.

Practice

Find the perimeter of each parallelogram or rectangle. Show your work. The first one is done for you.

1.

6 in.

9 in.

$P = \underline{6 + 6 + 9 + 9 = 30 \text{ in.}}$

2.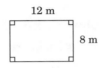

12 m

8 m

$P = \underline{\hspace{3cm}}$

3.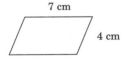

7 cm

4 cm

$P = \underline{\hspace{3cm}}$

4.

14 ft

12 ft

$P = \underline{\hspace{3cm}}$

5.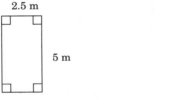

2.5 m

5 m

$P = \underline{\hspace{3cm}}$

6.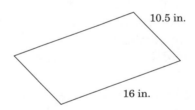

10.5 in.

16 in.

$P = \underline{\hspace{3cm}}$

Apply the Idea

7. Refer to the diagram at the top of page 126. The line segment across the middle of a basketball court is called the half-court line. How long is the half-court line? What is the perimeter of each half-court? $\underline{\hspace{3cm}}$

Write About It

8. Dani has 44 feet of fencing to use to make a rectangular dog pen. Give at least two possible combinations of length and width for the dog pen. Tell how you found the combinations.

$\underline{\hspace{10cm}}$

$\underline{\hspace{10cm}}$

◄5•2 Area of Parallelograms and Rectangles

◄IN THIS LESSON, YOU WILL LEARN

To find the area of parallelograms and rectangles

WORDS TO LEARN

Area *the measure of the surface a figure covers*

Base of a parallelogram *any side of a parallelogram*

Height of a parallelogram *the perpendicular distance between the bases*

Yolanda is making covers for her textbooks. She needs to cut pieces of paper that have a width of 12 inches and a length of 20 inches. What is the area of each book cover she makes?

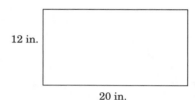

New Idea

The **area** (AIR-ee-uh) of a polygon is the measure of the surface it covers. The area of a rectangle can be found by multiplying the length and the width.

Area = length • width

$A = lw$

A **base of a parallelogram** (bays) can be any side. The **height of a parallelogram** (heyet) is the perpendicular distance between opposite bases. The area of a parallelogram can be found by multiplying the length of a base and the height.

Area = base • height

$A = bh$

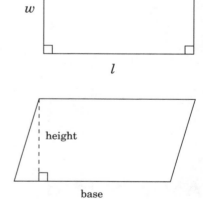

Examples: What is the area of each of Yolanda's book covers? The length of each book cover is 20 inches. The width is 12 inches.

$A = lw$

$A = 20 • 12$ ← Substitute 20 for l and 12 for w.

$A = 240$

The area of each book cover is 240 square inches, or 240 in.^{2}

What is the area of the parallelogram at the right?

$A = bh$

$A = 6 \cdot 4$ ← Substitute 6 for b and 4 for h.

$A = 24$

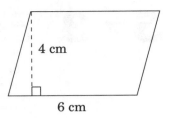

4 cm

6 cm

The area is 24 square centimeters, or 24 cm².

Focus on the Idea

The area of a rectangle is found by multiplying the length and the width. The area of a parallelogram is found by multiplying the base and the height.

Practice

Find the area of each parallelogram or rectangle. Show your work. The first two are done for you.

1.

7 cm

6 cm

$\underline{A = 7 \cdot 6 = 42 \ cm^2}$

2.

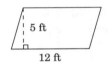

5 ft

12 ft

$\underline{A = 12 \cdot 5 = 60 \ ft^2}$

3.

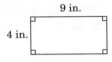

9 in.

4 in.

_____

4.

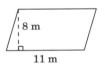

8 m

11 m

_____

5.

2.5 cm

6.5 cm

_____

6.

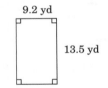

9.2 yd

13.5 yd

_____

Apply the Idea

7. Look back at the diagram of the basketball court on page 126. What is the area of the court? _____

Write About It

8. Can the area of a rectangle ever have the same number of units as its perimeter? Why or why not?

_____

_____

_____

↳5•3 Estimating Perimeter and Area

▸ **IN THIS LESSON, YOU WILL LEARN**

To estimate the perimeter and area of polygons

WORDS TO LEARN

Estimate *to make an educated guess about value*

To build support for endangered species, a wildlife foundation is holding a poster contest. Each poster must be shaped like a polygon. The back of the poster must be marked off in one-inch squares. The perimeter must be less than or equal to 100 inches. The area must be less than or equal to 100 square inches.

To make sure each poster meets the requirements, the contest judges must **estimate** (EHS-tuh-mayt), or guess, its perimeter and area.

New Idea

Sometimes you need only an approximate value for a perimeter or area. In these cases, you can estimate given certain information.

↪**Remember**

The symbol ≈ means "is approximately equal to."

Examples: How can the judges estimate the perimeter of this poster?

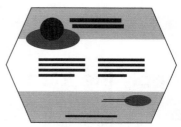

The judges use the grid on the back of the poster to estimate the length of each side. Then they add the lengths. They estimate that two of the sides measure 8 inches and four sides measure 5 inches.

$$P \approx 8 + 8 + 5 + 5 + 5 + 5 \approx 36$$

So, the perimeter is less than 100 inches.

How can the judges estimate the area of the poster?

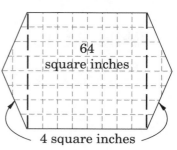

64 square inches

4 square inches

They count the number of squares inside the poster. Since the main part of the poster has 8 squares along the bottom and is 8 squares high, its area is 64 square inches. Each of the parts at the right and left sides of the poster adds at least another 4 square inches.

Area $\approx 64 + 4 + 4 \approx 72$

The approximate area, 72 in.^{2}, is less than 100 square inches. So, the poster meets the perimeter and area requirements of the contest.

◤ Focus on the Idea

Estimating is a good way to find approximate values for the area and perimeter of polygons.

Practice

Estimate the perimeter and area of each polygon shown on a grid. The first one is done for you.

1.

$P \approx$ ___20 units___

$A \approx$ ___18 square units___

2.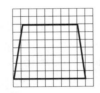

$P \approx$ _____

$A \approx$ _____

3.

$P \approx$ _____

$A \approx$ _____

4.

$P \approx$ _____

$A \approx$ _____

5.

$P \approx$ _____

$A \approx$ _____

6.

$P \approx$ _____

$A \approx$ _____

Apply the Idea

7. Work in a small group. Design an endangered species poster for the contest. Be sure to make your poster meet the shape and size requirements. Your polygon should have at least two different dimensions. Draw your design on a 1-inch grid.

✎ Write About It

8. How could you estimate the area of a figure that is not a polygon? Give an example.

_____

_____

5•4 Perimeter and Area of a Rhombus or a Square

IN THIS LESSON, YOU WILL LEARN

To find the perimeter and area of a rhombus and a square

WORDS TO LEARN

Rhombus *a four-sided figure with sides of equal length*

A community group, For the Neighborhood (FTN), is planning to make a vacant lot into a park. FTN decides to begin the work by laying sod over the entire lot and protecting it with a fence. To know how much fencing to buy, FTN needs to know the perimeter of the lot. To know how much sod to buy, FTN needs to know the area of the lot. The lot is shaped like a **rhombus**. (See Lesson 4•4.) What measurements does FTN need to find the perimeter and area of the lot?

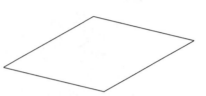

New Idea

To find the perimeter of a rhombus, multiply the length of one side by the number of sides, 4.

$$\text{Perimeter} = 4 \cdot \text{length of each side}$$
$$P = 4s$$

To find the area of a rhombus, use the formula for the area of a parallelogram.

$$A = bh$$

Examples: How much fencing does FTN need to buy?

$P = 4s$ ← Substitute 90 for s.
$P = 4 \cdot 90 = 360$

FTN needs to buy 360 feet of fencing.

How much sod does FTN need to buy?

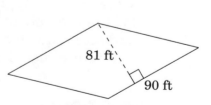

$A = bh$ ← Substitute 90 for b and 81 for h.

$A = 90 \cdot 81 = 7,290$

FTN needs to buy 7,290 square feet of sod.

Give the base and the height for each rhombus.

1.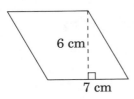

6 cm

7 cm

b = _____

h = _____

2.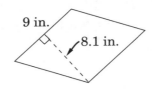

9 in.

8.1 in.

b = _____

h = _____

3.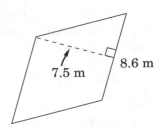

7.5 m

8.6 m

b = _____

h = _____

Focus on the Idea

The perimeter of a rhombus can be found by using the formula P = 4s. The area of a rhombus can be found using the formula for the area of a parallelogram, A = bh.

Practice

Find the perimeter and area of each rhombus. Show your work. The first one is done for you.

4.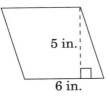

5 in.

6 in.

$P = \underline{4 \cdot 6 = 24}$ in.

$A = \underline{6 \cdot 5 = 30}$ in.²

5.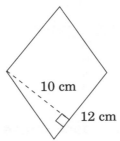

10 cm

12 cm

P = _____

A = _____

6.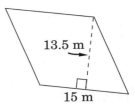

13.5 m

15 m

P = _____

A = _____

7.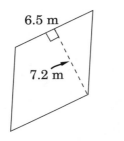

6.5 m

7.2 m

P = _____

A = _____

8.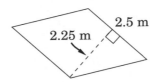

2.5 m

2.25 m

P = _____

A = _____

9.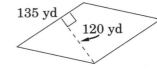

135 yd

120 yd

P = _____

A = _____

Extend the Idea

Recall that a square is a rhombus with four right angles. You can find the perimeter of a square the same way you find the perimeter of a rhombus, by using the formula $P = 4s$. Since all sides of a square are the same length, you can find the area of a square by multiplying one side by itself.

$A = \text{side} \cdot \text{side}$
$A = s^2$

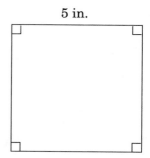

5 in.

Examples: Find the perimeter of the square at the right.

$P = 4s$ $\leftarrow$ Substitute 5 for s.
$P = 4 \cdot 5 = 20$

The perimeter of the square is 20 inches.

Find the area of the square at the right.
$A = s^2$ $\leftarrow$ Substitute 5 for s.
$A = 5^2 = 5 \cdot 5 = 25$

The area of the square is 25 square inches.

✓Check the Math

10. Margie says that the area of a square of a certain size is 36 square meters. Mario says that the area is 32.4 square meters. If the length of the sides of the square is a whole number, who is correct? Why?

_____

_____

🖩 Practice

Find the perimeter and the area of each square. Show your work. The first one is done for you.

11.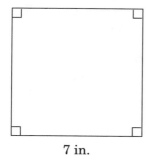

7 in.

$P = \underline{4 \cdot 7 = 28 \text{ in.}}$

$A = \underline{7 \cdot 7 = 49 \text{ in.}^2}$

12.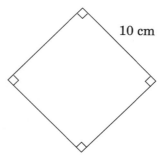

10 cm

$P = \underline{\hspace{3cm}}$

$A = \underline{\hspace{3cm}}$

13.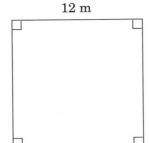

12 m

$P =$ _____

$A =$ _____

14.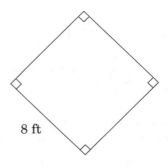

8 ft

$P =$ _____

$A =$ _____

15.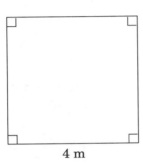

4 m

$P =$ _____

$A =$ _____

16.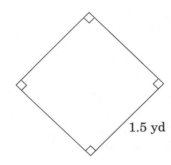

1.5 yd

$P =$ _____

$A =$ _____

Apply the Idea

17. The perimeter of a square garden is 56 feet. What is the area of the garden? _____

18. The area of a mirror shaped like a rhombus is 224 square inches. If the height of the mirror is 14 inches, what is the length of each side of the mirror? _____

19. Work with a partner to draw a rhombus. Cut out the shape. Then, find a way to cut the rhombus to make it into a rectangle that has the same area as the rhombus. Make a sketch of your work in the margin. What is the least number of cuts you can make to do this? _____

Write About It

20. The perimeter of a rhombus is 12 centimeters. Its area is 9 square centimeters. What must be true about this rhombus? How do you know?

_____

_____

5•5 Properties of the
Diagonals of a Rhombus

IN THIS LESSON, YOU WILL LEARN

*To find the area of a rhombus by using the measure
of its diagonal*

WORDS TO LEARN

Diagonal *the line segment that joins two
non-consecutive vertices of a polygon*

Norman is making rhombus-shaped party invitations. Each
rhombus needs to have diagonals with lengths of 5 inches
and 4.5 inches so that it will fit into an envelope of that size.
What is the area of each rhombus?

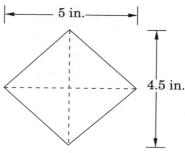

New Idea

The formula $A = bh$ is not the only formula for the area
of a rhombus. Another area formula uses the length of the **diagonal**.
(See Lesson 4•1.) The length of the diagonals is represented by d_1 and
d_2. The area of a rhombus is one-half times the product of d_1 and d_2.

Area = $\frac{1}{2}$ • (diagonal 1) • (diagonal 2)

$A = \frac{1}{2}d_1d_2$

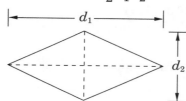

Example: Find the area of each rhombus Norman is making.

$A = \frac{1}{2}d_1d_2$

$A = \frac{1}{2} • 5 • 4.5$ ← Substitute 5 for d_1 and 4.5 for d_2.

$A = 11.25$ in.^{2} ← Simplify.

Focus on the Idea

*The area of a rhombus is one-half the product of the
lengths of its two diagonals.*

$A = \frac{1}{2}d_1d_2$

Practice

Find the area of each rhombus. The first one is done for you.

1.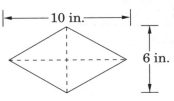

$$A = \tfrac{1}{2} \cdot 6 \times 10 = 30 \text{ in.}^2$$

2.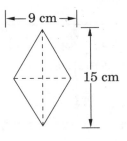

3.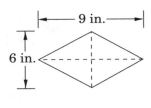

4.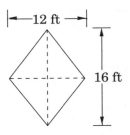

5.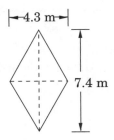

6.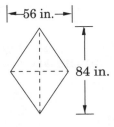

7. The area of a rhombus is 81 square feet. The length of one diagonal is 9 feet. How long is the other diagonal? _____

8. The area of a rhombus is 100 square meters. Give at least two possibilities for the lengths of the diagonals. _____

Apply the Idea

9. Norman decides to make a few invitations to fit into 9-inch by 4.5-inch envelopes. What is the area of the largest rhombus that will fit in these envelopes? _____

10. Recall that the diagonals of a rhombus are perpendicular to each other and that they bisect each other.

   a. What can you say about the four triangles formed by the two diagonals?

   _____

   b. If the area of a rhombus is 16 square inches, what is the area of each of the four triangles formed by the two diagonals? _____

Write About It

11. Do you think the formula for the area of a rhombus can be used to find the area of a square? Why or why not?

_____

_____

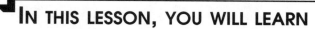

5•6 Area of Triangles

IN THIS LESSON, YOU WILL LEARN

To find the area of triangles

WORDS TO LEARN

Base of a triangle *any side of a triangle*

Height of a triangle *length of line segment drawn from a vertex so that it is perpendicular to the opposite base*

Caylah wants to wallpaper a triangular section of a wall. She needs to find the area of the section in order to know how much wallpaper to buy.

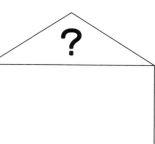

New Idea

The **base of a triangle** (bays uhv uh TRY-ang-guhl) is any side of the triangle. The **height of a triangle** (heyet uhv uh TRY-ang-guhl) is the length of the line segment drawn from a vertex perpendicular to the opposite base. The area of a triangle can be found by multiplying one-half times the base b and the height h.

Area $= \frac{1}{2} \cdot$ base $\cdot$ height

$A = \frac{1}{2}bh$

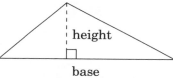

Example: What is the area of the base of Caylah's triangular wall section?

$A = \frac{1}{2}bh$

$A = \frac{1}{2} \cdot 12 \cdot 6$ ← Substitute 12 for b and 6 for h.

$A = 36$

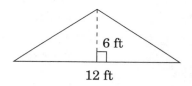

The area of the triangular wall section is 36 ft^2.

✓Check the Math

1. Paul says that the area of a triangle with base 16 meters and height 5 meters is 80 square meters. Paula says that the area is 40 square meters. Who is correct? How do you know?

◤ Focus on the Idea

To find the area of a triangle, find one-half the base times the height.

▦ Practice

Find the area of each triangle. Show your work. The first one is done for you.

2.
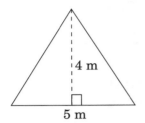
4 m
5 m

$A = \frac{1}{2}bh$
$A = \frac{1}{2} \cdot 5 \cdot 4$
$A = \frac{1}{2} \cdot 20$
$A = 10 \text{ m}^2$

3.
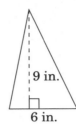
9 in.
6 in.

4.
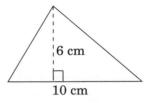
6 cm
10 cm

5.
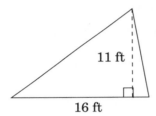
11 ft
16 ft

6.
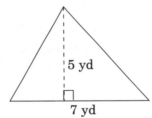
5 yd
7 yd

7.
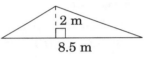
2 m
8.5 m

Apply the Idea

8. The area of a triangular mural is 15 square meters. Its height is 6 meters. What is the length of the base of the mural? _____

9. The area of a triangular park is 24 square kilometers. Give at least two possible pairs of measurements for the base and the height of the park. _____

✎ Write About It

10. Draw a parallelogram. How can you find its area? How could you find the area of a triangle by using the formula for the area of a parallelogram? Draw a picture as part of your answer.

_____

_____

Area of Trapezoids

> **IN THIS LESSON, YOU WILL LEARN**
>
> To find the area of trapezoids
>
> **WORDS TO LEARN**
>
> **Height of a trapezoid** *the perpendicular distance between the bases of the trapezoid*

Shaun is making a picture frame. Each of the four identical pieces of the frame is shaped like a trapezoid. Shaun wants to know the area of each piece so he can estimate how much veneer he will need to cover the pieces.

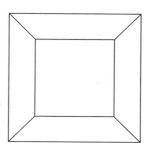

Remember

The two parallel sides of a trapezoid are called the bases.

New Idea

The **height of a trapezoid** (heyet uhv uh TRA-puh-zoyd) is the perpendicular distance between the bases. The area of a trapezoid can be found by multiplying $\frac{1}{2}$ the height by the sum of the bases.

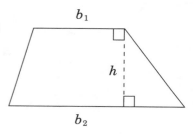

Area = $\frac{1}{2}$ • height • (base 1 + base 2)

$A = \frac{1}{2}h(b_1 + b_2)$

Example: How can Shaun find the area of each piece of the picture frame?

$A = \frac{1}{2}h(b_1 + b_2)$

$A = \frac{1}{2}(1)(3 + 5)$ ← Substitue 1 for h,
                             3 for b_1, and 5 for b_2.

$A = \frac{1}{2}(8)$

$A = 4$

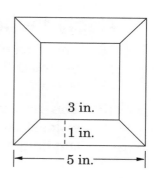

3 in.

1 in.

5 in.

The area of each piece of the frame is 4 in.^{2}

✓Check the Math

1. Fran said that the area of a trapezoid with a height of 4 centimeters and bases with lengths 6 centimeters and 8 centimeters is 20 square centimeters. Frank says the area is 28 square centimeters. Who is correct? How do you know?

Focus on the Idea

To find the area of a trapezoid, multiply half the height times the sum of the two bases.

$$A = \frac{1}{2}h(b_1 + b_2)$$

Practice

Find the area of each trapezoid. Show your work. The first one is done for you.

2.

2 cm

2 cm

4 cm

$A = \frac{1}{2}h(b_1 + b_2)$

$A = \frac{1}{2} \cdot 2(4 + 2)$

$A = 1 \cdot (6)$

$A = 6 \text{ cm}^2$

3.

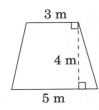

3 m

4 m

5 m

4.

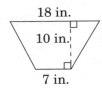

18 in.

10 in.

7 in.

5.

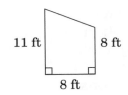

11 ft   8 ft

8 ft

6.

6 m

9 m

12 m

7.

14 yd

4.5 yd

8 yd

Apply the Idea

8. If the two nonparallel sides of a trapezoid have the same length, it is an *isosceles trapezoid*. The two dashed lines of this trapezoid show its height. Describe the three figures that make up this isosceles trapezoid. Be as specific as possible.

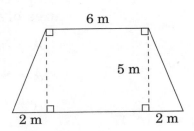

6 m

5 m

2 m   2 m

Write About It

9. How many line segments can you draw on a trapezoid to show its height? Should the segments all have the same length? Why or why not?

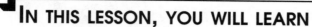 5•8 Perimeter and Area of Irregular Figures

IN THIS LESSON, YOU WILL LEARN

To find the perimeter and area of irregular figures

WORDS TO LEARN

Irregular figure *any shape than can be broken up into other recognizable shapes*

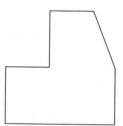

Maurice is covering his kitchen floor with tile. He needs to find the area of the floor in order to know how much tile to buy. The floor plan of his kitchen looks different from other geometric shapes he has seen. How can he find the area of the floor?

New Idea

An **irregular figure** (ihr-REHG-you-luhr FIHG-yuhr) is a shape that can be broken up into other recognizable shapes. You can often find the area of such a figure by first drawing lines to break up the figure into polygons such as rectangles, triangles, and trapezoids. Find the area of each polygon. Then add the areas of these polygons to find the area of the whole figure.

Example: How can Maurice find the area of the floor?

Add a dotted line to the floor plan, separating it into a rectangle and a trapezoid. Then find the area of each figure and add.

$A = lw$

$A = 8 \cdot 15$

$A = 120$ ← Area of rectangle

$A = \frac{1}{2}h(b_1 + b_2)$

$A = \frac{1}{2} \cdot 8(6 + 9)$

$A = (4)(15)$

$A = 60$ ← Area of trapezoid

The area of the kitchen floor is the sum of 120 ft^2 and 60 ft^2, which is 180 ft^2.

Each figure is separated into smaller polygons. Name the smaller polygons.

1.

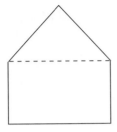

_____

2.

_____

3.

_____

4.

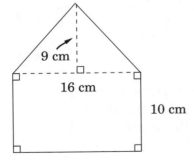

_____

◀ **Focus on the Idea**

One way to find the area of an irregular figure is to separate the figure into smaller familiar polygons. Then find the areas of the smaller polygons and find the sum of the areas.

🖩 **Practice**

Find the area of each irregular figure. The first one is done for you.

5.

9 cm

16 cm

10 cm

6.

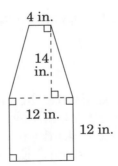

4 in.

14 in.

12 in.

12 in.

$A_1 = \frac{1}{2}bh$ $A_2 = lw$

$A_1 = \frac{1}{2}(16 \cdot 9)$ $A_2 = 16 \cdot 10$

$A_1 = 72 \text{ cm}^2$ $A_2 = 160 \text{ cm}^2$

$A = A_1 + A_2 = 72 + 160 = 232 \text{ cm}^2$

7.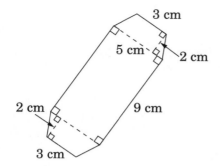

8.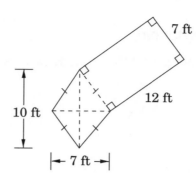

Extend the Idea

To find the perimeter of any figure, add the lengths of all the sides of the figure.

Example: Shaun wants to put molding along the base of the walls after installing his new kitchen floor. He needs to know the perimeter of the floor to know how much molding to buy.

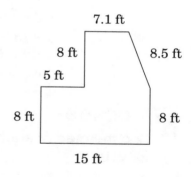

Add the measures of the sides.

$P = 7.1 + 8.5 + 8 + 15 + 8 + 5 + 8$

$P = 59.6$ ft

Shaun needs to buy approximately 60 feet of molding.

✓Check the Math

9. Jay draws an irregular figure that looks like a square on top of a rectangle. He says that if he knows the measure of one side of the square, he can find the area and the perimeter of the entire figure. Is he correct? Explain.

_____

_____

Practice

Find the perimeter of each irregular figure. The first one is done for you.

10.

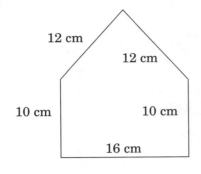

$P = 16 + 10 + 12 + 12 + 10$

$P = 60$ cm

11.

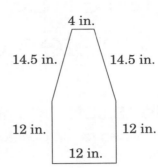

12.

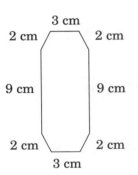

13.

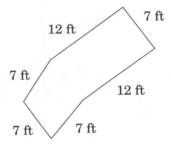

Apply the Idea

14. Look at the floor plan on page 142. Each floor tile has an area of 0.25 square feet. About how many tiles will be needed to cover the floor? _____

15. Janus is laminating the tabletop shown at the right.
   a. How many square feet of laminate will she need to cover the table? _____

   b. After Janus covers the table, she is going to put molding around the sides. How many feet of molding will she need? _____

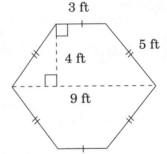

16. Work in a small group. Draw an irregular figure made up of polygons that has an area of 100 square centimeters. Use at least two different types of polygons.

Write About It

17. Suppose you are given the lengths of all the sides of an irregular figure. Can you find the perimeter of the irregular figure? Can you find its area? Why or why not?

_____

_____

5•9 Determining the Difference Between Perimeter and Area

IN THIS LESSON, YOU WILL LEARN

To know when to use perimeter or area to solve problems

WORDS TO LEARN

Linear distance *the length of a line segment or segments*

Theo is getting the pool at the local park ready for the summer. He needs to paint a stripe around the edge of the pool. He also needs to make a solar cover for the pool.

New Idea

It is important to know how to decide whether a problem involves the perimeter or the area of a figure. A problem that involves perimeter asks you to find the **linear distance** (LIHN-ee-er dis-TANS), or the length of the line segments, that make up the outside edge of a figure. A problem that involves area asks you to find the measure of the surface a figure covers.

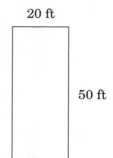

Examples: Theo finds that the width of the pool is 20 feet and the length is 50 feet. To determine how much tape he will need to mark a stripe that makes up the edge that he wants to paint, he will need to find the pool's perimeter.

$$P = 2l + 2w \qquad \leftarrow \text{Formula for the perimeter of a rectangle}$$

$$P = 2 \cdot 50 + 2 \cdot 20 = 100 + 40 = 140$$

Theo will need 140 feet of tape to mark the edge of the pool. To determine how large a cover he will need for the pool, Theo will need to find the pool's area.

$$A = lw \quad \leftarrow \text{Formula for the area of a rectangle}$$

$$A = 50 \times 20 = 1,000$$

Theo will need enough material to cover 1,000 ft², the area of the pool.

Focus on the Idea

When you need to know the distance around the outside edge of a figure, find the perimeter. When you need to know the measure of the flat region inside a figure, find the area.

Practice

Tell whether you need to use the *perimeter* or the *area* to find the amount of each material. The first two are done for you.

1. Caulking to seal around the outside edge of a window
   perimeter

2. Carpeting to cover the floor of a room ____area____

3. Molding to cover the edge of a door frame _____

4. Glass to repair a car window _____

5. Fabric to cover the seat of a chair _____

6. Edging to enclose a flower bed _____

7. Wallpaper to cover a wall _____

8. Gutter to go around the roof of a house _____

Apply the Idea

9. Rezi is planting a garden in the shape of a triangle. A drawing of the garden is shown at the right. She will cover the prepared ground with a plastic sheet before planting. She is also putting a fence around the garden.

   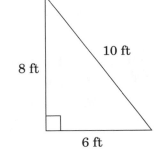

   a. How much plastic sheeting will she need?

   _____

   b. How much fencing will she need? _____

10. Jake is building a doghouse. The four sides of the doghouse will all be the same size. A drawing of a side of the doghouse is shown at the right.

    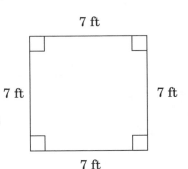

    a. How much wood does he need to make the frame for each side? _____

    b. How much plywood does he need to cover each side of the doghouse? _____

Write About It

11. How do the measurements 48 square meters and 48 meters differ? Give examples of figures that could have these measurements.

    _____

    _____

Chapter 5 Review

In This Chapter, You Have Learned
- To find the area and perimeter of parallelograms, rectangles, rhombuses, squares, triangles, and trapezoids
- To estimate the perimeter and area of a polygon
- To find the perimeter and area of some irregular figures
- To distinguish between when to use perimeter and when to use area to solve problems

Words You Know

From the lists of "Words to Learn," choose the word or phrase that best completes each statement.

1. The measure of the region a polygon covers is the
   _____.

2. The measure of the longer side of a rectangle is its
   _____; the measure of the shorter side is its
   _____.

3. The sum of the measures of all the sides of a polygon is called the _____.

More Practice

Find the perimeter and area of each parallelogram or rectangle. Show your work.

4.
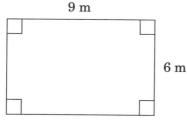
9 m

6 m

$P =$ _____ $A =$ _____

5.
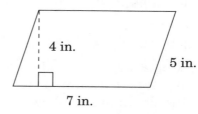
4 in.

5 in.

7 in.

$P =$ _____ $A =$ _____

6.
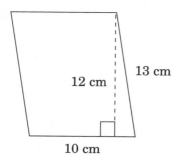
12 cm   13 cm

10 cm

$P =$ _____ $A =$ _____

7.
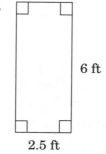
6 ft

2.5 ft

$P =$ _____ $A =$ _____

8.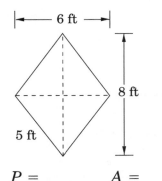

$P =$ _____ $A =$ _____

9.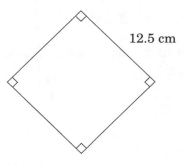

12.5 cm

$P =$ _____ $A =$ _____

Find the area of each figure.

10.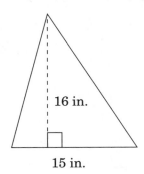

16 in.

15 in.

$A =$ _____

11.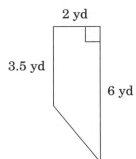

2 yd

3.5 yd

6 yd

$A =$ _____

12.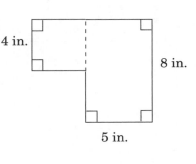

4 in.

8 in.

5 in.

$A =$ _____

Problems You Can Solve

13. Gerald is helping a group build a playground at a local park. The rectangular playground will be half sand and half grass. The length of the playground is 28 feet and the width is 25 feet.

   a. How much ground will the sand cover? _____

   b. How much fencing is needed to put around the playground? _____

14. Sharon has a stencil to make a rhombus with diagonals 3 inches and 4 inches long.

   a. What is the area of a rhombus of this size? _____

   b. Sharon draws six of the rhombuses next to one another to make a parallelogram. In the margin, draw a picture to show how she did this. What is the area of the parallelogram? _____

15. For Your Portfolio Research the size of a playing field for a sport other than basketball, such as tennis, baseball, football, or soccer. Suppose you want to add seating for fans to watch the games. In the margin, draw a diagram of the field and the necessary seats, labeling each part with the appropriate measurement. Find the total area of land needed for the field and the seats. _____

Find the perimeter and area of each figure.

1.

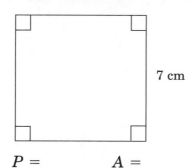

7 cm

P = _____   A = _____

2.

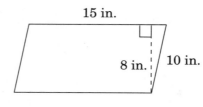

15 in.

8 in.   10 in.

P = _____   A = _____

3.

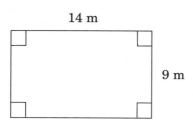

14 m

9 m

P = _____   A = _____

4.

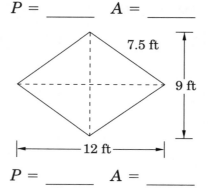

7.5 ft

9 ft

12 ft

P = _____   A = _____

Find the area of each figure shown.

5.

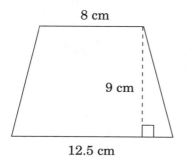

8 cm

9 cm

12.5 cm

A = _____

6.

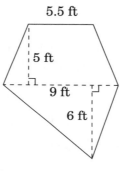

5.5 ft

5 ft

9 ft

6 ft

A = _____

Mr. Uzo is painting the ceiling of his living room. The room is a rectangle with a length of 15 feet and a width of 12 feet.

7. If Mr. Uzo needs one quart of paint for every 100 square feet of ceiling, how many quarts of paint will he need? _____

8. Mr. Uzo also decides to put molding around the ceiling. How much molding will he need?

_____

9. The diagram shows the size of the square bench Jerod is building around a tree. What is the area of each of the four pieces that form the surface of the bench? _____

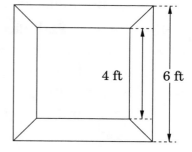

4 ft   6 ft

Chapter 6

Circles

OBJECTIVES:

In this chapter, you will learn

- *To identify and name the basic parts of a circle*
- *To identify and name lines and curves that meet to form a circle*
- *To find the circumference of a circle*
- *To find the area of a circle*
- *To identify inscribed and circumscribed polygons*
- *To find the measures of angles inscribed or circumscribed in a circle*

Circles are used in many different ways. One example is the ancient Aztec calendar. This calendar, also called the Sun Stone, is a circular calendar. It measures 3.6 meters across and weighs 24 metric tons. The face of the Aztec sun god is in the center of the circle. Other parts of the calendar that stand for the twenty days of the Aztec month are equally spaced around the calendar.

151

6•1 Parts of a Circle

---

IN THIS LESSON, YOU WILL LEARN

To identify and name the basic parts of a circle

WORDS TO LEARN

Circle *a set of points that are all the same distance from a given point called the center*

Radius *a line segment with one endpoint at the center of a circle and the other endpoint on the circle*

Diameter *a line segment that passes through the center of a circle with both endpoints on the circle*

Radii *the plural form of radius*

Look at a clock or wristwatch with a face that is shaped like a circle. The hands are attached at the center of the circle. A hand is like a radius of the circle. Two hands that are opposite rays forming one straight line are like a diameter of the circle.

New Idea

A **circle** (SER-kuhl) is the set of all points that are the same distance from a given point called the center. A **radius** (RAY-dee-uhs) is a line segment with one endpoint at the center of a circle and the other endpoint on the circle. A line segment that passes through the center of a circle with both endpoints on the circle is called a **diameter** (dy-AM-uht-uhr).

Example: Name the parts of the circle at the right.

The center of this circle is point P.
So, the circle is called circle P.
This can be written as $\odot P$.

$\overline{PQ}$, $\overline{MP}$, and $\overline{PN}$ are each a radius of the circle. $\overline{MN}$ is a diameter of the circle.

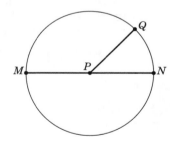

✓Check the Math

1. Garry drew circle T. He then drew a segment from T to a point W on the circle. He said that $\overline{TW}$ was a diameter of the circle. Is he correct? Why or why not? In the margin, draw and label a circle to illustrate your answer.

---

152 Chapter 6 *Circles*

Focus on the Idea

A circle is a set of all points that are the same distance from a point called the center. A radius is a line segment from the center of a circle to a point on the circle. A diameter is a line segment that passes through the center of the circle with both endpoints on the circle.

Practice

Draw and label the parts of the circle. The first one is done for you.

2. ⊙O with radius $\overline{OW}$

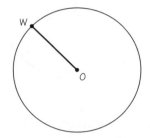

3. ⊙R with radius $\overline{RT}$

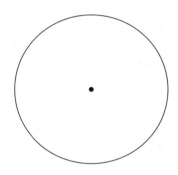

4. ⊙T with diameter $\overline{RS}$

5. ⊙M with diameter $\overline{LK}$ and radius $\overline{MQ}$

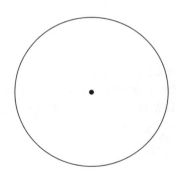

6. ⊙H with radius $\overline{HK}$ and diameter $\overline{BK}$

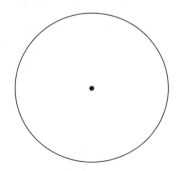

7. ⊙J with diameter $\overline{AB}$ and radius $\overline{JB}$

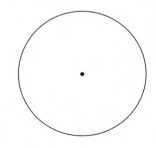

Extend the Idea

The plural of the word radius is **radii** (RAY-dee-eye). The lengths of all radii of the same circle are equal. The length of a diameter of a circle is twice the length of a radius of that circle.

You can use a compass to draw a circle with a given radius. First draw a line segment the length of the radius. Next, put the point of the compass on one endpoint of the line segment and open the compass to match the length of the segment. Then draw the circle.

Example: Draw a circle with a radius of 2 centimeters. Draw a line segment LV 2 centimeters long. Put the compass point on point V and open the compass so the pencil is on point L. Draw a circle with point V as the center. Draw a diameter through point V. The measure of the diameter is 4 centimeters.

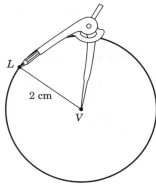

✓Check the Math

8. Anna drew a circle with a diameter of 12 inches. Kerry drew a circle with a radius of 6 inches. Kerry says that the circles are the same size. Is she right? Why or why not?

_____

_____

Practice

Write the missing measurement. Then use a centimeter ruler and a compass to draw the circle that is described. Be sure to label the parts of the circle. The first one is done for you.

9. $\odot T$ with radius $\overline{TR} = 3$ cm and diameter $\overline{SV} = $ _6 cm_

10. $\odot M$ with radius $\overline{MJ} = 1$ cm and diameter $\overline{LK} = $ _____

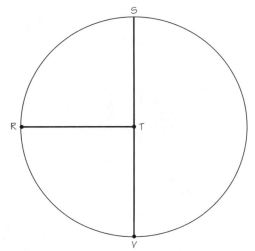

11. ⊙P with diameter $\overline{MN}$ = 4 cm and radius $\overline{PV}$ = _____

12. ⊙A with diameter $\overline{BC}$ = 5 cm and radius $\overline{AH}$ = _____

Apply the Idea

13. Look at a circular clock face. Mark this circle to look like the clock face. Label the center and both of the hands. What part of a circle do the hands suggest?

_____

_____

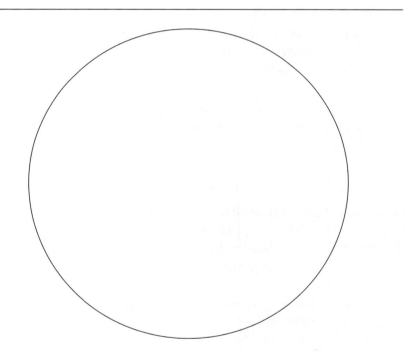

Write About It

14. How many radii does a circle have? How many diameters does a circle have? Explain.

_____

_____

_____

◀6•2 More Parts of a Circle

◀ IN THIS LESSON, YOU WILL LEARN

To identify and name lines and curves that meet in a circle

WORDS TO LEARN

Chord *a line segment with both endpoints on a circle*

Arc *part of a circle*

Central angle *an angle whose vertex is at the center of a circle and whose sides are radii*

Tangent *a line that touches a circle at exactly one point*

Secant *a line that intersects a circle in exactly two points*

Intercepted arc *a part of a circle that lies between the two sides of an angle*

Minor arc *part of a circle that lies between the two radii that form a central angle*

You may like to cook steaks and hamburgers on a grill. Many lines and curves that are associated with circles are shown by the grill top on the right.

New Idea

A **chord** (kawrd) is a line segment that connects any two points of a circle. An **arc** (ahrk) is part of the circle. It is named by two letters and the symbol ⌢. A **central angle** (SEHN-truhl ANG-guhl) is an angle whose sides are radii of a circle and whose vertex is at the circle's center.

A **tangent** (TAN-juhnt) is a line that touches a circle at exactly one point. A **secant** (SEE-kuhnt) is a line that intersects a circle in exactly two points.

Example: Name the parts of $\odot M$.

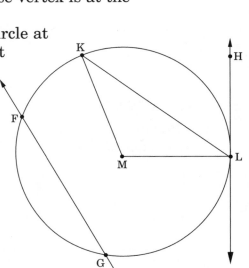

Chords: $\overline{KL}$ and $\overline{FG}$

Arcs: $\overset{\frown}{KL}$, $\overset{\frown}{LG}$, $\overset{\frown}{GF}$, $\overset{\frown}{FK}$

Central angle: $\angle KML$

Tangent: $\overleftrightarrow{HL}$

Secant: $\overleftrightarrow{FG}$

Use ⊙*M* on page 156 for exercises 1 to 5.

1. Draw $\overline{KF}$ on ⊙*M*. Is $\overline{KF}$ a chord? _____

2. Draw and name one other arc. _____

3. Draw and name one other central angle. _____

4. Draw and name one other tangent. _____

5. Draw and name one other secant. _____

Focus on the Idea

A chord is a line segment that connects any two points of a circle. An arc is part of a circle between two points on the circle. A central angle has its vertex at the center of a circle and sides that are radii. A tangent is a line that touches a circle at exactly one point. A secant is a line that touches a circle at exactly two points.

Practice

Draw and label the parts of the circle. The first one is done for you.

6. ⊙*O* with chord $\overline{AB}$ and tangent $\overleftrightarrow{PB}$

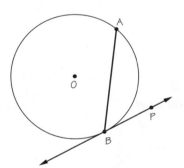

7. ⊙*P* with central angle ∠*MPN* and secant $\overleftrightarrow{RN}$

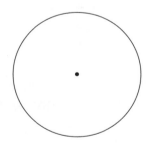

8. ⊙*B* with tangent $\overleftrightarrow{MN}$ and secant $\overleftrightarrow{ON}$

9. ⊙*M* with central angle ∠*CMR* and tangent $\overleftrightarrow{LR}$

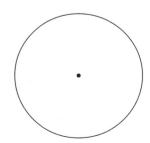

Extend the Idea

Each central angle of a circle forms an **intercepted arc** (ihn-tuhr-SEP-tuhd ahrk). The arc inside the central angle is called a **minor arc** (MY-nuhr ahrk). The measure of a minor arc is the same as the measure of its central angle. If two central angles in the same circle are congruent, then their minor arcs are congruent. If two minor arcs in the same circle are congruent, then their central angles are congruent.

Example: In $\odot P$, $\angle MPT \cong \angle RPS$.

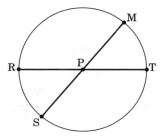

If $m\angle MPT = 50°$, find $m\angle RPS$.
Then find $m\widehat{MT}$ and $m\widehat{RS}$.

Since $\angle MPT \cong \angle RPS$, then $m\angle RPS = 50°$.

Since $\widehat{MT}$ is the minor arc intercepted by $\angle MPT$, then $m\widehat{MT} = m\angle MPT = 50°$.

Since $\widehat{MT}$ and $\widehat{RS}$ are intercepted by congruent central angles, then $m\widehat{MT} = m\widehat{RS} = 50°$.

✓ Check Your Understanding

Suppose that, in $\odot P$ above, $m\widehat{MR} = 130°$ and $m\widehat{MR} = m\widehat{ST}$.

10. Find $m\widehat{ST}$. _____

11. Find $m\angle MPR$. _____

12. Find $m\angle TPS$. _____

Practice

In $\odot X$, $m\angle AXB = 70°$, $m\angle BXC = 40°$, $m\widehat{CD} = 70°$, and $m\angle AXB = m\angle DXE$. Find the missing measures. The first one is done for you.

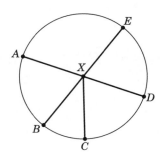

13. $m\angle AXE = $ _____110°_____

14. $m\angle DXE = $ _____

15. $m\angle CXD = $ _____

16. $m\widehat{AB} = $ _____

17. $m\widehat{BC} = $ _____

18. $m\widehat{DE} = $ _____

19. $m\widehat{AE} = $ _____

Apply the Idea

Here is an enlarged picture of the grill top shown on page 156.

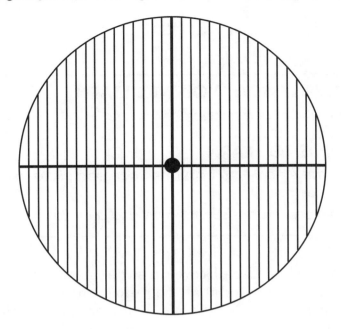

20. Label and name three chords. _____

21. Label and name three central angles. _____

22. Label and name three arcs. _____

23. Suppose all of the central angles pictured are congruent.

    a. What is the measure of each central angle? _____

    b. What is the measure of each minor arc intercepted by each of the four central angles?

    _____

Write About It

24. Can two arcs have the same degree measure and still have different lengths? Why or why not? Draw a picture as part of your answer.

_____

_____

_____

⬦6●3 Circumference of a Circle

In the third century B.C., Archimedes discovered some relationships between the parts of a circle. He found that the ratio of the distance around the outside of a circle to the length of a diameter of the circle is the same for all circles. This ratio represents a number and is called **pi** (peye). It is represented by the symbol π.

New Idea

The circumference of a circle is like the perimeter of a polygon. To find the **circumference** (suhr-KUHM-fuhr-uhns) of a circle, find the distance around the circle. One way to do this is with a long piece of string. Use as much of the string as you need to go around the circle exactly once. Then, straighten out the string you used and measure it.

Example: Find the circumference of the base of a can of green beans.

Wrap a piece of string around the circular base of the can. Then lay the string along the edge of a ruler and measure the string. The circumference of this can is about 23.5 centimeters.

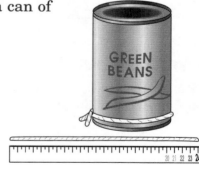

✓Check Your Understanding

Write *true* or *false* for each statement. If the statement is false, rewrite it to make it true.

1. The circumference of a circle is the distance across the circle.

   _____

2. The perimeter of a polygon is like the circumference of a circle.

   _____

Focus on the Idea

The circumference of a circle is the distance around it.

Practice

Use a piece of string to find the circumference of the circle to the nearest tenth of a centimeter. (You may want to use tape to hold the string in place on the circle.) Then, divide to find the ratio of the circumference to the diameter. The first one is done for you. Notice that, because you approximated the measure of the circumference, the answer is approximate ($\approx$) and is not an exact number.

3. diameter = 2 cm

circumference $\approx$ ___6.2 cm___

$\frac{\text{circumference}}{\text{diameter}} \approx$

$\frac{6.2}{2} \approx 3.1$ cm

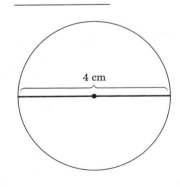

4. diameter = 3 cm

circumference $\approx$ _____

$\frac{\text{circumference}}{\text{diameter}} \approx$

_____

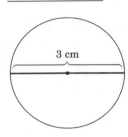

5. diameter = 4 cm

circumference $\approx$ _____

$\frac{\text{circumference}}{\text{diameter}} \approx$

_____

6. diameter = 5 cm

circumference $\approx$ _____

$\frac{\text{circumference}}{\text{diameter}} \approx$

_____

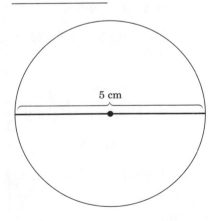

7. What do you notice about the ratios in exercises 3 to 6?

_____

_____

Extend the Idea

The ratio of the circumference of a circle to the diameter of the circle is a special ratio. The ratio is called pi (π), and it is the same for circles of all sizes. The approximate value of π is 3.14, or $\pi \approx 3.14$. Use this value to find the circumference of a circle *if you know the diameter*. The formula is given below.

$$\frac{\text{Circumference}}{\text{diameter}} = \pi$$

$$\frac{C}{d} = \pi \qquad C = \text{circumference}; \; d = \text{diameter}$$

$$C = \pi d$$

Because the diameter of a circle is twice the radius, you can find the circumference *if you know the radius*. This formula is given below.

$$C = \pi d \qquad d = 2r \; (r = \text{radius})$$

$$C = \pi(2r)$$

$$C = 2\pi r$$

Examples: The diameter of a circle is 8 inches. Find the circumference of the circle.

Use the formula $C = \pi d$. Substitute 8 for d and 3.14 for π. When you substitute the approximate value for π, then use $\approx$ instead of $=$ in the formula.

$$C = \pi d$$

$$C \approx 3.14 \cdot 8$$

$$C \approx 25.12$$

The circumference is about 25.12 inches.

The radius of a circle is 9 feet. Find the circumference of the circle.

Use the formula $C = 2\pi r$. Substitute 3.14 for π and 9 for r.

$$C = 2\pi r$$

$$C \approx 2 \cdot 3.14 \cdot 9$$

$$C \approx 56.52$$

The circumference is about 56.52 feet.

✓Check the Math

8. Hannah said that the circumference of a circle with a radius of 10 centimeters is 31.4 centimeters. Is she correct? Explain.

Practice

Find the circumference of each circle with the given radius or diameter. Show your work. The first two are done for you.

9. diameter = 9 m
$C = \pi d$

$C \approx 3.14 \cdot 9$

$C \approx 28.26$ m

10. radius = 4 ft
$C = 2\pi r$

$C \approx 2 \cdot 3.14 \cdot 4$

$C \approx 25.12$ ft

11. diameter = 11 in.
$C = \pi d$

12. radius = 15 cm
$C = 2\pi r$

13. radius = 7.5 ft
$C = 2\pi r$

14. diameter = 20.5 m
$C = \pi d$

15. diameter = 13.25 ft
$C = \pi d$

16. radius = 6π cm
$C = 2\pi r$

Apply the Idea

17. Marv wants to find the circumference of a wheel of his bicycle. If the diameter of the wheel is 26 inches, what is the circumference of the wheel to the nearest inch?

_____

18. To measure for new netting for a basketball hoop, find the circumference of a hoop with a diameter of 18 inches.

_____

Write About It

19. How would the circumference of a circle change if the radius were doubled? Explain your answer.

_____

_____

_____

6•4 Area of a Circle

IN THIS LESSON, YOU WILL LEARN
To find the area of a circle

WORDS TO LEARN
Area *the measure of the surface a figure covers*

Tija Mennala makes circular stained glass windows. She must find the area of a window to determine how much glass she will need to use.

New Idea

The **area** of a figure is the measure of the surface the figure covers. (See Lesson 5•2.) The area of a circle can be found by multiplying π by the square of the radius. The formula is given below.

$$\text{Area} = \pi \times \text{radius} \times \text{radius}$$

$$A = \pi r^2 \qquad (A = \text{area}; \ r = \text{radius})$$

Example: The radius of a circle is 5 centimeters. Find the area of the circle.

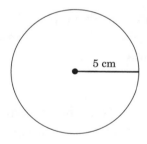

5 cm

Use the formula $A = \pi r^2$.

↷Remember

Since π is approximately 3.14 (and not exactly equal to 3.14), after you substitute the value 3.14 for π in the formula, you should use ≈ instead of =.

$$A = \pi r^2 \qquad \leftarrow \text{Substitute 3.14 for } \pi \text{ and 5 for } r.$$

$$A \approx 3.14 \cdot 5^2$$

$$A \approx 3.14 \cdot 25$$

$$A \approx 78.5 \ \text{cm}^2$$

 **Check the Math**

1. Jasken drew a square with an area of 16 square inches. Then he drew a circle that fit inside the square touching all four sides. He said that the area of the circle is half the area of the square. Is he correct? Explain your answer.

_____

_____

◀ Focus on the Idea

The area of a circle can be found by multiplying the value of π, 3.14, times the square of the radius.

Practice

Find the area of each circle with the given radius. Show your work. The first one is done for you.

2. radius = 7 cm

$A = \pi r^2$

$A \approx \underline{\quad 3.14 \cdot 7^2 \quad}$

$A \approx \underline{\quad 3.14 \cdot 49 \quad}$

$A \approx \underline{\quad 153.86 \ cm^2 \quad}$

3. radius = 4 in.

$A = \pi r^2$

$A \approx \underline{\qquad\qquad}$

$A \approx \underline{\qquad\qquad}$

$A \approx \underline{\qquad\qquad}$

4. radius = 10 m

$A = \pi r^2$

$A \approx \underline{\qquad\qquad}$

$A \approx \underline{\qquad\qquad}$

$A \approx \underline{\qquad\qquad}$

5. radius = 15 ft

$A = \pi r^2$

$A \approx \underline{\qquad\qquad}$

$A \approx \underline{\qquad\qquad}$

$A \approx \underline{\qquad\qquad}$

6. radius = 3.5 yd

$A = \pi r^2$

$A \approx \underline{\qquad\qquad}$

$A \approx \underline{\qquad\qquad}$

$A \approx \underline{\qquad\qquad}$

7. radius = 8.2 m

$A = \pi r^2$

$A \approx \underline{\qquad\qquad}$

$A \approx \underline{\qquad\qquad}$

$A \approx \underline{\qquad\qquad}$

Extend the Idea

You can use the formula for the area of a circle if you know the diameter of a circle. First, find the radius, which is half the diameter. Then use the formula $A = \pi r^2$ to find the area.

Example: The diameter of a circle is 22 feet. Find the area of the circle.

First, find the radius of the circle by finding half of the diameter.

$$r = 22 \div 2 = 11 \text{ feet}$$

Then substitute 3.14 for π in the area formula. Substitute 11 for r.

$$A = \pi r^2$$
$$A \approx 3.14 \cdot 11^2$$
$$A \approx 3.14 \cdot 121$$
$$A \approx 379.94$$

The area of the circle is about 379.94 square feet.

✓Check Your Understanding

Would you need to find half of the given measurement before using the area formula? Write *yes* or *no*.

8. radius = 4 cm

9. diameter = 4 ft

10. diameter = 6 in.

Practice

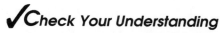 Find the area of each circle with the given diameter. Show your work. The first one is done for you.

11. diameter = 6 cm

radius = $\underline{6 \div 2 = 3 \text{ cm}}$

$A = \pi r^2$

$A \approx \underline{\quad 3.14 \cdot 3^2 \quad}$

$A \approx \underline{\quad 3.14 \cdot 9 \quad}$

$A \approx \underline{\quad 28.26 \text{ cm}^2 \quad}$

12. diameter = 14 ft

radius = _____

$A = \pi r^2$

$A \approx$ _____

$A \approx$ _____

$A \approx$ _____

13. diameter = 15 cm

radius = _____

$A = \pi r^2$

$A \approx$ _____

$A \approx$ _____

$A \approx$ _____

14. diameter = 10.2 in.

radius = _____

$A = \pi r^2$

$A \approx$ _____

$A \approx$ _____

$A \approx$ _____

Find the area of each circle with the given radius or diameter. Show your work.

15. diameter = 28 cm

$A = \pi r^2$

$A \approx$ _____

$A \approx$ _____

$A \approx$ _____

16. radius = 7.5 ft

$A = \pi r^2$

$A \approx$ _____

$A \approx$ _____

$A \approx$ _____

Apply the Idea

Think about the circular windows that Tija makes as you answer questions 17 and 18.

17. Suppose a window Tija is making has a diameter of 40 inches. What is the area of the window to the nearest tenth? _____

18. Suppose a window has a diameter of 100 inches. What is the area of the window to the nearest tenth? _____

19. The area of a circular table is given as approximately 28 square feet. What is the diameter of the table?

_____

Write About It

20. Imagine you wanted a glass top for a round table you were building. The diameter of the table is 4 feet. Glass costs $30 a square foot. How much money would you need to buy the glass? Explain how you found the answer.

_____

_____

_____

6•5 Circumscribed and Inscribed Polygons

IN THIS LESSON, YOU WILL LEARN
To identify inscribed and circumscribed polygons

WORDS TO LEARN
Inscribed polygon *a polygon whose vertices lie on a circle*

Circumscribed polygon *a polygon whose sides are tangent to a circle*

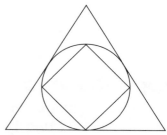

Decorative designs, like those on wallpaper, quilts, or clothing, often combine circles and other polygons. The design at the right contains a triangle, a circle, and a square.

New Idea

In the design above, the square is inside the circle. The square is an **inscribed polygon** (ihn-SKRYEBD PAHL-ih-gahn). All of the vertices of the square are on the circle, so it is said to be inscribed in the circle. The triangle in the design above is outside the circle. Each side of the triangle is tangent to the circle, so it is said to be circumscribed about the circle. The triangle is a **circumscribed polygon** (SER-kuhm-skryebd PAHL-ih-gahn).

Examples: Draw a hexagon inscribed in $\odot P$.

First, mark 6 points around the circle. Then connect the points to draw a hexagon. All of the vertices of the hexagon are on $\odot P$.

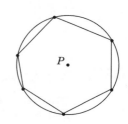

So, you can say that: a) the hexagon is inscribed in the circle; and b) the circle is circumscribed about the hexagon.

Draw a pentagon circumscribed about $\odot M$.

Mark 5 points on the circle. Then draw a tangent to the circle at each of the 5 points. The points at which these lines intersect are the vertices of the pentagon.

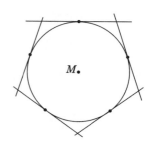

So, you can say that: a) the pentagon is circumscribed about $\odot M$; and b) $\odot M$ is inscribed in the pentagon.

◄ Focus on the Idea

If all the vertices of a figure are on a circle, then the figure is inscribed in the circle. If each side of a figure is tangent to a circle, then the figure is circumscribed about the circle.

Practice

Draw each of the figures described. The first one is done for you.

1. triangle circumscribed about ⊙A

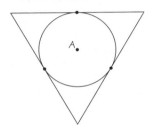

2. pentagon inscribed in ⊙V

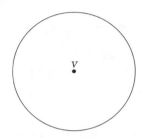

3. quadrilateral inscribed in ⊙C

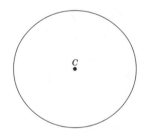

4. hexagon circumscribed about ⊙N

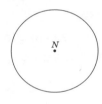

Apply the Idea

5. You can find the vertices of an inscribed polygon by folding a circular piece of paper. Get a pair of scissors and a ruler. Then draw a circle with a radius at least 4 inches. Cut out the circle and fold it in half. Fold it in half again. Unfold the circle. Draw chords to connect the endpoints formed by the folds. What inscribed polygon did you make? What is true about the sides of the polygon?

✏ Write About It

6. Look back at the design at the top of page 168. Trevor wants to transfer this design to the center of a poster. First, he needs to find the exact center of the circle. How can he do this? Draw on the design as part of your answer.

▾6•6 Measurement of Angles Circumscribed and Inscribed in a Circle

▾ IN THIS LESSON, YOU WILL LEARN

To find the measures of angles circumscribed about or inscribed in a circle

WORDS TO LEARN

Inscribed angle *an angle with its vertex on a circle and sides that are chords*

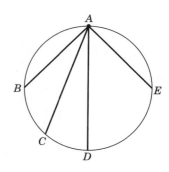

You are developing a screen saver for your personal computer. Your idea is a series of angles that all have the same vertex on a circle. You start with a right angle, $\angle BAE$. Then draw $\overline{AD}$ to bisect $\angle BAE$. Draw $\overline{AC}$ to bisect $\angle BAD$. To program your screen saver, you need to know about inscribed angles and the arcs they intercept.

New Idea

An angle with its vertex on a circle and sides that contain chords of the circle is called an **inscribed angle** (ihn-SKRYEBD ANG-guhl). The measure of an inscribed angle is equal to one-half the measure of the arc it intercepts. The sum of the measures of all the central angles of a circle is 360°. The sum of the measures of all the arcs is 360°.

Examples: Angle ABC is inscribed in $\odot P$. Arc AC is the arc intercepted by $\angle ABC$.

If $m\,\widehat{AC} = 60°$, find $m\angle ABC$.

Because $\widehat{AC}$ is intercepted by $\angle ABC$,

$m\angle ABC = \frac{1}{2}(m\widehat{AC})$.

$m\angle ABC = \frac{1}{2}(60°)$

$m\angle ABC = 30°$

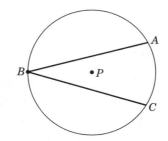

If $m\angle ABC = 40°$, find $m\overset{\frown}{AC}$.

$$m\angle ABC = \tfrac{1}{2}(m\overset{\frown}{AC})$$

$$40° = \tfrac{1}{2}(m\overset{\frown}{AC})$$

$$2(40°) = m\overset{\frown}{AC}$$

$$80° = m\overset{\frown}{AC}$$

 **Check the Math**

1. Hank said that the measure of an arc intercepted by a 90° inscribed angle is 45°. Is he correct? Why or why not?

_____

 Focus on the Idea

The measure of an inscribed angle is one-half the measure of the arc it intercepts.

Practice

In this figure, $m\angle XRY = 30°$, $m\overset{\frown}{YZ} = 30°$, $m\angle ZRW = 35°$, and $m\overset{\frown}{VW} = 20°$. Find each indicated measure. Show your work. The first one is done for you.

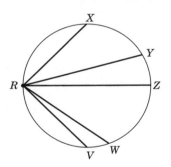

2. $m\overset{\frown}{XY} = \underline{\ 2(30°) = 60°\ }$

3. $m\angle YRZ = \underline{\hspace{2cm}}$

4. $m\overset{\frown}{ZW} = \underline{\hspace{2cm}}$

5. $m\angle WRV = \underline{\hspace{2cm}}$

$\angle MNP$ is inscribed in $\odot O$. Use the given measurement for each.

6. If $m\angle MNP = 65°$,

   $m\overset{\frown}{MP} = \underline{\hspace{2cm}}$.

7. If $m\overset{\frown}{MP} = 78°$,

   $m\angle MNP = \underline{\hspace{2cm}}$.

8. If $m\angle MNP = 26°$,

   $m\overset{\frown}{MP} = \underline{\hspace{2cm}}$.

9. If $m\overset{\frown}{MP} = 112°$,

   $m\angle MP = \underline{\hspace{2cm}}$.

Extend the Idea

From a point outside a circle, you can draw two lines tangent to the circle. The angle formed by two tangents to a circle intercepts two arcs. The measure of the angle is one-half the difference of the measures of the two intercepted arcs.

Example: In this figure, $\angle RST$ is formed by two tangents to $\odot P$. The arcs intercepted by $\angle RST$ are $\overset{\frown}{RT}$ and $\overset{\frown}{RQT}$.

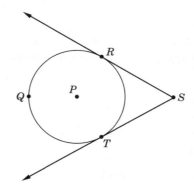

If $m\overset{\frown}{RT} = 120°$ and $m\overset{\frown}{RQT} = 240°$, find $m\angle RST$.

$m\angle RST = \frac{1}{2}(m\overset{\frown}{RQT} - m\overset{\frown}{RT})$

$m\angle RST = \frac{1}{2}(240° - 120°)$

$m\angle RST = \frac{1}{2}(120°)$

$m\angle RST = 60°$

✓ Check Your Understanding

Complete to make each statement true.

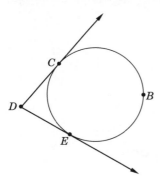

10. $m\angle CDE = \frac{1}{2}(m\overset{\frown}{CBE} - m\underline{\quad\quad})$

11. If $m\overset{\frown}{CE} = 100°$ and $m\overset{\frown}{CBE} = 260°$,

then $m\angle CDE = \frac{1}{2}(260° - \underline{\quad\quad})$

$= \frac{1}{2}(\underline{\quad\quad})$

$= \underline{\quad\quad}$

Practice

In this figure, $\overleftrightarrow{IH}$ and $\overleftrightarrow{IJ}$ are tangent to $\odot M$. Use the figure to find the measures in exercises 12 to 14. Show your work. The first one is done for you.

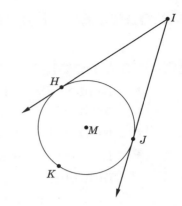

12. If $m\widehat{HJ} = 150°$ and $m\widehat{HKJ} = 210°$, then
$$m\angle HIJ = \tfrac{1}{2}(210° - 150°)$$
$$= \tfrac{1}{2}(60°)$$
$$= 30°$$

13. If $m\widehat{HJ} = 102°$ and $m\widehat{HKJ} = 258°$, then
$$m\angle HIJ =$$

14. If $m\widehat{HJ} = 94°$ and $m\widehat{HKJ} = 266°$, then
$$m\angle HIJ =$$

Apply the Idea

Look back at the screen saver diagram on page 170.

15. What is the measure of $\widehat{BDE}$? _____

16. What fraction of the circle is this arc? _____

17. What is the measure of $\widehat{CD}$? _____

18. What is the sum of $m\angle BAD$ and $m\angle DAE$? What are such angles called? _____

19. What is the measure of $\widehat{BC}$? _____

Write About It

20. Suppose you know the measure of one of the arcs intercepted by a right angle formed by two tangents to a circle. Describe how you can find the measure of the other intercepted arc.

_____

_____

Chapter 6   Review

In This Chapter, You Have Learned

- To identify and name lines and curves that are parts of a circle
- To find the circumference and area of a circle
- To identify inscribed and circumscribed polygons
- To find the measurements of angles inscribed and circumscribed in a circle

Words You Know

Write the letter of the phrase or formula in column 2 that best defines each word or phrase in column 1.

Column 1

1. diameter _____
2. radius _____
3. chord _____
4. secant _____
5. central angle _____
6. tangent _____
7. intercepted arc _____
8. circumference _____
9. pi _____
10. area _____
11. inscribed polygon _____
12. circumscribed polygon _____
13. inscribed angle _____

Column 2

a. Polygon whose vertices lie on a circle

b. Line segment that connects two points on a circle

c. Angle with its vertex at the center of a circle and sides that are radii

d. Distance around a circle

e. Angle with its vertex on a circle and with sides that are chords

f. Line that touches a circle at exactly one point

g. Line that intersects a circle at exactly two points

h. Length that is half of a diameter

i. Ratio of the circumference of a circle to its diameter

j. Part of a circle between the sides of an angle

k. πr^2

l. Polygon with each side tangent to a circle

m. Line segment through the center of a circle, connecting two points on the circle

More Practice

Draw and label the parts of each circle.

14. ⊙M with secant $\overleftrightarrow{KL}$

15. ⊙Q with tangent $\overleftrightarrow{RT}$

16. ⊙L with central angle KLM and inscribed angle KNM

17. ⊙F with circumscribed triangle ABC

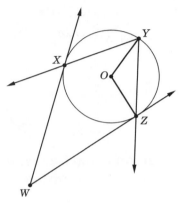

In ⊙O, m∠XYZ = 50° and m∠YOZ = 150°. Find each indicated measure.

18. $m\widehat{XZ}$ = _____

19. $m\widehat{YZ}$ = _____

20. $m\widehat{XY}$ = _____

21. $m\widehat{XYZ}$ = _____

22. $m\angle XWZ$ = _____

Find the circumference and area of each circle with the given radius or diameter.

23. radius = 8 cm

$C = 2\pi r \approx$ _____

$A = \pi r^2 \approx$ _____

24. diameter = 10 in.

$C = 2\pi r \approx$ _____

$A = \pi r^2 \approx$ _____

Problems You Can Solve

Tanya is making a quilt. She is cutting the fabric to make six pieces of equal size. Each piece is shaped like the one shown at the right. She will then put the pieces together to form a circle with a radius of 4 inches.

25. What is the measure of each angle? _____

26. What is the area of each completed circle? _____

27. What is the circumference of each completed circle?

_____

28. **For Your Portfolio** Use six large pieces of construction paper and make a sample circle for Tanya's quilt. Then make two other circles with radii of 3 inches and 6 inches. What is the same about the circles? What is different?

Draw and label the parts of each circle.

1. $\odot P$ with diameter $\overline{LT}$ and radius $\overline{PB}$

2. $\odot M$ with secant $\overline{RS}$ and tangent $\overline{OS}$

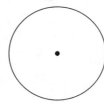

3. $\odot Q$ with central angle YQW and chord $\overline{YW}$

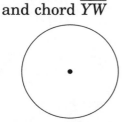

4. $\odot T$ with inscribed angle HIJ and secant $\overline{IJ}$

In the circle below, $m\angle RST = 70°$, $m\widehat{RT} = m\widehat{RS}$, and $m\widehat{ST} = 80°$. Find each measure.

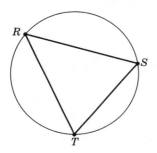

5. $m\widehat{RT} = $ _____

6. $m\widehat{RS} = $ _____

7. $m\angle SRT = $ _____

8. An angle formed by two tangents to $\odot H$ intercepts arcs of measures 140° and 220°. What is the measure of the angle?

_____

9. A circle has a radius of 20 centimeters. Find the circumference and area of the circle. _____

10. A circular tablecloth has an approximate area of 16 square feet. Will the tablecloth cover a circular table with a diameter of 6 feet? Explain your answer.

_____

_____

Chapter 7

Recognizing Three-Dimensional Shapes

OBJECTIVES:

In this chapter, you will learn

- *To identify polyhedra and their parts*
- *To identify cubes and rectangular prisms*
- *To identify pyramids and their parts*
- *To identify cylinders and cones and their parts*
- *To identify spheres and their parts*

Plato was a Greek philosopher. He was the first to describe in writing the three-dimensional shapes that can be made by putting together regular polygons. He identified five three-dimensional shapes, each of which can be created from a regular polygon. Because of Plato's influence, these three-dimensional shapes are sometimes called Platonic solids.

Tetrahedron
(4 faces)

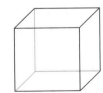
Hexahedron (Cube)
(6 faces)

Octahedron
(8 faces)

Dodecahedron
(12 faces)

Icosahedron
(20 faces)

7•1 Properties of Polyhedra

IN THIS LESSON, YOU WILL LEARN
To identify polyhedra and their parts

WORDS TO LEARN

Polyhedron *any three-dimensional shape made up of flat surfaces that are polygons*

Polyhedra *plural form of the word* polyhedron

Face *one of the polygons that makes up a polyhedron*

Edge *a line segment formed when two faces intersect*

Vertex *a point where three or more edges intersect*

Prism *a polyhedron with two congruent faces in parallel planes*

Base *one of the two congruent faces in the parallel planes of a prism*

Lateral face *a face in a prism that is not a base*

Lateral edge *an edge that two lateral faces have in common*

Altitude *a perpendicular line segment connecting both bases*

Height *the length of an altitude*

Origami (awr-uh-GAH-mee) is the Japanese art of creating three-dimensional paper figures. Each figure is made by folding paper without cutting, pasting, or decorating it. Some origami figures are animals, some are decorative designs, and others are geometric shapes.

New Idea

A three-dimensional shape formed by polygons is called a **polyhedron** (pahl-ih-HEE-druhn). Several different **polyhedra** (pahl-ih-HEE-druh) are shown here. Each of the polygons that form a polyhedron is called a **face** (fays). Two faces intersect, or meet, to form an **edge** (ehj). The point where three or more edges intersect is called a **vertex** (VER-tehks).

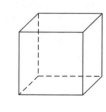

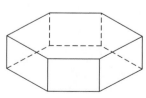

Example: The chart below lists the different parts of the polyhedron shown at the right.

Faces	Edges	Vertices
△AEB,	$\overline{AE}$, $\overline{BE}$,	A, B, C,
△BEC,	$\overline{CE}$, $\overline{DE}$,	D, E
△CED,	$\overline{AB}$, $\overline{BC}$,	
△DEA,	$\overline{CD}$, $\overline{DA}$	
ABCD		

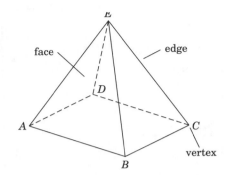

✓**Check Your Understanding**

1. Circle the three-dimensional shapes that are polyhedra.

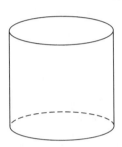 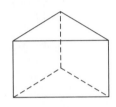  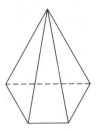

Focus on the Idea

Polyhedra are three-dimensional shapes formed by polygons. Each polygon is called a face. Each line segment formed where two faces meet is called an edge. Each point where three or more edges intersect is called a vertex.

Practice

Use the polyhedron at the right for exercises 2 to 7. Part of the second one is done for you.

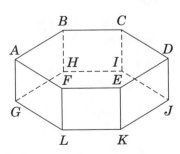

2. How many faces does the polyhedron have?
   _____

3. Name all the faces. AFLG, FEKL, EDJK, _____

4. How many edges does the polyhedron have?
   _____

5. Name all the edges. _____

6. How many vertices does the polyhedron have?
   _____

7. Name all the vertices. _____

8. Connect the dots to form a polyhedron. Use letters to label the vertices.

a. How many faces does the polyhedron have? _____

b. How many vertices does it have? _____

c. Name all the faces of the polyhedron.

   _____

Extend the Idea

Recall that a three-dimensional shape formed by polygons is a polyhedron. If a polyhedron has two congruent faces in parallel planes, it is called a **prism** (PRIHZ-uhm). Each congruent face in the parallel planes is called a **base** (bays). A face that is not a base is called a **lateral face** (LAT-uhr-uhl fays). An edge formed by a pair of lateral faces is called a **lateral edge** (LAT-uhr-uhl ehj). The **altitude** (AL-tuh-tood) is a perpendicular line segment connecting both bases. The length of an altitude is called the **height** (heyet).

Example: The polyhedron at the right is a prism.

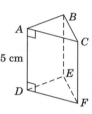

The bases of the prism are $\triangle ABC$ and $\triangle DEF$.
The lateral faces are $ADFC$, $CFEB$, and $BEDA$.
The lateral edges are $\overline{AD}$, $\overline{CF}$, and $\overline{BE}$.
An altitude of the prism is $\overline{AD}$.
The prism has a height of 5 centimeters.

✓Check the Math

9. Arturo said that a piece of pie is shaped like a prism. Do you agree? Explain your answer.

   _____

Practice

Use this prism for exercises 10 to 14. Part of the first one is done for you.

10. Name the bases of the prism.
    XYZW, RSTU, _____

11. Name the lateral faces of the prism.
    _____

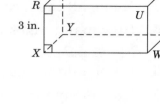

12. Name the lateral edges of the prism.
    _____

13. Name an altitude of the prism. _____

14. What is the height of the prism? _____

15. Complete the drawing of the prism with two square bases. Label each vertex.

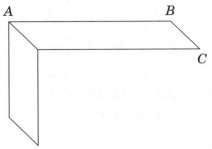

a. Name the bases. _____

b. Name the lateral faces. _____

c. Name the lateral edges. _____

d. Name an altitude. _____

16. If a prism has a base with six sides, how many edges does it have? _____

17. If a prism has seven faces, how many sides does each of its bases have? _____

Apply the Idea

18. Look around you. Find an object that is shaped like a polyhedron. Draw a picture of the object. Label each vertex.

a. Name all the faces. _____

b. Name all the edges. _____

c. Is the polyhedron a prism? Why or why not?

_____

Write About It

19. Is it possible for a prism to have four faces? Why or why not? Draw a picture to explain your answer.

_____

_____

7•2 Cubes and Rectangular Prisms

◀ IN THIS LESSON, YOU WILL LEARN

To identify cubes and rectangular prisms

WORDS TO LEARN

Rectangular prism *a prism in which all faces are rectangles*
Cube *a prism in which all faces are squares*

Karima works in a factory packing books in shipping cartons. The cartons arrive flattened. Before packing the books, Karima must set up each carton by folding it along fold lines, then taping the sides. As she folds, she notices that some of the cartons are made up of squares, and others are made up of rectangles.

New Idea

A prism in which the faces are rectangles is called a **rectangular prism** (rek-TANG-gyuh-luhr PRIHZ-uhm). A prism in which all the faces are squares is called a **cube** (kyoob). Because each of these figures has three pairs of parallel faces, any of the three pairs of faces can be the bases.

Examples: The prism at the right is a cube because all six of its faces are squares. The three possible pairs of bases are:

ABCD and *HEFG, ADGH* and *BCFE,*
ABEH and *DCFG.*

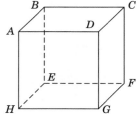

The prism at the right is a rectangular prism because all six of its faces are rectangles. The three possible pairs of bases are:

MNPQ and *RSTU, MNSR* and *QPTU,*
NSTP and *MRUQ.*

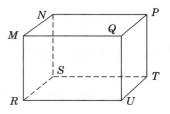

◀ Focus on the Idea

A rectangular prism has six rectangular faces. A cube is a prism with six square faces.

Practice

Label the vertices of each cube or rectangular prism. Name three possible pairs of bases. The first one is done for you.

1. cube with bases *JKLM* and *CDEF*

JKLM, CDEF; JCFM, KDEL;
JCDK, MFEL

2. rectangular prism with bases *STUW* and *DEFG*

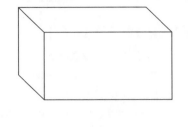

_____

_____

3. rectangular prism with two square bases

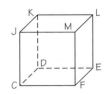

_____

_____

4. rectangular prism with four square bases

_____

_____

5. How many edges does a rectangular prism have?

_____

6. How many edges does a cube have? _____

Apply the Idea

7. Find two boxes, one shaped like a rectangular prism and one shaped like a cube. Measure each edge of each box. Record the measurements on the diagrams shown here. What can you say about the lengths of the edges of the rectangular prism? What can you say about the lengths of the edges of the cube?

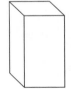

_____

_____

✏ Write About It

8. Use one of the boxes you used in exercise 7. Describe the shape of the pieces that made up the box. Describe how you can tell whether the box was a cube or a rectangular prism before unfolding the box.

_____

7•3 Pyramids

In about 2900 B.C., the Egyptians built the Great Pyramid of Giza, which is considered among the Seven Wonders of the World. It has a square base that covers an area of about 13 acres. It has an altitude of 450 feet.

New Idea

A **pyramid** (PIHR-uh-mihd) is a polyhedron with one base that is a polygon. All of the lateral faces of a pyramid are triangles that meet at a common vertex. A line segment drawn from the common vertex perpendicular to the base is called the altitude. If a pyramid has a base that is a regular polygon and congruent isosceles triangles as lateral faces, it is called a **regular pyramid** (REHG-yuh-luhr PIHR-uh-mihd). The **slant height of a pyramid** (slant heyet) is the length of an altitude of one of its lateral faces.

Example: The polyhedron at the right is a pyramid.

Its base is a regular hexagon. Its triangular lateral faces meet at vertex V. It is a regular pyramid because its base is a regular polygon and its lateral faces are congruent isosceles triangles.

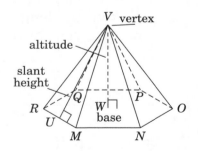

Base: regular hexagon $MNOPQR$
Lateral faces: $\triangle RVM$, $\triangle MVN$, $\triangle NVO$, $\triangle OVP$, $\triangle PVQ$, $\triangle QVR$
Altitude: $\overline{VW}$
Slant height: $\overline{VU}$

◢ Focus on the Idea

A polyhedron with one base that is a polygon and lateral faces that are triangles meeting at a common point is a pyramid. A regular pyramid has a regular polygon as its base and congruent isosceles triangles as its lateral faces.

Practice

**Use the pyramid at the right for exercises 1 to 5.
The first one is done for you.**

1. Name the base. _____ABCD_____

2. Name the lateral faces. _____

3. Name the altitude. _____

4. Is the pyramid regular? How do you know?

   _____

5. Draw and name a slant height on the pyramid.

6. Connect the dots to draw a regular pyramid with a triangular base. Label each vertex. Draw and label the altitude.

   a. Name the base. _____

   b. Name the lateral faces. _____

   c. Name the altitude. _____

   d. Name the slant height. _____

Apply the Idea

7. Imagine a use for a building shaped like a pyramid. Draw a picture of such a building. Label each vertex. Draw and label the altitude and slant height. Why is this shape right for your building?

   _____

   _____

✏ Write About It

8. Describe how pyramids and prisms are alike. Describe how they are different.

   _____

   _____

7•4 Cylinders and Cones

Petra is working at a hardware store stocking shelves. Some of the items are cans and cones, all of which have curved surfaces. Each can has two flat surfaces, so Petra can stack the cans. Each cone-shaped item has only one flat surface, so she cannot stack the cones.

New Idea

A **cylinder** (SIHL-uhn-duhr) has two congruent circular bases that lie in parallel planes and has a curved surface. An **altitude of a cylinder** (AL-tuh-tood) is a perpendicular line segment connecting the bases.

A **cone** (kohn) is like a rounded pyramid. It has only one circular base and a curved surface instead of lateral faces. The **altitude of a cone** (AL-tuh-tood) is the perpendicular line segment from the vertex of the cone to the base. The **slant height of a cone** (slant heyet) is the length of the line segment from the vertex to any point on the edge of the base.

Examples:

Cylinder

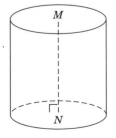

Bases: $\odot M$, $\odot N$
Altitude: $\overline{MN}$

Cone

Base: $\odot P$
Altitude: $\overline{QP}$
Slant height: $\overline{QR}$

▸ Focus on the Idea

A three-dimensional figure with two congruent circular bases and a curved surface connecting the edges is a cylinder. A three-dimensional figure with one circular base and a curved surface connecting the base edge to the vertex is a cone.

Practice

Label the parts of each cylinder or cone described. The first one is done for you.

1. cone with vertex *A* and an altitude drawn to the circular base at point *B*

    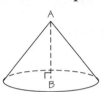

2. cylinder with bases ⊙*C* and ⊙*D*

3. cone with base ⊙*M* and altitude $\overline{MN}$

    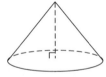

4. cylinder with bases ⊙*R* and ⊙*S* and altitude $\overline{RS}$

Apply the Idea

5. Look around you for a cone-shaped object.

    a. Draw a picture of the object. Draw and label the altitude, the base, and the slant height.

    b. Does the object have a circular base? Why or why not?

✎ Write About It

6. Think about the items Petra is putting on the shelves. What could be packed in containers shaped like cylinders? What items are cone-shaped? Why do you think different shapes are used for different types of items?

↳7•5 Spheres

↳ IN THIS LESSON, YOU WILL LEARN

To identify spheres and their parts

WORDS TO LEARN

Sphere *a three-dimensional figure with all of its points the same distance from a given point*

Center of a sphere *the point that is the same distance from all other points of the sphere*

Radius of a sphere *a line segment with one endpoint at the center of the sphere and the other endpoint on the sphere*

Diameter of a sphere *a line segment that passes through the center of a sphere and has both endpoints on the sphere*

Paul volunteers at the recreation center. He is in charge of the equipment closet. Some items in the closet, including soccer balls, basketballs, softballs, and volleyballs, are shaped like spheres.

New Idea

A sphere is similar in many ways to a circle. A **sphere** (sfeer) is a three-dimensional figure with all of its points the same distance from a given point called the **center of a sphere** (SEHNT-uhr). A line segment that connects the center of a sphere and a point on the sphere is called a **radius** (RAY-dee-uhs). A line segment that passes through the center and has both endpoints on the sphere is called a **diameter** (dy-AM-uht-uhr). The length of a diameter of a sphere is twice the length of the radius.

Example: The shape at the right is a sphere.

Center: point P
Radius: $\overline{PM}$ and $\overline{PN}$
Diameter: $\overline{MN}$
If $\overline{MN} = 8$, $\overline{PM} = 8 \div 2 = 4$.

↳ Focus on the Idea

The set of all points a given distance from a given point is a sphere. The given point is the center. A line segment from the center to the sphere is a radius. A line segment with endpoints on the sphere, passing through the center, is a diameter.

Practice

Draw and label the parts of each sphere described. The first one is done for you.

1. sphere with center C and radius $\overline{CD}$

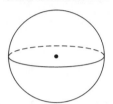

2. sphere with center M and diameter $\overline{LK}$

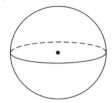

3. sphere with center R and radius $\overline{RT}$

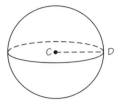

4. sphere with center Q and diameter $\overline{XY}$

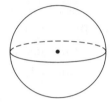

Find the radius (*r*) of each sphere, given the length of the diameter.

5. $d = 14$ m
$r =$ _____

6. $d = 6$ in.
$r =$ _____

7. $d = 18$ ft
$r =$ _____

8. $d = 15$ cm
$r =$ _____

9. $d = 9$ in.
$r =$ _____

10. $d = 2.5$ m
$r =$ _____

Apply the Idea

11. A knife slices through a sphere. Would the circle made by a cut through the center be larger or smaller than one made by a cut not through the center?

_____

12. A globe often is used to represent the earth. Draw a picture of a globe. Label the center of it. Draw and label a radius and a diameter. Longitude lines are drawn on a globe. What do you think is true about the longitude lines?

_____

Write About It

13. Describe a way to find the diameter of an object shaped like a sphere. Test your idea on a baseball or a tennis ball.

_____

_____

Chapter 7　Review

In This Chapter, You Have Learned
- To identify polyhedra and their parts
- To identify cubes and rectangular prisms
- To identify pyramids, cylinders, cones, spheres, and their parts

Words You Know

From the lists of "Words to Learn," choose the word or phrase that best completes each statement.

1. A(n) _____ is a three-dimensional shape with flat surfaces that are polygons.
2. A(n) _____ has one circular base.
3. A(n) _____ has all rectangular faces.
4. A(n) _____ is the set of all points in space a given distance from a given point.
5. A(n) _____ has two congruent polygons in parallel planes.
6. A(n) _____ has only one base that is a polygon.
7. A(n) _____ has two congruent circular bases.
8. A(n) _____ has all square faces.

More Practice

Identify and label each three-dimensional shape and its parts. Then name the parts.

9. **a.** Name the shape. _____
   b. Name the faces. _____
   c. Name the edges. _____
   d. Name the vertices. _____

10. **a.** Name the shape. _____
    b. Name the center. _____
    c. Name a radius. _____
    d. Name a diameter. _____

11. **a.** Name the shape. _____
    b. Name the base. _____
    c. Name the vertex. _____
    d. Name the altitude. _____
    e. Name the slant height. _____

12. **a.** Name the shape. _____

    b. Name the bases. _____

    c. Name the lateral faces. _____

    d. Name the lateral edges. _____

    e. Name the edges. _____

    f. Name the vertices. _____

13. **a.** Name the shape. _____

    b. Name the base. _____

    c. Name the altitude. _____

14. **a.** Name the shape. _____

    b. Name the bases. _____

    c. Name the altitude. _____

Problems You Can Solve

15. Miriam just took three tennis balls out of a can shaped like a cylinder.

    a. Compare the diameter of the base of the can to the diameter of a tennis ball.

    _____

    b. Compare the height of the can and the diameter of the tennis balls. What is the shortest length the can might have, in terms of the diameter of the balls? _____

16. **For Your Portfolio** Find a box that is not shaped like a rectangular prism. Cut the box apart at the edges. Describe and compare the pieces. Then tape the pieces together at some of the edges so that you can fold them to make the original box. Draw a picture of how the pieces look after you tape them together. Do you think there is more than one way to tape them together? Why or why not?

_____

_____

Write the letter of the figure.

a. 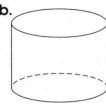 b.   c.   d. 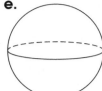 e.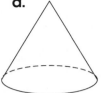

1. pyramid _____
2. cone _____
3. sphere _____
4. rectangular prism _____
5. cylinder _____

Draw a dotted line for any part of the figure not shown. Then label the figure.

6. A regular pyramid with a triangular base, altitude $\overline{RS}$ and slant height $\overline{RQ}$

7. A sphere with center O and radius $\overline{OP}$

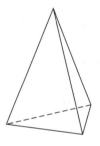

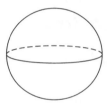

8. A cone with base $\odot N$, altitude $\overline{MN}$, and slant height $\overline{LK}$

9. A cylinder with altitude $\overline{AB}$ and bases $\odot A$ and $\odot B$

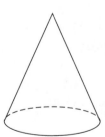

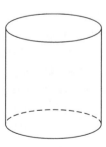

10. Harmon has a flat piece of cardboard. He wants to cut and fold the cardboard to make a box shaped like a cube. Draw an outline of the cardboard after he cuts it and draws lines for the folds.

Chapter 8

Surface Area of Three-Dimensional Shapes

OBJECTIVES:

In this chapter, you will learn

- *To find the surface area of a rectangular prism*
- *To find the lateral area and surface area of a cylinder*
- *To find the surface area of a rectangular pyramid*
- *To find the lateral area and surface area of a cone*
- *To find the surface area of a sphere*

The cost of an item can depend partly upon the cost of the material that covers it. Cars must be covered with paint. Buildings must be covered with materials such as wood, siding, stucco, bricks, or stones. Cans must be wrapped with labels. Floors must be covered with materials such as tile or carpet. The amount and the cost of material needed for each depends, in part, upon the area to be covered.

8•1 Surface Area of Rectangular Prisms

IN THIS LESSON, YOU WILL LEARN

To find the surface area of a rectangular prism

WORDS TO LEARN

Surface area *the total area of the outside of a three-dimensional figure*

Net *pattern that can be folded to form a three-dimensional figure*

Cara wants to buy sticky-backed paper to cover a box that will be used as a small table in her room. The box is shaped like a rectangular prism. In order to know how much paper to buy, she needs to find the area of the outside of the box. She decides to cut apart a model of the box and lay it open. Cara then measures the length and the width of each of the rectangles that form the faces of the box. How can she use this information to decide how much paper she needs to cover the box?

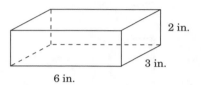

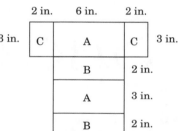

New Idea

The **surface area** (SER-fihs AIR-ee-uh) of a three-dimensional figure is the total area of the outside of the figure. In a rectangular prism, all the faces are rectangles. A flat pattern that can be folded to form a three-dimensional shape is called a **net** (neht). Cara can use the net she made of her box to help her find its surface area.

Example: Find the surface area of Cara's box.
The box is 6 inches long, 3 inches wide, and 2 inches high. You can see from the net that the box has six faces. There are three pairs of congruent faces. Pair A is 6 inches long and 3 inches wide. Pair B is 6 inches long and 2 inches wide. Pair C is 3 inches long and 2 inches wide. To find the area of each rectangle, multiply its length times its width.

Area of A	Area of B	Area of C
$A = lw$	$A = lw$	$A = lw$
$A = 6 \cdot 3$	$A = 6 \cdot 2$	$A = 3 \cdot 2$
$A = 18$	$A = 12$	$A = 6$

To find the surface area (*SA*), multiply the area of each rectangle by two. Then find the sum of the areas.

$$SA = 2(\text{area of A}) + 2(\text{area of B}) + 2(\text{area of C})$$

$$SA = 2(18) + 2(12) + 2(6)$$

$$SA = 36 + 24 + 12$$

$$SA = 72$$

The surface area of the box is 72 square inches, or 72 in.^{2} So Cara needs to buy at least 72 in.^{2} of paper to cover the box.

✓Check the Math

1. The areas of three faces of a rectangular prism are 2 cm^2, 4 cm^2, and 6 cm^2. Jackie says that the surface area of the rectangular prism is 12 cm^2. Josh says it is 24 cm^2. Who is correct? How do you know?

_____

_____

◀ Focus on the Idea

The total area of the outside of a three-dimensional object is called the surface area. A rectangular prism is a figure shaped like a brick. It has six rectangular faces.

▦ Practice

Draw and label a net for each rectangular prism with the given dimensions. Then find the surface area of the rectangular prism. The first one is done for you.

2. $l = 5$ cm, $w = 4$ cm, $h = 2$ cm   3. $l = 10$ ft, $w = 6$ ft, $h = 3$ ft

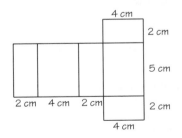

$SA = 2(5 \cdot 4) + 2(4 \cdot 2) + 2(5 \cdot 2)$ _____

$SA = 2(20) + 2(8) + 2(10)$ _____

$SA = 40 + 16 + 20 = 76 \text{ cm}^2$ _____

4. $l = 8$ in., $w = 7$ in., $h = 6$ in.   **5.** $l = 2.5$ m, $w = 1.5$ m, $h = 3$ m

_____   _____

_____   _____

_____   _____

Extend the Idea

A cube is a rectangular prism with six congruent, square faces. If you know the length of one of the edges of a cube, then you can find the surface area. First find the area of one of the faces. Then multiply that area by 6 to find the total surface area.

Example: Find the surface area of a cube with an edge that measures 8 cm.

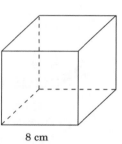

Area of one face: $A = s^2$
$$A = 8^2$$
$$A = 8 \cdot 8$$
$$A = 64 \text{ cm}^2$$

$$SA = 6 \cdot 64$$
$$SA = 384 \text{ cm}^2$$

8 cm

✓ Check Your Understanding

Write the letter that names the surface area of each cube.

6. cube with edge 2 cm _____   **a.** 6 cm^2

7. cube with edge 9 cm _____   **b.** 294 cm^2

8. cube with edge 1 cm _____   **c.** 24 cm^2

9. cube with edge 7 cm _____   **d.** 486 cm^2

Practice

Label each cube with the given dimensions. Then find its surface area. The first one is done for you.

10. edge = 5 in.   **11.** edge = 1.2 cm

5 in.

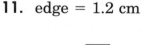
$5^2 = 25$; $6 \cdot 25 = 150$ in.^{2} _____

12. edge = 10 ft

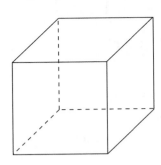

_____

13. edge = 0.5 m

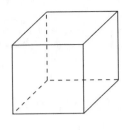

_____

Apply the Idea

14. Jake is painting all six faces of a large cube. It will be used as a prop for a school play.

   a. The cube has an edge that measures 3 feet. What is the area Jake needs to paint? _____

   b. A pint of paint covers about 32 square feet. How many pints of paint should Jake buy to paint the cube?

_____

✏ Write About It

15. Miguel has a box that is 22 inches long, 16 inches wide, and 6 inches high. He has three pieces of wrapping paper. Which piece of wrapping paper, **_a_**, **_b_**, or **_c_**, should Miguel use to wrap his box? Why? (Hint: Draw a net of the box to help you.)

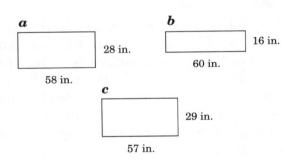

_____

_____

►8•2 Lateral and Surface Area of Cylinders

◄ IN THIS LESSON, YOU WILL LEARN

To find the lateral area and surface area of a cylinder

WORDS TO LEARN

Lateral area of a cylinder *the area of the curved surface of the cylinder*

Darla is making strawberry jam to sell at a neighborhood garage sale. She is using jars shaped like cylinders. She wants to put a label on each of the jars that will completely cover the curved surface. How much paper will she need for the label on each jar?

Darla's Jam

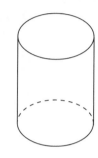

New Idea

Darla needs to find the area of the side, or the curved surface, of each jar. This area does not include the top and bottom of the jar. The area of the curved surface is called the **lateral area of a cylinder** (LAT-uhr-uhl AIR-ee-uh uhv uh SIHL-uhn-duhr). Notice that a net for the lateral area forms a rectangle. You already know that, to find the area of a rectangle, you multiply its length by its width. To find the lateral area, think of the length as the circumference of either of the circular bases and the width as the height of the cylinder. Because the diameter, d, is two times the radius, r, of a circle, the circumference can be calculated as πd or $2\pi r$.

Lateral Area = Circumference of a base • Height of cylinder

$LA = \pi d \quad • \quad h$

$LA = \pi dh$

Example: The height of one of Darla's jars is 12 cm and the diameter of each base is 10 cm. What is the lateral area of the jar?

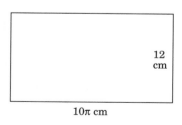

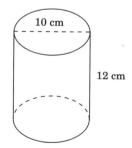

$LA = \pi dh$ ($\pi \approx 3.14$, $d = 10$, $h = 12$)
$LA \approx 3.14 • 10 • 12$
$LA \approx 376.8$

The lateral area of the jar is approximately 376.8 cm^2.
Darla will need about 377 cm^2 of paper for each label.

Check Your Understanding

1. What should be the length of each label Darla uses? _____

2. What should be the width of each label? _____

◀ Focus on the Idea

The lateral area of a cylinder is the area of the lateral, or curved, surface.

 Practice

Label each cylinder with the given dimensions. Then find its lateral area. The first one is done for you.

3. diameter = 6 in.
   height = 12 in.

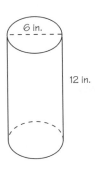

LA = πdh _____

≈ 3.14 • 6 • 12 _____

≈ 226.08 in.² _____

4. diameter = 8 m
   height = 5 m

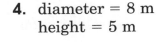
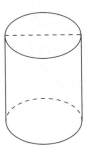

_____

_____

_____

5. diameter = 9 ft
   height = 7 ft

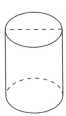

_____

_____

_____

6. diameter = 15 cm
   height = 10.5 cm

_____

_____

_____

Extend the Idea

You have learned that, in a three-dimensional figure, surface area is the total area of all surfaces. To find the surface area of a cylinder, add the lateral area to the area of each of the two congruent, circular bases. The formula for the surface area of a cylinder is given below.

Surface Area = Lateral area + 2(area of a base)

$$SA = 2\pi rh + 2\pi r^2$$

Diameter $d = 2r$; so lateral area = πdh or $2\pi rh$.

Example: The radius of a cylinder is 4 cm and the height is 6 cm. Find the surface area of the cylinder.

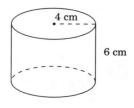

$SA = 2\pi rh + 2\pi r^2$

$SA \approx (2 \cdot 3.14 \cdot 4 \cdot 6) + (2 \cdot 3.14 \cdot 4^2)$

$SA \approx 150.72 + 100.48$

$SA \approx 251.2$

The surface area is approximately 251.2 cm².

✓ Check the Math

7. A cylinder has a radius of 4 inches and a height of 8 inches. Patrick found the surface area to be 301.44 square inches. Rachel says that the surface area is 200.96 square inches. Who is correct? How do you know?

_____

_____

🖩 Practice

Label each cylinder with the given dimensions. Then find its surface area. The first one is done for you.

8. radius = 10 in.
height = 4 in.

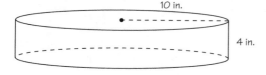

$SA = 2\pi rh + 2\pi r^2$

$SA \approx (2 \cdot 3.14 \cdot 10 \cdot 4) +$

$\quad (2 \cdot 3.14 \cdot 10^2)$

$SA \approx 879.2$ in.²

9. radius = 5 m
height = 6 m

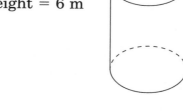

_____

_____

_____

_____

10. radius = 2 ft
height = 7 ft

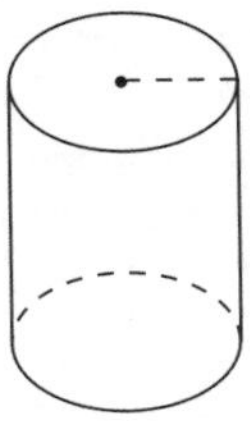

11. radius = 2.5 cm
height = 3 cm

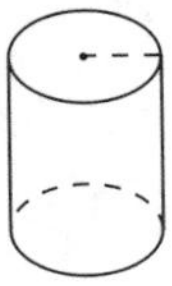

_____   _____

_____   _____

_____   _____

Find the surface area of each of the cylinders in exercises 3 to 6. (Remember, the radius is one-half the diameter.)

12. Exercise 3: $SA =$ _____

13. Exercise 4: $SA =$ _____

14. Exercise 5: $SA =$ _____

15. Exercise 6: $SA =$ _____

Apply the Idea

16. A water storage tank is shaped like a cylinder. It has a height of 75 meters and a radius of 25 meters.

   a. The curved surface of the tank needs to be painted. What is the area that will be painted? _____

   b. A gallon of paint covers 45 square meters. If two coats of paint are needed, about how many gallons of paint will be needed to paint the tank? _____

Write About It

17. Suppose that the height of a cylinder is doubled.

   a. What happens to the lateral area of the cylinder? Explain.

_____

_____

   b. Is the surface area of the cylinder also doubled? Explain.

_____

_____

8•3 Surface Area of Rectangular Pyramids

WORDS TO LEARN

Surface area of a square pyramid *the sum of the areas of the four triangular faces of a pyramid and its square base*

Surface area of a rectangular pyramid *the sum of the areas of the four triangular faces of a pyramid and its rectangular base*

Alayna is a commercial artist. She must create a package shaped like a rectangular pyramid. The base of the pyramid should be a square that measures 5 centimeters on a side. The slant height, which is the height of each triangular face, should measure 4 centimeters. How much cardboard will Alayna need to make her pyramid?

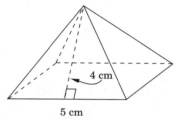

4 cm

5 cm

New Idea

A square pyramid is a **regular pyramid** with a square for its base. (See Lesson 7•3.) The **surface area of a square pyramid** (SER-fihs AIR-ee-uh uhv uh skwair PIHR-uh-mihd) is the sum of the lateral area and the area of the base. To find the lateral area of a square pyramid, first find the area of one of the lateral faces. Then multiply the area by the number of lateral faces, 4.

Example: Find the surface area of Alayna's pyramid.

Recall that the length of the base of the pyramid is 5 cm and the slant height is 4 cm. Each lateral face is a triangle.

$A = \frac{1}{2}bh$ ←Formula for area of lateral face

$A = \frac{1}{2} \cdot 5 \cdot 4$
$A = 10 \text{ cm}^2$ ←Area of one lateral face

$LA = 4 \cdot 10$
$LA = 40 \text{ cm}^2$ ←Total lateral area of four lateral faces

Find the area of the base.

$$A = 5^2$$
$$A = 5 \cdot 5$$
$$A = 25 \text{ cm}^2 \quad \leftarrow \text{Area of base}$$

The surface area is $40 + 25 = 65 \text{ cm}^2$.

✓ **Check Your Understanding**

Write a letter that names the surface area of each square pyramid.

1. base area = 4 cm², total lateral area = 8 cm² _____

2. base area = 9 cm², total lateral area = 24 cm² _____

3. base area = 1 cm², total lateral area = 8 cm² _____

4. base area = 16 cm², total lateral area = 26 cm² _____

a. 33 cm²

b. 42 cm²

c. 12 cm²

d. 9 cm²

 Focus on the Idea

To find the surface area of a pyramid, find the sum of the lateral area and the area of the base.

 Practice

Label each pyramid with the given dimensions. Then find its surface area. The first one is done for you.

5. base area = 16 in.²
   slant height = 5 in.
   length of side of base = 4 in.

6. base area = 36 ft²
   slant height = 7 ft
   length of side of base = 6 ft

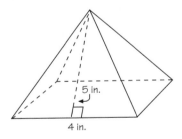

5 in.

4 in.

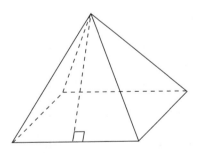

$LA = 4 \cdot (\frac{1}{2} bh)$ _____

$= 4 \cdot \frac{1}{2} \cdot 4 \cdot 5 = 40 \text{ in.}^2$ _____

$SA = 40 + 16 = 56 \text{ in.}^2$ _____

_____

_____

_____

7. base area = 49 m²
slant height = 9 m
length of side of base = 7 m

8. base area = 30.25 cm²
slant height = 6 cm
length of side of base = 5.5 cm

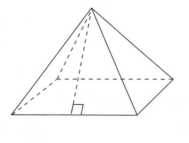

_____   _____

_____   _____

_____   _____

Extend the Idea

The **surface area of a rectangular pyramid** (SER-fihs AIR-ee-uh uhv uh rehk-TANG-gyuh-luhr PIHR-uh-mihd) is the sum of the areas of the four triangular faces of the pyramid and its rectangular base. If a pyramid has a rectangular base that is not a square, it has two pairs of congruent lateral faces.

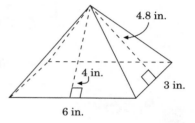

In the rectangular pyramid shown here, the rectangular base measures 6 inches by 3 inches. The slant height of two of the lateral faces is 4 inches. The slant height of the other two lateral faces is 4.8 inches.

Example: Find the surface area of the pyramid shown above.

Find the area of one pair of lateral faces.

$A = \frac{1}{2}bh = \frac{1}{2} \cdot 6 \cdot 4 = 12$ in.²

$LA = 2(12) = 24$ in.²

Find the area of the other pair of lateral faces.

$A = \frac{1}{2}bh = \frac{1}{2} \cdot 3 \cdot 4.8 = 7.2$ in.²

$LA = 2(7.2) = 14.4$ in.²

Total lateral area = 24 + 14.4 = 38.4 in.²

Find the area of the base.

$A = lw = 6 \cdot 3 = 18$ in.²

The surface area is the sum of the lateral area and the base area.

$SA = 38.4 + 18 = 56.4$ in.²

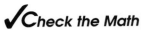

9. The base area of a rectangular pyramid is 24 cm². The slant heights of the lateral faces are 3 cm and 4.6 cm. Does this give you enough information to find the surface area? Explain.

_____

 Practice

Find the surface area of each pyramid. The first one is done for you.

10.

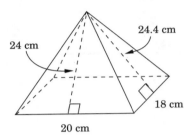

$LA = [2 \cdot (\frac{1}{2} \cdot 20 \cdot 24)] +$
_____

$[2 \cdot (\frac{1}{2} \cdot 18 \cdot 24.4)] = 919.2$ cm²

area of base $= 20 \cdot 18 = 360$ cm²

$SA = 919.2 + 360 = 1,279.2$ cm²

11.

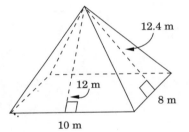

_____

_____

_____

_____

12.

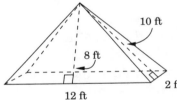

_____

_____

_____

_____

Apply the Idea

13. The Great Pyramid of Giza is a square pyramid. Each side of the base is 231 meters long. It has a slant height of 187 meters. What is the surface area of the pyramid? _____

✏ Write About It

14. Suppose you are given only the lengths of all the edges of a rectangular pyramid. Can you find the surface area of the pyramid? Why or why not?

_____

_____

8•4 Lateral and Surface Area of Cones

The Museum of Natural History is creating a Native American exhibit. The curator wants to make a teepee of the sort used in the past by some Native American people for shelter. She must find the lateral area of the teepee so her employees will know how much material to use. She knows that a teepee is shaped like a cone, so she draws a net of the cone and its base to help her find the lateral area of the teepee.

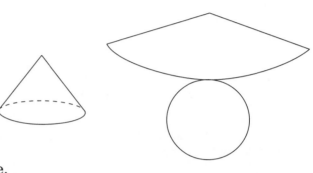

New Idea

The **lateral area of a cone** (LAT-uhr-uhl AIR-ee-uh uhv uh kohn) is the area of the cone's curved surface. A net for the lateral area of a cone forms a sector of a circle. The length of the sector is the slant height of the cone. To find the lateral area of a cone, use the formula $LA = \pi rs$ where r is the radius of the base of the cone and s is the slant height.

Example: Find how much material the museum will need to buy for the teepee.

The radius of the base of the teepee is 6 feet. The slant height is 15 feet.

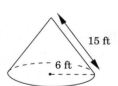

$$LA = \pi rs \qquad \leftarrow \text{Substitute 6 for } r \text{ and } 15 \text{ for } s.$$

$$LA \approx 3.14 \cdot 6 \cdot 15 \leftarrow \text{Simplify.}$$

$$LA \approx 282.6$$

The lateral area of the teepee is approximately 282.6 square feet. So the museum will need about 283 square feet of material for the teepee.

Check Your Understanding

Write a letter that names the lateral area of each cone.

1. radius = 4 cm, slant height = 5 cm _____   **a.** 43.96 cm^2

2. radius = 2 cm, slant height = 7 cm _____   **b.** 84.78 cm^2

3. radius = 3 cm, slant height = 9 cm _____   **c.** 62.8 cm^2

4. radius = 5 cm, slant height = 8 cm _____   **d.** 125.6 cm^2

Focus on the Idea

To find the lateral area of a cone, use the formula LA = πrs, where r is the radius of the base and s is the slant height.

Practice

Label each cone with the given dimensions. Then find its lateral area. The first one is done for you.

5. radius = 7 cm
   slant height = 12 cm

12 cm

7 cm

LA = πrs ≈ 3.14 • 7 • 12

LA ≈ 263.76 cm^2

6. radius = 10 in.
   slant height = 15 in.

_____

_____

7. radius = 13 ft
   slant height = 20 ft

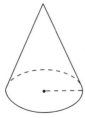

_____

_____

8. radius = 14 m
   slant height = 18.5 m

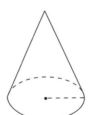

_____

_____

Extend the Idea

The total surface area of a cone can be found by adding the area of the circular base to the lateral area. The formula is given below.

Surface Area = Area of base + Lateral Area

$$SA = \pi r^2 \qquad + \pi rs$$

Example: Find the surface area of a cone with a radius of 9 cm and a slant height of 12 cm.

$$SA = \pi r^2 + \pi rs$$

$$SA \approx (3.14 \cdot 9^2) + (3.14 \cdot 9 \cdot 12)$$

$$SA \approx 254.34 + 339.12$$

$$SA \approx 593.46$$

The surface area of the cone is approximately 593.46 cm².

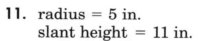

✓Check the Math

9. Niki says that she can find the surface area of a cone if she knows the diameter of the base and the slant height. Is she correct? Explain.

_____

_____

🖩 Practice

Label each cone with the given dimensions. Then find its surface area. The first one is done for you.

10. radius = 8 cm
    slant height = 10 cm

11. radius = 5 in.
    slant height = 11 in.

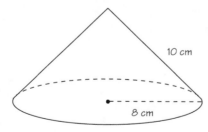

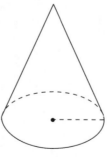

SA = πr² + πrs

SA ≈ 3.14 • 8² + 3.14 • 8 • 10

SA ≈ 452.16 cm²

_____

_____

_____

12. radius = 12 ft
slant height = 13 ft

13. radius = 2.5 m
slant height = 3.5 m

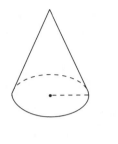

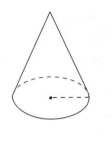

_____

_____

_____

_____

_____

_____

Find the surface area of each cone described in exercises 5 to 8.

14. Exercise 5: $SA =$ _____

15. Exercise 6: $SA =$ _____

16. Exercise 7: $SA =$ _____

17. Exercise 8: $SA =$ _____

Apply the Idea

18. Think about the teepee for the museum exhibit.

    a. What will be the area of the floor of the teepee?

    _____

    b. The museum curator decides not only to make the teepee but also to cover the teepee's floor. How much material will the museum need altogether? _____

19. The factory at which Janis works makes funnels. The most popular funnel has a radius of 3 inches and a slant height of 5 inches. The tin to make funnels costs about $0.02 per square inch. Disregarding the hole, approximately how much does the tin for each funnel cost? _____

Write About It

20. For any cone, which is greater—the lateral area or the area of the base? Explain.

_____

_____

_____

 8•5 Surface Area of Spheres

> ◤ **IN THIS LESSON, YOU WILL LEARN**
>
> *To find the surface area of a sphere*
>
> **WORDS TO LEARN**
>
> **Surface area of a sphere** *the area of the curved surface of the sphere*

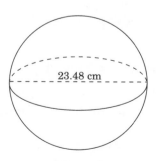

Both baseballs and basketballs are usually covered with leather. How much leather is needed to cover a baseball? How much is needed to cover a basketball?

New Idea

The curved surface of a sphere is the surface area. The **surface area of a sphere** (SER-fihs AIR-ee-uh uhv uh sfihr) with radius r can be found using the formula $SA = 4\pi r^2$.

If, instead of the radius, the diameter of the sphere is given, find half of the diameter to get the radius. Then use the formula to find the surface area.

Examples: Find the surface area of a baseball.

A baseball has a radius of approximately 1.5 in.

$SA = 4\pi r^2$ ←Substitute 1.5 for r.

$SA \approx 4 \cdot 3.14 \cdot 1.5^2$

$SA \approx 28.3$ in.^{2}

1.5 in.

Baseball

The surface area of the baseball is approximately 28.3 in.^{2}

Find the surface area of a basketball with a diameter of 23.48 cm.

First, find the radius:

$r = \dfrac{d}{2}$

$r = \dfrac{23.48}{2}$ ←Substitute 23.48 for d.

$r = 11.74$ cm

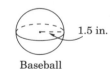

23.48 cm

Basketball

Then use the formula for surface area:

$$SA = 4\pi r^2$$

$$SA \approx 4 \cdot 3.14 \cdot 11.74^2$$

$$SA \approx 1{,}731 \text{ cm}^2$$

The surface area of the basketball is approximately 1,731 cm².

◤ Focus on the Idea

You can find the surface area of a sphere using the formula SA = 4πr², where r is the radius of the sphere.

Practice

Find the surface area of each sphere with the given radius or diameter. The first two are done for you.

1. radius = 7 ft

$$SA = 4\pi r^2$$

$$SA \approx 4 \cdot 3.14 \cdot 7^2$$

$$SA \approx 615.44 \text{ ft}^2$$

2. diameter = 10 m

$$SA = 4\pi r^2$$

$$SA \approx 4 \cdot 3.14 \cdot 5^2$$

$$SA \approx 314 \text{ m}^2$$

3. radius = 14 in.

_____

_____

_____

4. diameter = 18 mm

_____

_____

_____

5. radius = 2.5 m

_____

_____

_____

6. diameter = 3.5 cm

_____

_____

_____

Apply the Idea

7. A softball has a diameter of about 3.8 in.

a. What is the surface area of the softball? _____

b. How much greater is the surface area of a softball than that of a baseball? _____

✎ Write About It

8. The diameter of the earth is about 4 times the diameter of the moon. How do the surface areas of the earth and the moon compare? Explain.

_____

_____

Chapter 8　Review

In This Chapter, You Have Learned

- To find the surface area of a rectangular prism, a rectangular pyramid, and a sphere
- To find the lateral area and surface area of a cylinder and a cone

Words You Know

From the lists of "Words to Learn," choose the word or phrase that best completes each statement.

1. A(n) _____ is a pattern used to form a three-dimensional figure that has at least one flat surface.

2. The formula πdh gives the _____.

3. The area of all the surfaces of a three-dimensional figure is called the _____.

More Practice

Label each figure described. Then find the surface area of the figure. Show your work.

4. rectangular prism with length 6 cm, width 5 cm, and height 2 cm

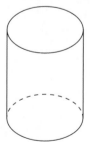

$SA = 2(lw + lh + wh)$
$SA = $ _____

5. cube with edge of 11 in.

$SA = 6s^2$
$SA = $ _____

6. cylinder with diameter 10 ft and height 7 ft

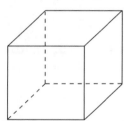

$LA = \pi dh$
$LA \approx $ _____
$SA = LA + 2\pi r^2$
$SA \approx $ _____

7. square pyramid with base area 4 m², slant height 4 m, and length of edge of base = 2 m

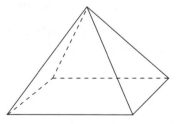

$LA = 4(\frac{1}{2}bh)$
$LA = $ _____
$SA = LA + \text{area of base}$
$SA = $ _____

8. cone with radius 9 ft and slant height 10 ft

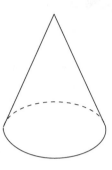

$LA = \pi rs$

$LA \approx$ _____

$SA = LA + \pi r^2$

$SA \approx$ _____

9. sphere with radius 20 mm

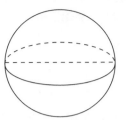

$SA = 4\pi r^2$

$SA \approx$ _____

Problems You Can Solve

10. Kamil is using a full sheet of paper that measures 8.5 inches by 11 inches to cover the lateral surface of a cylinder.

   a. What is the lateral area of the cylinder? _____

   b. Could Kamil cover the lateral surfaces of different cylinders using paper that measures 8.5 inches × 11 inches? How many different cylinders could he cover? Explain.

   _____

   _____

   _____

11. A water cup is shaped like a cone. It has a radius of 4 cm and a slant height of 10.8 cm. How much paper is used to form the cup? _____

12. **For Your Portfolio** Find several large pieces of cardboard of the same size. Or, cut three pieces so that they are the same size. Make a different three-dimensional shape from each piece of cardboard, using as much of that piece as possible. Find the surface area of each shape you make. Make a drawing of each shape and describe how you made it.

   _____

   _____

   _____

   _____

Chapter 8   Practice Test

Find the surface area of each figure described. (First find the lateral area, if necessary.) Show your work in the margin.

1. cube with edge of 6 cm

    $SA = 6s^2$

    $SA =$ _____

2. cylinder with diameter 5 in. and height 6 in.

    $LA = \pi r h$

    $LA \approx$ _____

    $SA = LA + 2\pi r^2$

    $SA \approx$ _____

3. square pyramid with base area 9 ft², slant height 8 ft, and length of base 3 ft

    $LA = 4(\frac{1}{2}bh)$

    $LA =$ _____

    $SA = LA + \text{base}$

    $SA =$ _____

4. cone with radius 15 cm and slant height 18 cm

    $LA = \pi r s$

    $LA \approx$ _____

    $SA = LA + \pi r^2$

    $SA \approx$ _____

5. sphere with diameter of 12 m

    $SA = 4\pi r^2$

    $SA \approx$ _____

Solve.

6. A can has a height of 12 cm and a diameter of 8 cm. How much metal is used to make the can? _____

7. A box is shaped like a rectangular prism. It has a length of 5 in., a width of 3 in., and a height of 2 in. How much paper is needed to cover the box? _____

8. Mars is shaped like a sphere, with a radius of 3,400 km. What is the surface area of Mars? _____

9. An ice-cream cone has a slant height of about 5.2 in. and a diameter of 2.5 in. What is the lateral area of the ice-cream cone? _____

10. A fish tank is shaped like a rectangular prism. It has a length of 4 ft, a width of 2 ft, and a height of 3 ft. If all five sides are made of glass, how much glass is used for the fish tank? _____

Chapter 9

Volume of Three-Dimensional Shapes

OBJECTIVES:

In this chapter, you will learn

- *To find the volume of a rectangular prism*
- *To find the volume of a cylinder*
- *To find the volume of a rectangular pyramid*
- *To find the volume of a cone*
- *To find the volume of a sphere*
- *To decide whether a problem involves surface area or volume*

Manufacturers use containers of many different shapes and sizes to pack their products. The containers are made to hold a certain number of products. Manufacturers test different types of containers to determine which one is the best for a certain product.

The cost of materials to make the containers also must be considered. Different containers may hold the same amount of the product. Manufacturers usually prefer containers that hold the correct amount and cost the least.

What else do you think manufacturers may need to consider when deciding on packaging containers?

▶9•1 Volume of Rectangular Prisms

Mandie is an assistant manager of a tropical fish store. She often helps customers choose the correct fish for their tanks. Mandie needs to know how much water a fish tank will hold so she can suggest the right number and kind of fish. One customer has a fish tank that measures 20 inches by 12 inches by 10 inches. Mandie can use these dimensions to find how much water the fish tank will hold.

New Idea

The amount of space enclosed by a three-dimensional object is called the **volume** (VAHL-yoom). You can think about the volume of a rectangular prism as being the number of cubic units that will fill the prism.

The rectangular prism at the right is filled with cubes that measure 1 centimeter on a side. So, each cube is 1 cubic centimeter, or 1 cm^3. The length of the prism is 4 cm, the width is 2 cm, and the height is 3 cm. To find the volume of the prism, you could count the cubic centimeters. You also could multiply length times width times height, or $4 \cdot 2 \cdot 3 = 24 \text{ cm}^3$.

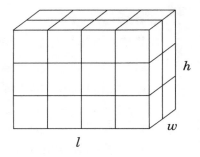

The formula for the volume of a rectangular prism is given below.

Volume = length • width • height

$$V = l \cdot w \cdot h$$
$$V = lwh$$

Example: Find the volume of Mandie's customer's fish tank. Use the formula $V = lwh$. Substitute 20 in. for l, 12 in. for w, and 10 in. for h.

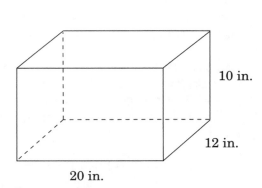

$$V = lwh$$

$$V = 20 \cdot 12 \cdot 10$$

$$V = 2,400$$

The volume of the fish tank is 2,400 in.^{3}

1. Gamon says that the volume of a box with length 6 centimeters, width 4 centimeters, and height 5 centimeters is 24 cm³. Garnet says the volume is 120 cm³. Who is correct? How do you know?

_____

Focus on the Idea

The number of cubic units needed to fill a shape is the volume of the shape. The formula for the volume of a rectangular prism is V = lwh.

Practice

Label each rectangular prism with the given dimensions. Then find the volume of the rectangular prism. The first one is done for you.

2. length = 4 cm
   width = 2 cm
   height = 5 cm

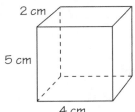

   2 cm

   5 cm

   4 cm

   V = lwh

   V = 4 • 2 • 5

   V = 40cm³

3. length = 9 ft
   width = 8 ft
   height = 5 ft

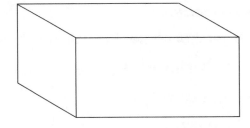

4. length = 12 in.
   width = 11 in.
   height = 9 in.

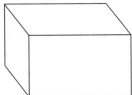

5. length = 3.5 m
   width = 2.5 m
   height = 4 m

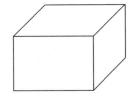

Find the volume of each rectangular prism with the given measurements.

6. length = 10 cm
   width = 5 cm
   height = 6 cm

7. length = 4.5 ft
   width = 3.9 ft
   height = 8 ft

Extend the Idea

If you know the length of one edge of a cube, then you can find the volume of the cube. Because the length, width, and height of a cube all have the same measure, the volume is found by raising that number to the third power. Let s be the length of an edge. Then the volume is given by the formula below.

$$V = s \cdot s \cdot s = s^3$$

Example: Find the volume of a cube with each side measuring 6 centimeters.

$$V = s^3 = 6^3 = 216$$

The volume is 216 cm^3.

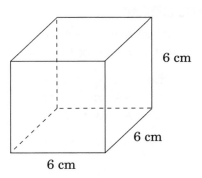

6 cm

6 cm

6 cm

✓Check Your Understanding

Write the letter that names the volume of each cube.

8. cube with edge 7 cm _____

9. cube with edge 11 cm _____

10. cube with edge 9 cm _____

11. cube with edge 8 cm _____

a. 512 cm^3

b. 729 cm^3

c. 343 cm^3

d. 1,331 cm^3

Practice

Label each cube with the given dimension. Then find the volume of the cube. The first one is done for you.

12. edge = 4 cm

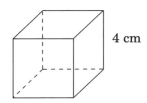

4 cm

$V = s^3$

$V = 4^3 = 4 \cdot 4 \cdot 4$

$V = 64$ cm^3

13. edge = 13 in.

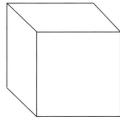

14. edge = 10 ft

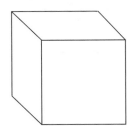

15. edge = 4.5 m

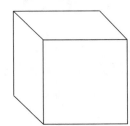

Apply the Idea

16. A storage shed needs a sand floor for drainage. The length of the floor is 5 feet, the width is 2.5 feet, and the height is 1 foot. What is the volume of the sand floor? _____

17. A fish pond is shaped like a rectangular prism. It has a length of 10 feet, a width of 8 feet, and a depth of 6 feet.

   a. What is the volume of water that the pond can hold?

   _____

   b. One cubic foot holds about 7.5 gallons of water. How many gallons of water can the pond hold? _____

18. The volume of Mandie's customer's fish tank is 2,400 cubic inches. The recommended living space for each fish of a certain size is 160 cubic inches. What is the greatest number of these fish that Mandie can sell for the tank? _____

Write About It

19. Visit a store that sells appliances. Take along a tape measure. Find the volume, or capacity, of a refrigerator. (This information usually can be found on a label attached to the refrigerator.) Then measure the length, width, and height of the refrigerator. Calculate the volume of the refrigerator. Is the volume you calculated the same as the volume on the label? Explain your answer.

_____

_____

_____

_____

_____

9•2 Volume of Cylinders

> ### IN THIS LESSON, YOU WILL LEARN
> To find the volume of a cylinder
>
> ### WORDS TO LEARN
> **Cylindrical** *having the shape of a cylinder*

Ms. Mechanick has two gasoline engines that run lawn mowers. One engine has a cylinder with a radius of 4 centimeters and a height of 6 centimeters. The other engine has a cylinder with a radius of 3 centimeters and a height of 7 centimeters. Ms. Mechanick thinks that both cylinders hold the same amount of gasoline. Her nephew, Kaleb, says she can find the volumes of the cylinders to see if this is true.

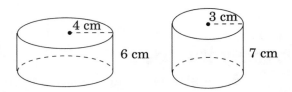

New Idea

A **cylindrical** (suh-LIHN-drih-kuhl) container is shaped like a cylinder. To find the volume of a cylindrical container, multiply the area of the base by the height. The base of a cylinder is a circle. If the radius of the base is r, the area of the base is πr^2. The formula for the volume of a cylinder is given below.

$$\text{Volume} = \text{Base area} \cdot \text{height}$$
$$V = \pi r^2 \cdot h$$
$$V = \pi r^2 h$$

Example: Find the volume of Ms. Mechanick's engine cylinders. Use the formula $V = \pi r^2 h$.

For the first cylinder, substitute 4 for r and 6 for h.

$$V = \pi r^2 h$$

$$V \approx 3.14 \cdot 4^2 \cdot 6$$

$$V \approx 3.14 \cdot 16 \cdot 6$$

$$V \approx 301.44 \text{ cm}^3$$

For the second cylinder, substitute 3 for r and 7 for h.

$$V \approx 3.14 \cdot 3^2 \cdot 7$$

$$V \approx 3.14 \cdot 9 \cdot 7$$

$$V \approx 197.82 \text{ cm}^3$$

Because 301.44 cm^3 is greater than 197.82 cm^3, the volume of the first cylinder is greater than the volume of the second cylinder.

✓Check the Math

1. Kareem bought a can of car wax with a radius of 5 centimeters and a height of 10 centimeters. He says the volume of the can is 314 cubic centimeters. Jay says the volume is 785 cubic centimeters. Who is correct? Explain.

_____

_____

◀Focus on the Idea

To find the volume of a cylinder, use the formula V = πr²h, where r is the radius of the base and h is the height.

Practice

Label each cylinder with the given dimensions. Then find the volume of the cylinder, using *V = πr²h*. The first one is done for you.

2. radius = 9 in.
   height = 2 in.

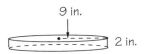
9 in.   2 in.

V = πr²h

V ≈ 3.14 • 9² • 2

V ≈ 508.68 in.³

3. radius = 6 ft
   height = 8 ft

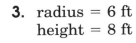

4. radius = 12 m
   height = 15 m

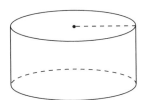

5. radius = 3.5 cm
   height = 9 cm

Extend the Idea

You can find the volume of a cylinder if you are given the height of the cylinder and the diameter of the base. First divide the diameter by two to get the radius. Then use the formula for the volume of a cylinder, $V = \pi r^2 h$.

Example: Find the volume of a cylinder with a diameter of 22 centimeters and height of 6 centimeters. The diameter is 22 centimeters, so the radius is 22 ÷ 2, or 11 centimeters.

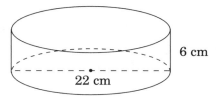

6 cm

22 cm

$$V = \pi r^2 h$$

$$V \approx 3.14 \cdot 11^2 \cdot 6 \quad \leftarrow \text{Substitute 11 for } r \text{ and 6 for } h.$$

$$V \approx 3.14 \cdot 121 \cdot 6$$

$$V \approx 2{,}279.64$$

The volume is 2,279.64 cm^3.

✓Check Your Understanding

Write the letter that names the volume of each cylinder.

6. diameter = 8 cm, height = 8 cm _____

7. diameter = 14 cm, height = 5 cm _____

8. diameter = 10 cm, height = 6 cm _____

a. 401.92 cm^3

b. 769.3 cm^3

c. 471 cm^3

Practice

Find the volume of each of the following cylinders using $V = \pi r^2 h$. The first one is done for you.

9. diameter = 20 in.
height = 7 in.

$$r = \frac{d}{2} = \frac{20 \text{ in.}}{2} = 10 \text{ in.}$$
$$V = \pi r^2 h$$
$$V = 3.14 \cdot 10^2 \cdot 7$$
$$V = 2{,}198 \text{ in.}^3$$

10. diameter = 24 ft
height = 9 ft

11. diameter = 44 mm
height = 20 mm

12. diameter = 11 m
height = 6 m

Apply the Idea

13. A cylindrical fuel storage tank has a diameter of 6 meters and a height of 10 meters. Find the volume of the tank.
_____

14. A cylindrical pipe in an oil refinery is 200 feet long. The diameter of the pipe is 0.5 feet. How many cubic feet of oil can this pipe hold? _____

15. A drinking glass shaped like a cylinder has a radius of 2.5 centimeters and a height of 12 centimeters.

    a. Find the volume of the drinking glass. _____

    b. A cubic centimeter of water has a mass of 1 gram. Suppose the drinking glass is filled with water. What is the mass of the water? _____

16. Find a container that is shaped like a cylinder. Make a drawing of your container.

    a. Find the diameter and radius of the container. Label these on your drawing. Which was easier to find, the diameter or radius? Why?

    _____

    b. Find the height of your container. Label your drawing.

    _____

    c. Find the volume of your container.

    _____

✎ Write About It

17. Think about some real objects that are shaped like cylinders.

    a. Why do you think each object is shaped that way?

    _____

    _____

    b. Do you think each object was designed to have a specific volume? Why or why not?

    _____

    _____

◢9•3 Volume of Rectangular Pyramids

◤ IN THIS LESSON, YOU WILL LEARN

To find the volume of a rectangular pyramid

WORDS TO LEARN

Volume of a pyramid *the amount of space enclosed by a pyramid*

A pyramid in Cholula, Mexico, called Quetzalcoatl, is 177 feet tall. It has a base that covers about 1,960,200 square feet. What is the volume of this pyramid?

New Idea

Look at the pyramid within the rectangular prism shown at the right. The pyramid and the prism have the same base. The top of the pyramid touches the opposite base of the prism.

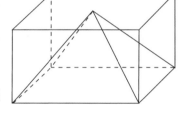

The **volume of a pyramid** (VAHL-yoom, PIHR-uh-mihd), the amount of space enclosed by the pyramid, is one-third of the volume of a prism. To find the volume of any pyramid, find $\frac{1}{3}$ of the volume of the rectangular prism that has the same base area, B, and height, h. The formula is given below.

Volume of pyramid $= \frac{1}{3} \cdot Bh$

Since B, the area of the base, is equal to the length times the width (lw), another way to write this formula is given below.

$V = \frac{1}{3} \cdot B \cdot h = \frac{1}{3} \cdot lw \cdot h = \frac{1}{3}lwh$

Example: Find the volume of a pyramid with a base that is 6 centimeters long, 3 centimeters wide, and 8 centimeters high.

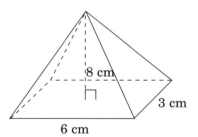

The dimensions of the base are given, so use the formula $V = \frac{1}{3}lwh$, where $l = 6$ cm, $w = 3$ cm, and $h = 8$ cm.

$V = \frac{1}{3}lwh$

$V = \frac{1}{3} \cdot 6 \cdot 3 \cdot 8$

$V = 48$

The volume is 48 cm³.

◣ Focus on the Idea

To find the volume of a rectangular pyramid, use one of these formulas:

$V = \frac{1}{3}Bh$, where B is the area of the base and h is the height

$V = \frac{1}{3}lwh$, where l is the length of the base, w is the width of the base, and h is the height

Practice

Label each pyramid with the given dimensions. Then find the volume of the pyramid, using $V = \frac{1}{3}Bh$ or $V = \frac{1}{3}lwh$. The first one is done for you.

1. $B = 9 \text{ ft}^2$
   $h = 5 \text{ ft}$

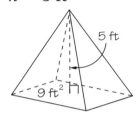

5 ft

9 ft²

$V = \frac{1}{3}Bh$

$V = \frac{1}{3} \cdot 9 \cdot 5$

$V = 15 \text{ ft}^3$

2. $l = 5 \text{ m}$
   $w = 3 \text{ m}$
   $h = 4 \text{ m}$

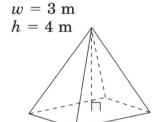

3. $B = 18 \text{ in.}^2$
   $h = 9 \text{ in.}$

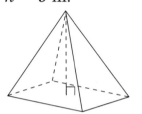

Find the volume of each pyramid with the given dimensions.

4. $l = 12 \text{ cm}$
   $w = 7 \text{ cm}$
   $h = 15 \text{ cm}$

5. $B = 14 \text{ in.}^2$
   $h = 10 \text{ in.}$

6. $l = 5 \text{ m}$
   $w = 5 \text{ m}$
   $h = 13 \text{ m}$

Apply the Idea

7. Look back at page 224. Find the volume of the Quetzalcoatl pyramid. _____

8. The Great Pyramid of Giza is in Egypt. Each side of its square base is about 756 feet long. Its height, when first built, was 481 feet. Find the volume of the pyramid. _____

✐ Write About It

9. Suppose a pyramid has the same base area as a rectangular prism and a height that is half the height of the rectangular prism. Imagine filling the pyramid with sand. How many times would you need to fill the pyramid with sand to completely fill the prism? Explain.

9•4 Volume of Cones

IN THIS LESSON, YOU WILL LEARN

To find the volume of a cone

WORDS TO LEARN

Conical *having the shape of a cone*
Volume of a cone *the amount of space enclosed by a cone*

Your bottled-water company delivers 20-liter containers to customers. A single-serving, cone-shaped cup is 8 centimeters tall and has a 3-centimeter radius. Approximately how many cups will one container fill? (Note: 20 liters = 20,000 cubic centimeters.)

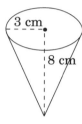

New Idea

You can find the volume of a cone-shaped, or **conical** (KAHN-ih-kuhl) container, by comparing it with a cylinder. Look at the cone within the cylinder shown at the right. The cone and the cylinder have the same base. The **volume of a cone** (VAHL-yoom, kohn), the amount of space enclosed by the cone, is one-third of the volume of a cylinder. To find the volume of any cone, find $\frac{1}{3}$ of the volume of the cylinder that has the same base area, B, and the same height, h. The formula is given below.

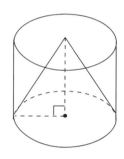

Volume of cone = $\frac{1}{3}$ • Volume of cylinder

$$V = \tfrac{1}{3}\pi r^2 h$$

Since πr^2 gives the area of the base (B), another way to write this formula is given below.

$$V = \tfrac{1}{3} \bullet \pi r^2 \bullet h = \tfrac{1}{3} \bullet B \bullet h = \tfrac{1}{3}Bh$$

Examples: Find the volume of the conical water cup.

$$V = \tfrac{1}{3}\pi r^2 h$$

$$V \approx \tfrac{1}{3} \bullet 3.14 \bullet 3^2 \bullet 8 \quad \leftarrow \text{Substitute 3 for } r \text{ and 8 for } h.$$

$$V \approx 75.36$$

The volume of the water cup is about 75.36 cm^3.

To find about how many cups can be filled by the 20-liter container, divide 20,000 by 75:
    20,000 ÷ 75 = 266.67

About 267 cups can be filled.

Focus on the Idea

To find the volume of a cone, use one of these formulas:
$V = \frac{1}{3}Bh$, *where B is the area of the base and h is the height*
$V = \frac{1}{3}\pi r^2 h$, *where r is the radius of the base and h is the height*

 ## Practice

Label each cone with the given dimensions. Then find the volume of the cone. The first one is done for you.

1. $B = 6$ m^2
   $h = 8$ m

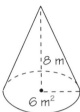

8 m
6 m²

$V = \frac{1}{3} \cdot 6 \cdot 8$
$V = 16$ m^3

2. $r = 3$ ft
   $h = 5$ ft

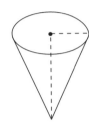

$V = \frac{1}{3}Bh$

3. $B = 18$ ft^2
   $h = 7$ ft

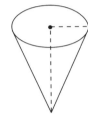

Find the volume of a cone with the given dimensions.

4. $r = 11$ mm
   $h = 21$ mm

5. $B = 78.5$ cm^2
   $h = 13$ cm

6. $r = 14$ in.
   $h = 16$ in.

Apply the Idea

7. A funnel is conical. The larger open end of the funnel has a radius of 4 centimeters. The height of the funnel's cup is 9 centimeters. Find the volume of the funnel's cup.

_____

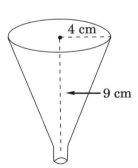

4 cm

9 cm

 ## Write About It

8. The area of the base of Cone A is 80 square centimeters and its height is 6 centimeters. The area of the base of Cone B is 160 square centimeters and its height is 12 centimeters. How does the volume of Cone B compare to the volume of Cone A?

_____

_____

9•5 Volume of Spheres

Your company makes glass globes for lamps that are **spherical** (SFER-ih-kuhl), or shaped like a sphere. Each one has a radius of 4 inches. Will a globe fit in a cube-shaped box with a volume of 300 cubic inches?

New Idea

The **volume of a sphere** (VAHL-yoom uhv uh sfihr), the amount of space enclosed by a sphere, can be found using the formula given below.

$$\text{Volume} = \tfrac{4}{3} \cdot \pi \cdot r^3$$
$$V = \tfrac{4}{3}\pi r^3$$

Example: To decide whether a glass globe will fit into the box whose volume is 300 in.³, find the volume of the glass globe.

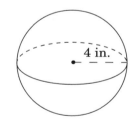

4 in.

$$V = \tfrac{4}{3}\pi r^3 \qquad \leftarrow \text{Substitute 4 for } r.$$

$$V \approx \tfrac{4}{3} \cdot 3.14 \cdot 4^3$$

$$V \approx \tfrac{4}{3} \cdot 3.14 \cdot 64$$

$$V \approx 267.9$$

The volume of a glass globe is about 267.9 in.³ Because the volume of the globe is less than the volume of the 300-in.³ box, the globe will fit in the box.

 ## Focus on the Idea

To find the volume of a sphere with radius r, use the formula $V = \tfrac{4}{3}\pi r^3$.

Practice

Label each sphere with the given dimension. Then find the volume of the sphere, using $\frac{4}{3}\pi r^3$. The first one is done for you.

1. radius = 3 ft

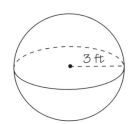

$V = \frac{4}{3}\pi r^3$

$V \approx \frac{4}{3} \cdot 3.14 \cdot 3^3$

$V \approx 113.04 \text{ ft}^3$

2. diameter = 8 cm
(Hint: Find the radius first.)

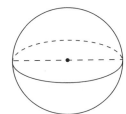

3. $r = 9$ in.

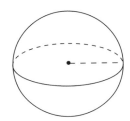

4. $d = 16$ mm

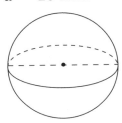

Find the volume of the sphere with the given dimensions.

5. $r = 5.5$ m   **6.** $d = 25$ in.   **7.** $r = 15$ ft   **8.** $d = 12.5$ m

Apply the Idea

9. A spherical water tank is half full of water. Its diameter is 12 feet. How much water is in the tank? _____

Write About It

10. The volume of Sphere A is 420 cubic centimeters. The volume of Sphere B is 140 cubic centimeters. Is the radius of Sphere A three times the radius of Sphere B? Explain.

_____

_____

9•6 Distinguishing Between Surface Area and Volume

> ## IN THIS LESSON, YOU WILL LEARN
> *To decide whether a problem involves surface area or volume*
>
> ## WORDS TO LEARN
> **Surface area** *the total area of the outside of a three-dimensional figure*

Teri's company makes large wooden planters in two shapes: cubes and cylinders. After the planters are built, the insides must be coated with preservative. Each planter then is labeled with its capacity, given in cubic feet.

New Idea

You have learned about surface area and volume. (See Lesson 8•1.) It is important to know the difference between a problem that involves surface area and one that involves volume. A problem involves **surface area** when it asks about the area of the surfaces of a three-dimensional shape. A problem involves volume when it asks about the amount of space enclosed by a three-dimensional shape.

Examples: One cylindrical planter has a diameter of 18 inches and a height of 10 inches. To determine how much preservative Teri will need to coat the bottom and the sides of the cylinder, she will need to calculate part of the surface area.

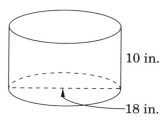

Area of the bottom $= \pi r^2 \approx 3.14 \cdot 9^2 \approx 254.3$

Lateral area $= 2\pi rh \approx 2 \cdot 3.14 \cdot 9 \cdot 10 \approx 565.2$

The area Teri will coat $\approx 254.3 + 565.2 \approx 819.5$ in.^{2}

To determine the capacity of the cylinder, Teri needs to find the volume:
Volume $= \pi r^2 h \approx 3.14 \cdot 9^2 \cdot 10 \approx 2{,}543.4$

The planter will hold about 2,543.4 in.^{3} of soil.

► Focus on the Idea

When you need to calculate the area of the surfaces of a three-dimensional object, find the surface area. When you need to calculate the amount of space enclosed by a three-dimensional object, find the volume.

Practice

Write whether you should calculate the *surface area* or the *volume* for each. The first two are done for you.

1. paper needed to make a cup and a lid   *surface area*
2. juice that will fill a cup   *volume*
3. food that will fit inside a cooler   _____
4. fabric needed to cover a pillow   _____
5. stuffing needed to fill a pillow   _____
6. wrapping paper needed to cover a box   _____
7. packing material needed to put inside a box   _____

Apply the Idea

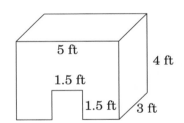

8. Verna is building a doghouse. It is a rectangular prism 5 feet long, 3 feet wide, and 4 feet high. The opening on the front of the doghouse is 1.5 feet wide and 1.5 feet high.

   a. How much wood will Verna need to build the doghouse, including the floor? _____

   b. How much space is there inside the doghouse?

   _____

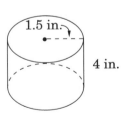

9. Miguel works at the local greenhouse. Some of the flower pots have a radius of 1.5 inches and a height of 4 inches.

   a. Miguel wants to paint the curved surface of each pot. How much surface is he going to paint on each pot? _____

   b. How much potting soil will he need to fill each pot? _____

✏ Write About It

10. What is the difference between these measurements: 52 square meters and 52 cubic meters? Give examples of figures that could have these measurements.

_____

_____

In This Chapter, You Have Learned

- To find the volume of rectangular prisms, cylinders, rectangular pyramids, cones, and spheres
- To determine whether a problem involves surface area or volume

Words You Know

Write the letter of the formula or phrase in Column 2 that best defines each word or phrase in Column 1.

Column 1

1. volume _____
2. spherical _____
3. cylindrical _____
4. volume of a rectangular prism _____
5. volume of a cube _____

Column 2

a. $V = lwh$

b. amount of space enclosed by a three-dimensional shape

c. shaped like a sphere

d. $V = s^3$

e. shaped like a cylinder

More Practice

Label each figure with the given dimensions. Then find the volume of the figure.

6. rectangular prism with length 8 ft, width 3 ft, and height 5 ft

7. cube with edge 9 cm

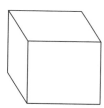

8. cylinder with radius 6 in. and height 7 in.

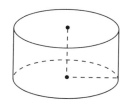

9. rectangular pyramid with length 4 m, width 1.5 m, and height 5 m

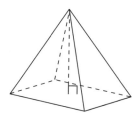

10. cone with height
12 ft and diameter 8 ft

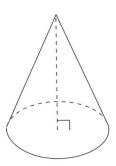

11. sphere with radius 11 cm

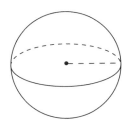

Problems You Can Solve

12. A container is shaped like a rectangular prism. It has a length of 15 centimeters, a width of 15 centimeters, and a height of 20 centimeters. It is half full of water.

   a. What is the volume of the container? _____

   b. What is the height of the water? _____

   c. What is the volume of the water? _____

   d. Disinfectant is poured into the container. It raises the water level by 3 centimeters. What is the volume of the water and the disinfectant? _____

13. Maurice makes copper plumbing pipes. He received an order to make 20 pipes. Each pipe must be 40 inches long and have a diameter of 9 inches.

   a. How much copper will Maurice need to make the pipes?

   _____

   b. What is the capacity of each pipe? _____

14. **For Your Portfolio**   Design a box that has a volume of 216 cubic feet and that uses the least amount of cardboard possible. Write a plan for your design. Be sure your plan includes a sketch of your box with its dimensions labeled. Explain why your design works.

_____

_____

_____

Chapter 9   Practice Test

Label each figure with given dimensions. Then find the volume of each figure described. Show your work.

1. rectangular prism with length 7 cm, width 6 cm, and height 4 cm

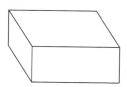

_____

2. cube with edge 10.5 m

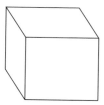

_____

3. cylinder with diameter 16 ft and height 9 ft

_____

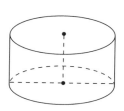

Find the volume of each of the following figures.

4. rectangular pyramid with base area 56 in.^{2} and height 12 in.

_____

5. cone with radius 7 cm and height 6 cm

_____

6. sphere with diameter 28 in. _____

7. A cylindrical swimming pool has a radius of 10 feet and a depth of 6 feet. How much water will the pool hold?

_____

An ice-cream cone has a radius of 5 centimeters and a height of 15 centimeters. Kimi puts a scoop of ice cream that has a diameter of 10 centimeters on top of the cone.

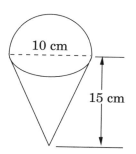

10 cm

15 cm

8. What is the volume of the cone? _____

9. What is the volume of the ice-cream scoop? _____

10. If the ice cream melts, will the cone overflow? Explain.

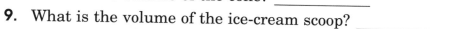

_____

Glossary

A

Acute angle an angle that measures less than 90° (2•1)

Acute triangle a triangle with three acute angles (3•2)

Adjacent angles two angles with one vertex and a common side (1•6)

Alternate exterior angles two exterior angles that lie on opposite sides of a transversal and are outside two lines (1•5)

Alternate interior angles angles that lie on opposite sides of a transversal and are enclosed between two lines (1•5)

Altitude a perpendicular line segment connecting both bases (7•1)

Altitude of a cone the perpendicular line segment connecting the vertex of the cone to the base (7•4)

Altitude of a cylinder the perpendicular line segment connecting the two bases (7•4)

Angle a figure formed by two rays that have the same endpoint (1•3)

Angle bisector a ray that divides an angle into two congruent angles (2•7)

Angle-Side-Angle Postulate (ASA) postulate that states if two angles and the common side of these angles of one triangle are congruent to the corresponding angles and side of a second triangle, then the two triangles are congruent (3•4)

Arc part of a circle (6•2)

Area the measure of the surface a figure covers (5•2)

B

Base angle each angle that has a base as a side (4•5)

Base of a parallelogram any side of a parallelogram (5•2)

Base of a prism one of the two congruent faces in the parallel planes of a prism (7•1)

Base of a triangle any side of a triangle (5•6)

Bases of a trapezoid the two parallel sides of a trapezoid (4•5)

Bisects divides into two equal parts (2•6)

Bisector a line that divides an angle or a line segment into two equal parts (2•6)

C

Center of a sphere the point that is the same distance from all other points of the sphere (7•5)

Central angle an angle whose vertex is at the center of a circle and whose sides are radii (6•2)

Chord a line segment with both end points on a circle (6•2)

Circle a set of points that are all the same distance from a given point called the center (6•1)

Circumference the distance around a circle (6•3)

Circumscribed polygon a polygon whose sides are tangent to a circle (6•5)

Collinear points three or more points that lie in a straight line (1•1)

Compass a tool used to draw circles and arcs (2•6)

Complementary angles two angles whose measures have a sum of 90° (2•2)

Cone a three-dimensional figure that has a circular base and a curved surface connecting the vertex and the edge of the base (7•4)

Congruent figures that have the same size and shape (2•5)

Congruent angles angles that have the same measure or size (2•5)

Congruent line segments line segments that are the same length (2•5)

Congruent polygons polygons that have the same size and shape (4•7)

Congruent triangles triangles that have the same size and shape (3•3)

Conical having the shape of a cone (9•4)

Coordinate one of the numbers in an ordered pair (4•9)

Coordinate plane a grid where every point can be located by using two numbers (4•9)

Coplanar points points that lie in the same plane (1•1)

Corresponding angles two angles that lie on the same side of a transversal; one is an interior angle and one is an exterior angle (2•8)

Corresponding parts a side or angle of one triangle that is exactly the same size as a side or angle of another triangle (3•3)

Corresponding parts of a polygon the matching pairs of sides and angles of two congruent polygons (4•7)

Cube a prism in which all faces are squares (7•2)

Cylinder a three-dimensional figure that has two congruent circular bases that are in parallel planes and a curved surface connecting the bases (7•4)

Cylindrical having the shape of a cylinder (9•2)

D

Degrees units of measure for angles, each of which is equal to $\frac{1}{360}$ of a circle (2•4)

Diagonal the line segment that joins two nonconsecutive vertices of a polygon (4•1)

Diameter a line segment that passes through the center of a circle with both endpoints on the circle (6•1)

Diameter of a sphere a line segment that passes through the center of a sphere and has both endpoints on the sphere (7•5)

E

Edge a line segment formed when two faces intersect (7•1)

Endpoints points that represent the starting point of a ray or one of the two points that represents the ends of a line segment (1•2)

Equilateral triangle a triangle with three sides of equal length (3•2)

Estimate to make an educated guess about value (5•3)

Exterior all points outside a figure (3•1)

Exterior angle of a polygon an angle that lies outside a polygon, but forms a linear pair with an interior angle of the polygon (4•6)

Exterior angles angles outside two lines crossed by a transversal (1•5)

F

Face one of the polygons that makes up a polyhedron (7•1)

H

Half plane part of a plane made up of one line, called the edge, and all points on one side of the edge (1•7)

Height the length of an altitude (7•1)

Height of a parallelogram the perpendicular distance between the bases (5•2)

Height of a trapezoid the perpendicular distance between the bases of the trapezoid (5•7)

Height of a triangle length of line segment drawn from a vertex so that it is perpendicular to the opposite base (5•6)

Hypotenuse the side of a right triangle opposite the right angle (3•6)

I

Inequality a statement that two expressions are not equal (3•8)

Inscribed angle an angle with its vertex on a circle and sides that are chords (6•6)

Inscribed polygon a polygon whose vertices lie on a circle (6•5)

Intercepted arc a part of a circle that lies between the two sides of an angle (6•2)

Interior all points inside a figure (3•1)

Interior angle of a polygon angle within a polygon formed by two sides of the polygon (4•6)

Interior angles angles that are enclosed between two lines crossed by a transversal (1•5)

Interior angles of a triangle angles formed by the sides in the interior of the triangle (3•5)

Intersecting lines two lines that meet, or cross, at exactly one point (1•4)

Intersecting planes planes that meet in one line (1•7)

Irregular figure any shape that can be broken up into other recognizable shapes (5•8)

Isosceles trapezoid a trapezoid with congruent legs (4•5)

Isosceles triangle a triangle with at least two sides of equal length (3•2)

L

Lateral area of a cone the area of the curved surface of the cone (8•4)

Lateral area of a cylinder the area of the curved surface of the cylinder (8•2)

Lateral edge an edge that two lateral faces have in common (7•1)

Lateral face a face in a prism that is not a base (7•1)

Legs the two sides of a right triangle that form the right angle (3•6)

Legs the two sides of a trapezoid that are not parallel (4•5)

Length of a rectangle the longer pair of sides (5•1)

Line a set of many points that extends with no end in opposite directions (1•1)

Line segment a part of a line that consists of two points and all the points between them (1•2)

Linear distance the length of a line segment or segments (5•9)

Linear pair two adjacent angles whose noncommon sides form a straight line (1•6)

M

Midpoint a point that divides a line segment into two equal parts (2•6)

Median a line segment that connects the midpoints of the legs of a trapezoid (4•5)

Minor arc part of a circle that lies between the two radii that form a central angle (6•2)

N

Net pattern that can be folded to form a three-dimensional figure (8•1)

Noncollinear points points that do not lie in a straight line (1•1)

Nonconsecutive vertices any two vertices that are not next to one another (4•1)

Noncoplanar points points that lie in different planes (1•1)

O

Obtuse angle an angle that measures greater than 90° but less than 180° (2•1)

Obtuse triangle a triangle with one obtuse angle (3•2)

Ordered pair two numbers that tell the x-coordinate and y-coordinate of a point (4•9)

Origin the meeting point of the x-axis and the y-axis (4•9)

P

Parallel lines lines in the same plane that do not meet; they are always the same distance apart (1•4)

Parallel planes planes that do not intersect (1•7)

Parallelogram a quadrilateral with two pairs of parallel sides (4•2)

Perimeter the distance around a polygon (5•1)

Perpendicular lines lines that meet at a right angle (1•4)

Pi (π) the ratio of the circumference of a circle to its diameter (6•3)

Plane a flat surface that extends in all directions with no end (1•1)

Point a location in space represented by a dot (1•1)

Polygon a closed figure formed by joining three or more line segments at their endpoints (4•1)

Polyhedra plural form of the word *polyhedron* (7•1)

Polyhedron any three-dimensional shape made up of flat surfaces that are polygons (7•1)

Postulate a rule in mathematics (3•4)

Prism a polyhedron with two congruent faces in parallel planes (7•1)

Proportion a statement that two ratios are equal (3•7)

Protractor a tool that is used to measure angles in degrees (2•3)

Pyramid a polyhedron with one base and triangular lateral faces that meet at a common vertex (7•3)

Pythagorean Theorem theorem that states that in a right triangle, the sum of the squares of the lengths of the two legs equals the square of the length of the hypotenuse (3•6)

R

Radii the plural form of radius (6•1)

Radius a line segment with one endpoint at the center of a circle and the other endpoint on the circle (6•1)

Radius of a sphere a line segment with one endpoint at the center of the sphere and the other endpoint on the sphere (7•5)

Ratio comparison of two numbers (3•7)

Ray the part of a line that starts at one point and extends endlessly in one direction (1•2)

Rectangle a parallelogram with four right angles (4•3)

Rectangular prism a prism in which all faces are rectangles (7•2)

Reflection flip of a figure over a given line (4•9)

Regular polygon polygon with all sides and all angles congruent (4•6)

Regular pyramid a pyramid with a regular polygon as its base and congruent isosceles triangles as its lateral faces (7•3)

Regular tessellation pattern formed by tessellating one regular polygon (4•10)

Rhombus a parallelogram with four congruent sides (4•4)

Right angle an angle with a measure of 90° (1•4)

Right triangle a triangle with one right angle (3•2)

Rotation turn of a figure (4•9)

S

Scale drawing a drawing of a structure that is too big or too small to be drawn actual size (3•7)

Scalene triangle a triangle with no equal sides (3•2)

Secant a line that intersects a circle in exactly two points (6•2)

Side-Angle-Side Postulate (SAS) postulate that states that if two sides and the angle formed by these sides of one triangle are congruent to the corresponding sides and angle of a second triangle, then the two triangles are congruent (3•4)

Side-Side-Side Postulate (SSS) postulate that states that if three sides of one triangle are congruent to three sides of a second triangle, then the two triangles are congruent (3•4)

Sides the two rays that form an angle (1•3)

Sides the line segments that form a figure (3•1)

Similar polygons polygons that are the same shape and have corresponding sides that are in proportion (4•8)

Similar triangles triangles that are the same shape but not necessarily the same size (3•7)

Skew lines lines that do not intersect and are not in the same plane (1•7)

Slant height of a cone the length of a line segment from the vertex to any point on the edge of the base (7•4)

Slant height of a pyramid altitude of one of the lateral faces (7•3)

Sphere a three-dimensional figure with all of its points the same distance from a given point (7•5)

Spherical shaped like a sphere (9•5)

Square a rectangle with four congruent sides (4•4)

Straight angle an angle that measures 180° and whose sides form a straight line (2•1)

Straightedge a tool used to draw straight lines (2•6)

Supplementary angles two angles whose measures have a sum of 180° (2•2)

Surface area the total area of the outside of a three-dimensional figure (8•1)

Surface area of a rectangular pyramid the sum of the areas of the four triangular faces of a pyramid and its rectangular base (8•3)

Surface area of a square pyramid the sum of the areas of the four triangular faces of a pyramid and its square base

Surface area of a sphere the area of the curved surface of the sphere (8•5)

T

Tangent a line that touches a circle at exactly one point (6•2)

Tessellation pattern of repeating polygons that completely covers an area without any gaps or overlaps (4•10)

Theorem a mathematical statement that can be proved (3•6)

Transformations movements of a figure from one place to another (4•9)

Translation slide of a figure (4•9)

Transversal a line that intersects two or more lines (1•5)

Trapezoid a quadrilateral with exactly one pair of parallel sides (4•5)

Triangle figure formed by three line segments (3•1)

The Triangle Inequality Theorem states that for any triangle, the sum of the lengths of any two sides is greater than the length of the remaining side (3•8)

V

Vertex the point at which two line segments intersect (3•1)

Vertex of an angle the point at which the sides of an angle meet (1•3)

Vertex of a polyhedron a point where three or more edges intersect (7•1)

Vertical angles pairs of angles formed by lines that intersect (1•5)

Vertices more than one vertex (3•1)

Volume amount of space enclosed by a three-dimensional object (9•1)

Volume of a cone the amount of space enclosed by a cone (9•4)

Volume of a pyramid amount of space enclosed by a pyramid (9•3)

Volume of a sphere the amount of space enclosed by a sphere (9•5)

W

Width of a rectangle the shorter pair of sides (5•1)

X

x-axis the horizontal number line used on a coordinate plane (4•9)

x-coordinate the number of units that a point is right or left of the origin (4•9)

Y

y-axis the vertical number line used on a coordinate plane (4•9)

y-coordinate the number of units that a point is up or down from the origin (4•9)

Answers

Chapter 1   Introduction to Basic Elements

1•1   Points, Lines, Planes

1. Point *M* and point *N*; a line is named by two points on the line.

3. $\overleftrightarrow{EF}$ 5. $\overleftrightarrow{BC}$

7. Points *H*, *I*, and *J*; plane *HIJ*

9. Points *T*, *U*, and *V*; plane *TUV*

11. Drawing should show a four-sided plane with the corners labeled and two dotted diagonal lines inside the plane.   **a.** Possible answer: Point *F*, point *G*, point *R*, point *S*; plane *FGRS*   **b.** six   **c.** Possible answer: $\overleftrightarrow{FG}$, $\overleftrightarrow{GR}$, $\overleftrightarrow{RS}$, $\overleftrightarrow{SF}$, $\overleftrightarrow{FR}$, $\overleftrightarrow{GS}$

13. $\overleftrightarrow{DF}$
    a. Possible answer: *ABCDF*
    b. Possible answer: Points *B*, *A*, and *F*
    c. Possible answer: Points *A*, *F*, and *D*

15. Drawing should show the cage with points *A*, *B*, and *C* on the front corners and point *D* on one of the rear corners.   **a.** Yes, plane *ABC*
    b. Plane *ABC*, plane *BCD*, plane *ACD*

1•2   Line Segments and Rays

1. Yes, the endpoint is *N*. The endpoint is always named first.

3. Drawing should show $\overrightarrow{GF}$ with *G* as the endpoint.

5. Ray *FG*

7. Line segment *XY* (or *YX*)

1•3   Angles

1. Yes; when three letters are used to name an angle, the middle letter (*I*) is the letter at the vertex.

3. Drawing in text shows an angle with sides $\overrightarrow{GF}$ and $\overrightarrow{GH}$ and vertex *G*

5. Drawing should show an angle with sides $\overrightarrow{JH}$ and $\overrightarrow{JK}$ and vertex: *J*

7. c   9. d   11. b

1•4   Parallel and Perpendicular Lines

1. Marie could tell from the names of lines *CD* and *CB* that the lines had one point in common, point *C*. This meant that the lines intersected, so they could not be parallel.

3. Drawing should show lines *XY* and *ZY* intersecting at point *Y*. Both lines should extend in two directions after intersecting.

5. Drawing should show line *KL* with a point near the middle, *I*, where line *IJ* begins.

7. Line *PY* is parallel to line *MZ*. $\overleftrightarrow{PY} \parallel \overleftrightarrow{MZ}$

9. Line *QL* is parallel to line *MN*. $\overleftrightarrow{QL} \parallel \overleftrightarrow{MN}$

11. a   13. c

15. Possible answer: $\overleftrightarrow{AB}$ and $\overleftrightarrow{AD}$, $\overleftrightarrow{BD}$ and $\overleftrightarrow{EC}$

17. $\overleftrightarrow{AB} \parallel \overleftrightarrow{EC}$

1•5   Angles Formed by Intersecting Lines

1. Drawing in text shows lines *MN* and *TV* intersecting at point *X*. ∠*MXT* and ∠*VXN*, ∠*MXV* and ∠*TXN*

3. Drawing should show lines *CD* and *EF* intersecting at point *P*. ∠*EPC* and ∠*DPF*, ∠*EPD* and ∠*CPF*

5. Possible answer: **a.** ∠3, ∠4, ∠5, and ∠6   **b.** ∠1, ∠2, ∠7, and ∠8

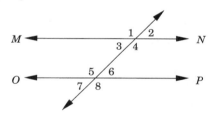

7. ∠2, ∠6, ∠3, and ∠7

9. Possible answer: **a.** ∠2 and ∠8, ∠3 and ∠5   **b.** ∠1 and ∠7, ∠4 and ∠6

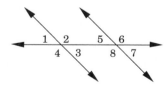

11. ∠1 and ∠8, ∠4 and ∠5

1•6 More Pairs of Angles

1. Adjacent angles are ∠*PSQ* and ∠*QSR*, and ∠*XWY* and ∠*YWZ*.
3. Yes 5. No
7. Drawing should show 2 separate angles, having no common elements.
9. Drawing should show two adjacent angles whose noncommon sides form a straight line.

1•7 Intersecting and Parallel Planes

1. a, b, and d 3. Parallel planes
5. Intersecting planes 7. e 9. a 11. b 13. *GH*
15. *XZ* 17. 3

Chapter 1 Review

1. angle 2. intersecting
3. right 4. skew
5. linear pair 6. plane
7. perpendicular
8. ∠1 and ∠3, ∠2 and ∠4, ∠5 and ∠7, ∠6 and ∠8
9. ∠3 and ∠5, ∠4 and ∠6
10. ∠1 and ∠7, ∠2 and ∠8
11. e 12. g 13. a
14. i 15. c 16. b
17. d 18. h 19. f
20. **a.** They are parallel lines. **b.** They are parallel lines. **c.** They are perpendicular lines.

Chapter 2 Angles

2•1 Classifying Angles

1. Yes, an acute angle must be greater than 0° and less than 90°.
3. obtuse 5. right 7. acute
9. Drawing should show an obtuse angle.
11. Drawing should show an angle of 180°.
13. none 15. none
17. ∠*SMR*, ∠*ZMT*
19. ∠*SMV*, ∠*VMT*
21. Possible answer: ∠*CGF*
23. Possible answer: ∠*CAD*

2•2 Recognizing Complementary and Supplementary Angles

1. Yes. A right angle has a measure of 90°.
   90° + 90° = 180°, so the angles are supplementary.
3. supplementary 5. complementary 7. a
9. Yes. 44 + 46 = 90. Two angles whose measures have a sum of 90° are complementary angles.
11. Drawing should show two angles whose measures have a sum of 180°.
13. 65° 15. ∠*A* and ∠*C*, ∠*B* and ∠*D*
17. Possible answer: ∠*CAE* and ∠*AEB*

2•3 Using a Protractor to Measure Angles

1. $m\angle ABC = 40°$
3. $m\angle S = 145°$
5. $m\angle T = 40°$
7. **a.** 70° **b.** 80° **c.** 100° **d.** 110°

2•4 Using a Protractor to Draw Angles

1. Drawing in text shows $m\angle ABC = 100°$.
3. Drawing should show $m\angle LMN = 150°$.
5. Drawing should show $m\angle QRS = 20°$.
7. **a.** Possible answer: Put the center point of a protractor on point E and line up the 0° line on the inner scale of the protractor with the top leg of $\angle DEF$. Mark the point on the inner scale labeled 40. Remove the protractor and draw a line from point E to the 40° mark. This is the uncommon side of your new 40° angle. **b.** Drawings should show $m\angle DEF = 40°$ and an adjacent angle of 40°.

2•5 Recognizing Congruent Line Segments and Angles

1. $\overline{TR} \cong \overline{HJ}$ 3. $\overline{LR} \cong \overline{OK}$
5. $\overline{AX} \cong \overline{XB}, \overline{DX} \cong \overline{XC}, \overline{XB} \cong \overline{XD}, \overline{AC} \cong \overline{BD}$
7. Possible answer: $\overline{AB}$ and $\overline{BC}$ at the top of the trellis appear to be congruent. To check this, I would measure both line segments.

2•6 Bisecting Line Segments

1. Point T is the midpoint of $\overline{JK}$ and $\overline{RS}$. This is true because point T divides both line segments equally.
3. Point R 5. Point E 7. $\overline{PR} \cong \overline{RQ}$ 9. $\overline{CE} \cong \overline{EB}$
11. A
13. more than $\frac{1}{2}$ the length of $\overline{AB}$
15. Drawing should show arcs intersecting above and below $\overline{RT}$, and a line drawn between the points where the arcs intersect, intersecting $\overline{RT}$ at point P. $\overline{RP} \cong \overline{PT}$
17. Drawing should show arcs intersecting above and below $\overline{XY}$, and a line drawn between the points where arcs intersect, intersecting $\overline{XY}$ at point P. $\overline{XP} \cong \overline{PY}$

2•7 Bisecting Angles

1. **a.** 45° **b.** A right angle has a measure of 90°, and half of 90° is 45°.
3. $\overrightarrow{OP}$ 5. $\overrightarrow{MP}$ 7. $\angle NOP \cong \angle POQ$
9. $\angle LMP \cong \angle PMN$
11. Drawing should show a ray bisecting $\angle ABC$ into two 50° angles.
13. Drawing should show an arc intersecting both sides of $\angle DJF$, two arcs intersecting in the middle of the angle, and a midpoint drawn from that intersection to point J, bisecting $\angle DJF$ into two 37° angles.
15. Possible answer: Use a protractor to measure the angle and divide it in half. Drawing should show four line segments all perpendicular to each other and two additional line segments perpendicular to each other and forming 45° angles with the other four line segments.

2•8 Using Parallel Lines

1. $\angle 3$ and $\angle 5$, $\angle 4$ and $\angle 6$ 3. $\angle 3 \cong \angle 5$, $\angle 2 \cong \angle 8$
5. **a.** 140° **b.** 40° **c.** 40° **d.** 140° **e.** 140° **f.** 40°
7. 100° 9. 80° 11. 100°
13. $\angle 1$ and $\angle 6$, $\angle 2$ and $\angle 5$, $\angle 3$ and $\angle 8$, $\angle 4$ and $\angle 7$
15. 105° 17. 125° 19. 105° 21. 75° 23. 55°
25. 125° 27. 75°
29. **a.** Possible answer: AB, CD, and EF **b.** Possible answer: GH and IJ **c.** Possible answer: $\angle 5$ and $\angle 10$, $\angle 6$ and $\angle 9$, $\angle 7$ and $\angle 12$, $\angle 8$ and $\angle 11$, $\angle 13$ and $\angle 18$, $\angle 14$ and $\angle 17$, $\angle 15$ and $\angle 20$, $\angle 16$ and $\angle 19$ **d.** Possible answer: $\angle 1$ and $\angle 9$, $\angle 2$ and $\angle 10$, $\angle 3$ and $\angle 11$, $\angle 4$ and $\angle 12$, $\angle 13$ and $\angle 21$, $\angle 14$ and $\angle 22$, $\angle 15$ and $\angle 23$, $\angle 16$ and $\angle 24$
e. Possible answer: $\angle 1$ and $\angle 6$, $\angle 2$ and $\angle 5$, $\angle 3$ and $\angle 8$, $\angle 4$ and $\angle 7$, $\angle 9$ and $\angle 14$, $\angle 10$ and $\angle 13$, $\angle 11$ and $\angle 16$, $\angle 12$ and $\angle 15$, $\angle 17$ and $\angle 22$, $\angle 18$ and $\angle 21$, $\angle 19$ and $\angle 24$, $\angle 20$ and $\angle 23$ **f.** Possible answer: $\angle 1$ and $\angle 2$, $\angle 5$ and $\angle 6$, $\angle 1$ and $\angle 5$, $\angle 2$ and $\angle 6$

Chapter 2 Review

1. degrees 2. acute 3. bisector
4. measure 5. complementary
6. supplementary 7. straight
8. protractor 9. bisect 10. compass 11. midpoint
12. 35°; acute 13. 110°; obtuse 14. 90°; right
15. Drawing should show an angle of 80° bisected into two angles of 40°.
16. Drawing should show $\overline{FG}$ with the midpoint marked.
17. 55° 18. 55° 19. 55°
20. 125° 21. 125°
22. 125° 23. 125°
24. Possible answer: Using a ruler or a compass and straightedge, Miriam should measure the board and find the midpoint. This will tell her where to cut the board to get two equal pieces.
25. Possible answer: Timi could use a protractor to measure the size of the angle formed by the piece of pie. Then she could divide the number of degrees by 2 to determine what size half of the angle would be. Using a protractor, she could determine where a bisector would divide the piece of pie into two equal pieces.

Chapter 3 Triangles

3•1 Identifying the Line Segments that Form Triangles

1. $\triangle WXY$; Sides: $\overline{WX}$, $\overline{XY}$, $\overline{YW}$;
Vertices: Points W, X, Y
3. a. $\overline{DF}$, $\overline{FN}$, $\overline{ND}$ b. Points D, F, N
5. Possible answer: tripods for the cameras of photographers, for stability in bridge construction, in roofs of houses for stability and water runoff

3•2 Classifying Triangles

1. Yes. An isosceles triangle has at least two congruent sides. Since Roberto's triangle had three congruent sides, it was also an equilateral triangle.
3. Equilateral 5. isosceles; 5 m
7. Drawing must be a triangle with at least two congruent sides.
9. equilateral, isosceles, and acute
11. right 13. right 15. obtuse
17. 45°; 90°; 45°; right

3•3 Identifying Congruent Triangles

1. ABC 3. TUV 5. $\angle S$ 7. $\angle T$ 9. $\overline{RS}$
11. $\triangle QPL \cong \triangle RST$ 13. 6 cm; 8 cm; 12 cm

3•4 Proving Triangles Congruent

1. a, b
3. $\overline{RT} \cong \overline{QX}$, $\overline{RW} \cong \overline{QZ}$, $\overline{TW} \cong \overline{XZ}$
5. $\overline{RS} \cong \overline{NO}$, $\overline{RT} \cong \overline{NP}$, $\overline{ST} \cong \overline{OP}$
7. Yes; $\triangle RLK \cong \triangle RMB$
9. No 11. Yes; SAS 13. Yes; ASA
15. $\angle I \cong \angle L$, $\overline{IG} \cong \overline{LJ}$, $\angle G \cong \angle J$
17. $\overline{JL} \cong \overline{MP}$, $\angle L \cong \angle P$, $\overline{LK} \cong \overline{PN}$

3•5 Angles of a Triangle

1. 180°; 30°; 180°; 80°; 180°; 180°; 80°; 100°
3. 180°; 180°; 110°; 180°; 180°; 110°; 70°
5. 90° Possible answer: Since the right angle measures 90°, the two acute angles must have a sum of $180° - 90° = 90°$.
7. 30° 9. 58° 11. 120°; 60°; 120°
13. 80° 15. 105°

3•6 Right Triangles

1. Yes. Possible answer: $\overline{MP}$ is the third side, and the two legs have already been named.
3. legs: $\overline{XW}$ and $\overline{WV}$; hypotenuse: $\overline{XV}$
5. legs: $\overline{PQ}$ and $\overline{PR}$; hypotenuse: $\overline{QR}$
7. n and l; m 9. 8^2, 6^2, 64; 36; 100; 10
11. 8.9 13. 15.6 15. 18.4
17. a. Home plate to first base is a; first base to second base is b; home plate to second base is c.
b. 127.3 ft

3•7   Similar Triangles

1. Yes, because corresponding angles of similar triangles are congruent
3. *GFH*   5. *DFE*
7. Drawings will vary. $\overline{GH} \leftrightarrow \overline{CD}, \overline{GI} \leftrightarrow \overline{CB}, \overline{HI} \leftrightarrow \overline{DB}$
9. Drawings should show $\triangle MNP \sim \triangle QNR$. $\overline{MN} \leftrightarrow \overline{QN}, \overline{MP} \leftrightarrow \overline{QR}, \overline{NP} \leftrightarrow \overline{NR}$
11. $\overline{GH}; \overline{HI}; \overline{IG}$
13. $d = 15; e = 12$ 15. $m = 10; n = 18$
17. **a.** 2.5 in.   **b.** Triangle should have two sides each 2.5 in. long and one side 1.5 in. long.

3•8   Using Inequalities for Sides and Angles of a Triangle

1. Yes. Possible answer: The sum of the lengths of any two sides is greater than the length of the third side.
3. $\overline{MN} + \overline{NO} > \overline{MO}; \overline{MO} + \overline{ON} > \overline{MN}; \overline{MO} + \overline{MN} > \overline{ON}$
5. $\overline{LM} + \overline{LK} > \overline{MK}; \overline{MK} + \overline{LK} > \overline{LM}; \overline{ML} + \overline{MK} > \overline{KL}$
7. No   9. Yes
11. No   13. Yes
15. Yes. Since the sides are all equal in length, the angles should all have the same measure.
17. $\angle Q; \angle S; \angle R$
19. $\overline{GH}; \overline{FG}; \overline{FH}$
21. $\angle G$
23. Possible answer: No. It is at most 8 blocks from school to the library, and at most 10 blocks from the library to the skating path. So Morte could only have walked at most 18 blocks.

Chapter 3 Review

1. equilateral   2. size, shape
3. scalene   4. corresponding parts
5. obtuse   6. legs
7. similar   8. isosceles
9. $\overline{AB} \cong \overline{XY}, \angle A \cong \angle X, \overline{AC} \cong \overline{XZ}$
10. $\angle M \cong \angle R, \overline{MP} \cong \overline{RT}, \angle P \cong \angle T$
11. Yes   12. No   13. No
14. 85°   15. 45°   16. 140°
17. 40°   18. 18.0 m   19. 7.9 in.
20. $x = 8$ m; $\overline{NM} = 3$ m
21. 8 ft
22. $\angle J > \angle N$ 23. $\angle M < \angle J$
24. 12 ft

Chapter 4   Polygons

4•1   Types of Polygons

1. sides: $\overline{LM}, \overline{MN}, \overline{NO}, \overline{OP}, \overline{PL}$; vertices: L, M, N, O, P; diagonals: $\overline{MP}, \overline{NP}$
3.

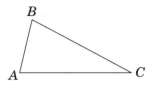

5.

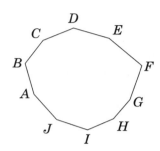

7. Possible answer: Perhaps a blackboard, or floor is tiled—quadrilateral. Watch face may be octagon.

4•2   Properties of Parallelograms

1. **a.** Rico is correct. Both pairs of opposite sides must be parallel to have a parallelogram. If only one pair of opposite sides are parallel, it may be a trapezoid, not a parallelogram.
b.

3. sides: $\overline{LM} \cong \overline{ON}; \overline{NM} \cong \overline{OL}$; angles: $\angle L \cong \angle N; \angle M \cong \angle O$
5. $\overline{NM} = 5$ cm   7. $m\angle M = 135°$
9. line segments: $\overline{XY} \cong \overline{ZW}, \overline{YZ} \cong \overline{WX}, \overline{XA} \cong \overline{AZ}, \overline{YA} \cong \overline{AW}$; triangles: $\triangle YXW \cong \triangle WZY, \triangle XYZ \cong \triangle ZWX$
11. line segments: $\overline{JK} \cong \overline{LM}, \overline{KL} \cong \overline{MJ}, \overline{JN} \cong \overline{LN}, \overline{KN} \cong \overline{MN}$; triangles: $\triangle JKL \cong \triangle LMJ, \triangle JKM \cong \triangle MLK$

4•3   Rectangles

1. No, it is not a rectangle; it is not a parallelogram.

3. Yes, it is a rectangle. It is a parallelogram with 4 right angles.

5. Yes, the diagonals of a rectangle are congruent and the diagonals of a parallelogram bisect each other. Halves of equals are equal.

7. $\overline{DE} = 8$ in.

9. 8 ft

4•4   Rhombuses and Squares

1.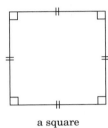

a square

3.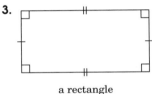

a rectangle

5. $m\angle 9 = m\angle 10 = m\angle 11 = m\angle 12$, 90°

7. $m\angle 3 = m\angle 4$, 45°

9. **a.** $m\angle 1 = m\angle 2$, 30°   **b.** $m\angle KLH = m\angle HJK$, 60°
   c. $m\angle 5 = m\angle 6$, 30°

4•5   Trapezoids

1. A trapezoid is a quadrilateral with exactly one pair of opposite sides parallel, and no sides that are necessarily congruent.

3. Isosceles trapezoid; It has two parallel sides and its legs are congruent.

5. Neither: There are no pair of parallel sides.

7. No. The sum of the interior angles of a quadrilateral is 360°, so you could not have 4 acute angles in a trapezoid.

9. No, if 3 sides are congruent, the 4th side would also be congruent.

11. No, congruent parallel bases will automatically make the legs congruent and parallel, forming a parallelogram, not a trapezoid.

13. 15 cm   **15.** 10.5 in.   **17.** 6 cm

19. Possible answer: Trapezoid $ABCD$; bases: $\overline{AB}$ and $\overline{CD}$, legs: $\overline{AD}$ and $\overline{BC}$, base angles: $\angle D$ and $\angle C$ are a pair and $\angle A$ and $\angle B$ are another pair.

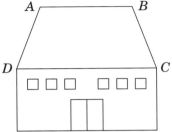

21. Answers should be about 16 mm ± 2 mm.

4•6   Regular Polygons

1. No, a rhombus has all 4 sides congruent but is not a regular polygon. All sides are congruent and all angles are congruent in a regular polygon.

3. 180°   **5.** 540°   **7.** 60°   **9.** 108°   **11.** 7 sides

13. Richard is correct. You need to know the sum of the measures of the interior angles. As the following exercises show, the sum of the exterior angles is 360 degrees for all polygons.

15. 90°; 360°   **17.** 45°; 360°

4•7   Congruent Polygons

1. $\overline{FG} \cong \overline{PQ}$ 3. $\overline{HJ} \cong \overline{RS}$ 5. $\overline{TP} \cong \overline{KF}$

7. $\angle G \cong \angle Q$ 9. $\angle S \cong \angle J$

11.

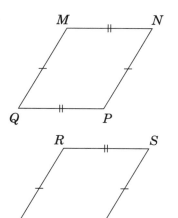

13. Possible answer:

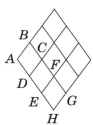

The rhombuses are congruent.

$ABCD \cong EFGH$

4•8   Similar Polygons

1. No, they cannot both be correct. One angle, $\angle D$, must correspond to only one angle, either $\angle J$ or $\angle K$. $\angle F \cong \angle L$ and $\angle G \cong \angle M$. One of the two people is correct, not both.

3. $\angle S \cong \angle X$, $\angle T \cong \angle Y$, $\angle U \cong \angle Z$, $\angle R \cong \angle W$, $\overline{RS} \leftrightarrow \overline{WX}$, $\overline{ST} \leftrightarrow \overline{XY}$, $\overline{TU} \leftrightarrow \overline{YZ}$, $\overline{UR} \leftrightarrow \overline{ZW}$

5. No, the polygons must have the corresponding angles congruent also.

7. $XY = 12$, $ZY = 10$, $RU = 12$

9. $CD = 14$, $KL = 3$, $MN = 3$

4•9   Drawing Polygons on the Coordinate Plane

1. Yes, a point on the x-axis has y-coordinate 0.

3. W at $(4, 1)$, X at $(2, 0)$, Y at $(2, 1)$, Z at $(3, 4)$

5. JFK is a triangle.

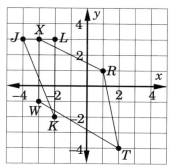

Drawing should include both polygons (5) and (6) on the same coordinate plane given.

7. translation to the right 3 units

9. reflection over x-axis

11. F'' at $(3, -3)$, G'' at $(4, -1)$, H'' at $(0, -2)$

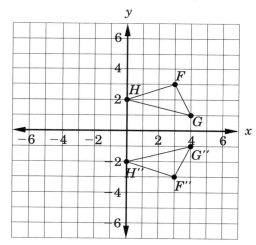

4•10 Tessellations of Regular Polygons

1. The first and third figures should be circled.
3. equilateral triangles, squares, rhombuses
5. isosceles triangles
7. Yes; a tessellation is formed by translating, reflecting, or rotating one or more of the same polygons, which means the sides of one are congruent to many others.
9. Possible answer:

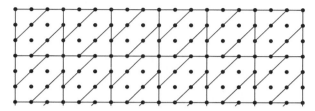

11. Possible answer: The pattern is of repeated polygons. The pattern was formed by tessellating the polygons around one another. Inside, rhombuses were used. See drawing.

Chapter 4 Review

1. polygon **2.** tessellation **3.** parallelogram
4. quadrilateral **5.** rhombus **6.** congruent
7. ordered pair **8.** pentagon **9.** hexagon
10. triangle **11.** quadrilateral **12.** rhombus
13. trapezoid **14.** square **15.** parallelogram
16. 105° **17.** 75° **18.** 3 **19.** $\triangle ABD \cong \triangle CDB$
20. 6 **21.** 4 **22.** 8
23. $m \angle XQY = m \angle YQZ = m \angle ZQW = m \angle WQX = 90°$
24. **a.** 8 **b.** 135°
25.

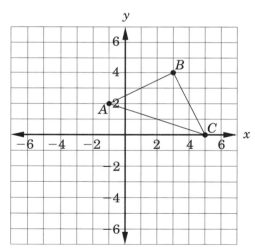

26.

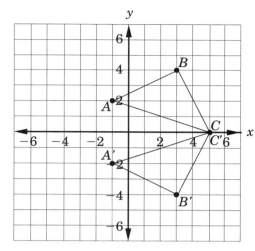

27. Possible answer: Given sides: 3, 4.5, 6, 2.5. Side proportional to 3 will be 5.

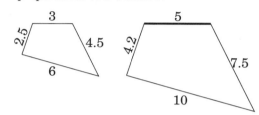

Chapter 5   Area and Perimeter of Polygons

5•1   Perimeter of Parallelograms and Rectangles

1. $2(6) + 2(9) = 12 + 18 = 30$ in.
3. $7 + 7 + 4 + 4 = 22$ cm
5. $2(2.5) + 2(5) = 5 + 10 = 15$ m
7. 50 ft; 194 ft

5•2   Area of Parallelograms and Rectangles

1. $A = 6 \cdot 7 = 42$ cm^2 **3.** $A = 9 \cdot 4 = 36$ in.^{2}
5. $A = 6.5 \cdot 2.5 = 16.25$ cm^2 **7.** 4,700 ft^2

5•3 Estimating Perimeter and Area

1. $P \approx 20$ in.; $A \approx 18$ in.^{2}
3. $P \approx 26$ in.; $A \approx 34$ in.^{2}
5. $P \approx 16$ in.; $A \approx 18$ in.^{2}
7. See drawing. Make sure that the poster meets the size requirements.

5•4 Perimeter and Area of a Rhombus or a Square

1. $b = 7$ cm, $h = 6$ cm **3.** $b = 8.6$ m, $h = 7.5$ m
5. $P = 4 \cdot 12 = 48$ cm; $A = 12 \cdot 10 = 120$ cm^2
7. $P = 6.5 \cdot 7.2 = 26$ m; $A = 7.2 \cdot 6.5 = 46.8$ m^2
9. $P = 4 \cdot 135 = 540$ yd; $A = 135 \cdot 120 = 16{,}200$ yd^2
11. $P = 4 \cdot 7 = 28$ in.; $A = 7^2 = 49$ in.^{2}
13. $P = 4 \cdot 12 = 48$ m; $A = 12^2 = 144$ m^2
15. $P = 4 \cdot 4 = 16$ m; $A = 4^2 = 16$ m^2
17. 196 ft^2 **19.** 2; Sketches will vary.

5•5 Properties of the Diagonals of a Rhombus

1. $A = (\frac{1}{2}) \cdot 6 \cdot 10 = 30$ in.^{2}
3. $A = (\frac{1}{2}) \cdot 9 \cdot 6 = 27$ in.^{2}
5. $A = (\frac{1}{2}) \cdot 7.4 \cdot 4.3 = 15.91$ m^2
7. 18 ft
9. 20.255 in.^{2}

5•6 Area of Triangles

1. Paula is correct, because the area is half the base, or 8 m, times the height, 5 m, or 40 m^2.
3. $A = (\frac{1}{2}) \cdot 6 \cdot 9 = 27$ in.^{2}
5. $A = (\frac{1}{2}) \cdot 16 \cdot 11 = 88$ ft^2
7. $A = (\frac{1}{2}) \cdot 8.5 \cdot 2 = 8.5$ m^2
9. Possible answer: 6 km and 8 km; 4 km and 12 km

5•7 Area of Trapezoids

1. Frank is correct; the formula says find half of the height and multiply that times the sum of the lengths of the bases. $(\frac{1}{2})(4)(6 + 8) = 28$.
3. $A = (\frac{1}{2})(4)(3 + 5) = 16$ m^2
5. $A = (\frac{1}{2})(8)(8 + 11) = 76$ ft^2
7. $A = (\frac{1}{2})(4.5)(14 + 8) = 49.5$ yd^2

5•8 Perimeter and Area of Irregular Figures

1. triangle, rectangle **3.** 2 trapezoids, 1 rectangle
5. $A = (16 \cdot 10) + (\frac{1}{2}) \cdot 16 \cdot 9) = 232$ cm^2
7. $A = [2 \cdot (\frac{1}{2})(2)(3 + 5)] + (5 \cdot 9) = 61$ cm^2
9. No, he also needs to know the measures of the two sides of the rectangle.
11. $P = 14.5 + 4 + 14.5 + 12 + 12 + 12 = 69$ in.
13. $P = 12 + 7 + 12 + 7 + 7 + 7 = 52$ ft
15. a. 48 ft^2 **b.** 26 ft

5•9 Determining the Difference Between Perimeter and Area

1. perimeter **3.** perimeter **5.** area **7.** area
9. a. 24 ft^2 **b.** 24 ft

Chapter 5 Review

1. area **2.** length; width **3.** perimeter
4. $P = 2(9) + 2(6) = 30$ m; $A = 9 \cdot 6 = 54$ m^2
5. $P = 2(7) + 2(5) = 24$ in.; $A = 4 \cdot 7 = 28$ in.^{2}
6. $P = 2(13) + 2(10) = 46$ cm; $A = 12 \cdot 10 = 120$ cm^2
7. $P = 2(6) + 2(2.5) = 17$ ft; $A = 6 \cdot 2.5 = 15$ ft^2
8. $P = 4 \cdot 5 = 20$ ft; $A = (\frac{1}{2}) \cdot 6 \cdot 8 = 24$ ft^2
9. $P = 4 \cdot 12.5 = 50$ cm; $A = 12.5^2 = 156.25$ cm^2
10. $A = (\frac{1}{2}) \cdot 15 \cdot 6 = 120$ in.^{2}
11. $(2)(3.5) + [(\frac{1}{2})(2)(2.5)] = 9.5$ yd^2
12. $4^2 + (8)(5) = 56$ in.^{2}
13. a. 350 ft^2 **b.** 106 ft
14. a. 12 in.^{2} **b.** 72 in.^{2}

Chapter 6   Circles

6•1   Parts of a Circle

1. No, $\overline{TW}$ would be the radius since one endpoint is at the center of the circle and the other is on the circle. Drawing should show $\odot T$ with radius $\overline{TW}$.
3. Drawing should show $\odot R$ with radius $\overline{RT}$.
5. Drawing should show $\odot M$ with diameter $\overline{LK}$ and radius $\overline{MQ}$.
7. Drawing should show $\odot J$ with diameter $\overline{AB}$ and radius $\overline{JB}$.
9. 6 cm. Drawing should show $\odot T$ with a 6 cm diameter $\overline{SV}$ and a 3 cm radius $\overline{TR}$.
11. 2 cm. Drawing should show $\odot P$ with a 4-cm diameter $\overline{MN}$ and a 2-cm radius $\overline{PV}$.
13. Drawing should show a clock with a labeled center and hands. The hands suggest the radii of the circle.

6•2   More Parts of a Circle

1. Yes. Drawing should show $\overline{KF}$ drawn on $\odot M$.
3. Possible answer: Draw radius $\overline{MD}$. One other central angle is $\angle LMD$.
5. Possible answer: Draw line connecting L and G. One other secant is $\overleftrightarrow{LG}$.
7. Drawing should show $\odot P$ with central $\angle MPN$ and secant $\overleftrightarrow{RN}$.
9. Drawing should show $\odot M$ with central $\angle CMR$ and tangent $\overleftrightarrow{LR}$.
11. 130°   13. 110°
15. 70°   17. 40°   19. 110°
21. Possible answer: $\angle AGB$, $\angle BGC$, $\angle CGD$
23. a. 90°   b. 90°

6•3   Circumference of a Circle

1. False. The circumference is the distance around the circle.
3. 6.2 cm; 3.1 cm   5. 12.4 cm; 3.1 cm
7. The ratios all equal 3.1 cm.
9. 28.26 m   11. 34.54 in.   13. 47.1 ft
15. 41.605 ft   17. 82 in.

6•4   Area of a Circle

1. Jasken is incorrect. Since the area of the square is 16 in², then each side of the square is 4 in., making the diameter of the circle also 4 inches. The area of the circle would be 12.56 in.². The area of the circle is not half the area of the square.
3. 50.24 in.²   5. 706.50 ft²   7. 211.1336 m²
9. Yes   11. 3 cm; 28.26 cm²   13. 7.5 cm; 176.625 cm²
15. 615.44 cm²   17. 1256 in²   19. approximately 6 ft

6•5   Circumscribed and Inscribed Polygons

1. Drawing should show a triangle circumscribed about $\odot A$.
3. Drawing should show a quadrilateral inscribed in $\odot C$.
5. The inscribed polygon is a square. The sides of the polygon are all equal.

6•6   Measurement of Angles Circumscribed and Inscribed in a Circle

1. Hank is incorrect; the measure of an arc intercepted by a 90° inscribed angle is 180°.
3. 15°   5. 10°   7. 39°   9. 56°   11. 100°; 160°; 80°
13. 78°   15. 180°   17. 45°   19. 45°

Chapter 6 Review

1. m   2. h   3. b   4. g   5. c   6. f   7. j   8. d   9. i
10. k   11. a   12. l   13. e
14. Drawing should show $\odot M$ with secant $\overleftrightarrow{KL}$.
15. Drawing should show $\odot Q$ with tangent $\overleftrightarrow{RT}$.
16. Drawing should show $\odot L$ with central angle KLM and inscribed angle KNM.
17. Drawing should show $\odot F$ with circumscribed triangle ABC
18. 100°   19. 130°   20. 130°   21. 260°   22. 80°
23. 50.24 cm; 200.96 cm²   24. 31.4 in.; 78.5 in.²
25. 60°   26. 50.24 in.²   27. 25.12 in.

Chapter 7 Recognizing Three-Dimensional Shapes

7•1 Properties of Polyhedrons

1. The second and fourth shapes should be circled.
3. *AFLG, FEKL, EDJK, DCIJ, CBHI, BAGH, ABCDEF, GHIJKL*
5. $\overline{AB}, \overline{BC}, \overline{CD}, \overline{DE}, \overline{EF}, \overline{FA}, \overline{GH}, \overline{HI}, \overline{IJ}, \overline{JK}, \overline{KL}, \overline{LG}, \overline{AG}, \overline{BH}, \overline{CI}, \overline{DJ}, \overline{EK}, \overline{FL}$
7. *A, B, C, D, E, F, G, H, I, J, K, L*
9. No. A piece of pie cannot be a prism because the crust is curved. A polygon cannot be curved.
11. *RSYX, STZY, UTZW, RUWX, RSTU, XWZY*
13. Possible answer: $\overline{RX}$
15. **a–d.** Answers will vary according to the label of each vertex.
17. 5

7•2 Cubes and Rectangular Prisms

1. *JKLM, CDEF; JCFM, KDEL; JCDK, MFEL*
3. Answers will vary according to the vertex labels.
5. 12
7. Answers will vary according to the sizes of the chosen boxes. The length, width, and height of the edges of the rectangular prism should be different. The lengths of the edges of a cube are all equal.

7•3 Pyramids

1. *ABCD*
3. *EF*
5. Answers will vary according to the second chosen variable. However, the first chosen variable should be *E*. Possible answer: *EP*.
7. Answers will vary according to the chosen building and its vertex labels. Answer should include the labeled altitude, slant height, and the reason why the building was shaped as it was.

7•4 Cylinders and Cones

1. The vertex should be labeled *A* and the circle should be labeled *B*.
3. The base should be labeled *M* and the altitude should be labeled *MN*.
5. **a.** Answers will vary according to the chosen object and the measurements of the cone. **b.** Possible answer: If the object was an ice-cream cone, then the object would not have a circular base because that is where the ice cream is placed.

7•5 Spheres

1. The center should be labeled *C*, and *D* should be an endpoint on the sphere, forming a radius *CD*.
3. The center should be labeled *R*, and *T* should be an endpoint on the sphere, forming radius *RT*.
5. 7 m **7.** 9 ft **9.** 4.5 in.
11. The size of the circle cut through the center is larger than the circle cut anywhere else.

Chapter 7 Review

1. polyhedron **2.** cone **3.** rectangular prism
4. sphere **5.** prism **6.** rectangular pyramid
7. cylinder **8.** cube
9. **a.** cube **b–d.** Answers will vary according to the chosen labels.
10. **a.** sphere **b–d.** Answers will vary according to the chosen labels.
11. **a.** pyramid **b–e.** Answers will vary according to the chosen labels.
12. **a.** rectangular prism **b–f.** Answers will vary according to the chosen labels.
13. **a.** cone **b–c.** Answers will vary according to the chosen labels.
14. **a.** cylinder **b–c.** Answers will vary according to the chosen labels.
15. **a.** The diameter of the base of the can must be slightly larger than the diameter of the tennis ball. **b.** The height of the can must be slightly larger than three times the diameter of the tennis ball.

Chapter 8 Surface Area of Three-Dimensional Shapes

8•1 Surface Area of Rectangular Prisms

1. Josh is correct. Since a rectangular prism has six sides, the lengths of the three sides must each be multiplied by two so that $2(2) + 2(4) + 2(6) = 24$ cm^2.

3. Drawing should show a net rectangular prism with length = 10 ft, width = 6 ft, and height = 3 ft. Surface area = 216 ft^2

5. Drawing should show a net rectangular prism with length = 2.5 m, width = 1.5 m, and height = 3 m. Surface area = 31.5 m^2

7. d **9.** b **11.** 8.64 cm^2 **13.** 1.5 m^2

8•2 Lateral and Surface Area of Right Cylinders

1. 10π cm **3.** 226.08 in.^{2} **5.** 197.82 ft^2

7. Patrick is correct. The surface area = $(2)(3.14)(4)(8) + (2)(3.14)(4^2) = 301.44$ in.^{2}

9. 345.4 m^2 **11.** 86.35 cm^2 **13.** 226.08 m^2

15. 847.8 cm^2

8•3 Surface Area of Rectangular Pyramids

1. c **3.** d **5.** 56 in.^{2} **7.** 175 m^2

9. No, you would also need to know the measurements of the two rectangular bases.

11. 299.2 in.^{2} **13.** 139,755 m^2

8•4 Lateral and Surface Area of Cones

1. c **3.** b **5.** 263.76 cm^2 **7.** 816.4 ft^2

9. Yes; Since half of the diameter equals the radius, all Niki needs to do is divide the diameter by two.

11. 251.2 in.^{2} **13.** 47.1 m^2 **15.** 785 in.^{2}

17. 1,428.7 m^2 **19.** 94.2 cents

8•5 Surface Area of Spheres

1. 615.44 ft^2 **3.** 2,461.76 in.^{2} **5.** 78.5 m^2

7. **a.** 45.3416 in.^{2} **b.** 17.0416 in.^{2}

Chapter 8 Review

1. net **2.** lateral area **3.** surface area

4. 104 cm^2 **5.** 726 in.^{2} **6.** 219.8 ft^2; 376.8 ft^2

7. 16 m^2; 20 m^2 **8.** 282.6 ft^2; 536.94 ft^2

9. 5024 mm^2

10. **a.** 93.5 in.^{2} **b.** Kamil could cover a total of two cylinders; one that had the measurements of 8.5 inches for the circumference and 11 inches for the height of the cylinder, or one that had the measurements of 11 inches for the circumference of the base and 8.5 inches for the height of the cylinder.

11. 135.648 cm^2

Chapter 9 Volume of Three-Dimensional Shapes

9•1 Volume of Rectangular Prisms

1. Garnet is correct. The volume of the box is
   (6 cm)(4 cm)(5 cm) = 120 cm^3.
3. 360 ft^3 5. 35 m^3 7. 140.4 ft^3 9. d   11. a
13. 2,197 in.^{3} 15. 91.125 m^3
17. **a.** 480 ft^3 **b.** approximately 3,600 gallons

9•2 Volume of Cylinders

1. Jay is correct. The volume of the can is
   (3.14)(5 cm)^2(10 cm) = 785 cm^3.
3. 904.32 ft^3 5. 346.185 cm^3 7. b   9. 2,198 in.^{3}
11. 30,395.2 mm^3 13. 282.6 m^3
15. **a.** 235.5 cm^3 **b.** 235.5 g

9•3 Volume of Rectangular Pyramids

1. 15 ft^3 3. 54 in.^{3} 5. $46\frac{2}{3}$ in.^{3} 7. 115,651,800 ft^3

9•4 Volume of Cones

1. 16 m^3 3. 42 ft^3 5. ≈ 340.17 cm^3 7. 150.72 cm^3

9•5 Volume of Spheres

1. 133.04 ft^3 3. 3,052.08 in.^{3} 5. 696.56 m^3
7. 14,130 ft^3 9. 452.16 ft^3
10. No. Possible answer: If the radius sas three times
    as long, the volume would be 27 times as great.

9•6 Distinguishing Between Surface Area and Volume

1. surface area   3. volume   5. volume   7. volume
9. **a.** 37.68 in.^{2} **b.** 28.26 in.^{3}

Chapter 9 Review

1. b   2. c   3. e   4. a   5. d
6. 120 ft^3 7. 729 cm^3 8. 791.28 in.^{3} 9. 10 m^3
10. 200.96 ft^3 11. ≈ 5,572.45 cm^3
12. **a.** 4,500 cm^3 **b.** 10 cm^3 **c.** 2,250 cm^3
    d. 2,925 cm^3
13. **a.** 22,608 in.^{2} **b.** 2,543.4 in.^{3}